Hayden White

Published:

Hayden White

The Historical Imagination

Herman Paul

polity

First published in 2011 by Polity Press

Polity Press
65 Bridge Street
Cambridge CB2 1UR, UK

Polity Press
350 Main Street
Malden, MA 02148, USA

ISBN-13: 978-0-7456-5013-5
ISBN-13: 978-0-7456-5014-2(pb)

A catalogue record for this book is available from the British Library.

Typeset in 10.5 on 12 pt Palatino
by Toppan Best-set Premedia Limited
Printed and bound in Great Britain by MPG Books Group Limited, Bodmin, Cornwall

The publisher has used its best endeavours to ensure that the URLs for external websites referred to in this book are correct and active at the time of going to press. However, the publisher has no responsibility for the websites and can make no guarantee that a site will remain live or that the content is or will remain appropriate.

For further information on Polity, visit our website: www.politybooks.com

Contents

Acknowledgments

It is hard to say whether this is my first or second book on Hayden White. Originally, I planned this study to be a reworked version of my 2006 Ph.D. dissertation, which traced how White's philosophy of history was shaped by existentialist concerns about human dignity and moral responsibility in a world believed to be meaningless in itself. However, the revisions to the thesis gradually became so thorough that the outcome is an almost entirely new book. In marked contrast to its unpublished predecessor, the present book is first and foremost an introduction to White. Written for an audience unfamiliar with his work, it explains White's views as clearly as possible, while offering an interpretation that I claim to be more accurate than the sort of *Wikipedia* wisdom ("history is a form of fiction") that many seem to associate with his name. What has not changed, though, is my historicizing approach, as evidenced, among other things, by the chronological organization of this study and the use of past tense forms throughout the book. This is not to suggest that White's interventions belonged to an age now long gone – even though *Metahistory* appeared well before I was born – but to show how his (often changing) views on history were rooted in specific historical situations, social structures, political realities, and generational sensitivities.

The greatest debt I have incurred in the course of writing this book is to Hayden White himself, who immediately took me out for coffee and pizza when I reluctantly knocked on his office door at Stanford University in the Fall of 2002. Ever since, he has been a stimulating conversation partner, generous with his time and ideas, always prepared to answer my questions or to recommend a new historical novel, but fierce in his insistence that I should write "with" rather than "about" his work. Although this was not precisely what I had in mind with the current book, I trust my other work in the field of historical theory testifies that my ideas are often shaped in conversation with White's. Also, I am most grateful to my former doctoral advisors, Frank Ankersmit and Chris Lorenz, for their support and many helpful suggestions. I cannot imagine how I would have entered the historical profession without the encouragement and scholarly example of especially Frank Ankersmit.

Furthermore, I owe a word of thanks to Peter Novick, who read my Ph.D. thesis in 2006 and responded with a nine-page letter that was as friendly as it was useful in preparing the present book. In addition, I have benefited from stimulating conversations with Mark Bevir, Ewa Domańska, Brian Fay, Thomas L. Haskell, Martin Jay, Hans Kellner, Dominick LaCapra, Raymond Martin, Allan Megill, Annie van den Oever, Rik Peters, Paul A. Roth, Eelco Runia, Richard T. Vann, John H. Zammito, Eugen Zeleňák, and other colleagues near and abroad.

My editors at Polity Press, Emma Hutchinson and David Winters, have been wonderful to work with. At home, my wife Esther gave me invaluable support and encouragement to finish this project. Thanks so much, my dear! Finally, I should like to dedicate this book to my parents, Mart-Jan and Nelleke Paul, as a sign of my gratitude and love towards them.

Parts of Chapter 1 appeared previously in "A Weberian Medievalist: Hayden White in the 1950s," *Rethinking History*, 12, no. 1 (2008), pp. 75–102. This material is reprinted here by kind permission of the publisher, Taylor & Francis Ltd. Chapter 3 quotes heavily from Hayden White, *Metahistory: The Historical Imagination in Nineteenth-Century Europe*, pp. ix, x, xi, xii, 2, 5, 7, 15, 22–3, 29, 31, 33, 37, 42, 50, 52, 66–7, 69, 167, 173, 176, 177, 179, 186, 222, 226–7, 276–7, 283, 334, 346, 355–6, 372–3, 402, 415, 427–8, 431, 433–4. © 1973 The Johns Hopkins University Press. These quotations are reprinted with permission of The Johns Hopkins University Press. The same press also granted me permission to quote brief passages from White's essay collections, *Tropics of Discourse*, *The Content of the Form*, and *The Fiction of Narrative*.

Introduction: How to Read Hayden White

"No one writing in this country at the present time has done more to wake historians from their dogmatic slumber than has Hayden White," wrote Dominick LaCapra.[1] In a sense, these words aptly describe how White, the American scholar best classified as a philosopher of history, spent a good part of his career explaining why historians are unjustified in thinking they have privileged access to the past. Over the years, in both his writing and teaching, White invested considerable energy in challenging the conventional wisdom that archival research and historical analysis enable historians to offer "better" accounts of the past than, say, historical novels or films. In expressive and often ironic prose, he fired volleys of questions: Who is to decide what counts as better? Better for what purposes? By whose standards? In whose interest? The word "history," in particular, often aroused White's critical attention. What does it mean to write history, to classify an event as historical, or to say that a phenomenon must be explained historically? What is it that historians and the general public in the West take as "history?" And what reasons could one possibly have for preferring this way of looking at history, this view of what counts as history, over alternatives proposed in other times and places? Like David Hume, the Scottish philosopher whom Immanuel Kant famously declared had awakened him from his "dogmatic slumber," White raised a number of difficult questions disturbing the peaceful sleep of those assuming that the only way of doing history was taking notes in an archive and "getting the facts straight."

Yet, in so far as LaCapra, in the words just quoted, implied that White's wake-up calls were heard or answered by these note-taking historians, there was no small amount of wishful thinking in his claim. Who was White after all? Presumably, by the time LaCapra wrote his favorable review, in 1976, few American historians had ever tried to read White. They might have recognized his name as the director of Wesleyan's Center for the Humanities or as a history professor who had taught at Wayne State, Rochester, and UCLA. But it is unlikely that more than a few historians ever reached the last page of White's often long and difficult essays, published in such high-brow journals as *History and Theory* and *New Literary History*. Admittedly, by 1976, the leading historical journal in the United States had welcomed White's path-breaking study, *Metahistory: The Historical Imagination in Nineteenth-Century Europe* (1973), as "a daring, ingenious, and sometimes bewildering tour de force."[2] But nor does that count as an indicator of the sort of influence that LaCapra seems to detect. Only by the 1980s did *Metahistory* begin to acquire fame and notoriety.[3] LaCapra's statement is therefore best understood as a friendly encouragement, or as the enthusiastic endorsement of a program that LaCapra – himself a soon-to-be-famous theorist – considered healthy for historians still suffering from faith in truth and objectivity.[4]

Much, though, has changed in the meantime. Hayden White hardly needs a word of introduction today. His essays, collected in *Tropics of Discourse* (1978), *The Content of the Form* (1987), *Figural Realism* (1999), and *The Fiction of Narrative* (2010), are required reading for graduate students throughout the humanities. Friends and foes alike consider White a major spokesman of "narrativist" or "postmodernist" approaches to the study of history. Wherever historians refer to the "linguistic turn" in their profession, they mention the name of White. In the English-speaking world, his views have dominated the research agenda of philosophers of history ever since the early 1970s. Of course, wherever White goes, or wherever his texts are discussed in class, he receives negative feedback, especially from historians who see their "craft" threatened by the language of discourse and representation. Yet, whereas in earlier decades the mere mention of White's name was sufficient to ensure vigorous debate, younger generations of historians have increasingly absorbed the "tropes" and "plots" from *Metahistory* – as have literary scholars, who have learned from White how to treat historical writing as discourse.

In this way, White has become a short-hand reference to "literary analyses of historical texts" or "narrativist philosophy of history," much in the way that Hans-Georg Gadamer represents hermeneutics and Jacques Derrida symbolizes deconstruction. Arguably, no other philosopher of history since Robin G. Collingwood, in the second quarter of the twentieth century, has had such a profound impact on historical thinking. Indeed, "[n]o one writing in this country [the United States] at the present time" has done more to revolutionize the way we reflect upon history.

Narrativist philosophy of history

White's achievement

How has White managed to achieve this? According to many, his work challenges three conventional distinctions, or demarcations between fields that are often believed to differ significantly. Take, first of all, the field, or activity, called "philosophy of history."[5] Since the eighteenth century, philosophy of history has traditionally been identified with the study of the laws of historical development. A prime example of this tendency is Saint Augustine, who depicted the process between Creation and Judgment Day as a constant war between the City of God and the City of Man. Other examples could include G. W. F. Hegel, for whom history was the gradual self-realization of the spirit, and Karl Marx, who believed that history would eventually culminate in a Socialist society. By the mid twentieth century, however, this type of thought was almost unanimously dismissed as speculative and unscientific (also, one might add, because many saw the Fascist and National-Socialist regimes in 1930s Europe as illustrating the potentially dangerous political implications of such philosophies of history).[6] The only legitimate sort of philosophy of history, William Walsh and others argued, was the analytical philosophy found in, for instance, the early volumes of the journal *History and Theory*. This kind of philosophy did not study the historical process, but historical scholarship. It did not offer grandiose syntheses, but scrupulous reflections on what can be accepted as valid historical explanations, or the relative faults and merits of competing concepts of causality.[7]

One can imagine the consternation caused by White's provocative claim that this distinction between "speculative" and "analytical" philosophy of history conceals as much as it reveals. White argued that the former only makes explicit what the latter chooses

#1

to leave implicit. Obviously, he did not say that philosophers of history in the analytic branch tacitly subscribe to Augustinian, Hegelian, or Marxist theories of historical development. Nonetheless, in White's view, it is impossible for them to study historical scholarship without making substantive assumptions about what "history" is, what counts as "past" and "present," what a historical "agent" is, or how historical events are "caused." There can be no reflection on historical scholarship that is metaphysically neutral. Therefore, analytical philosophy of history may pretend to be detached, impersonal, and devoid of the metaphysical speculation often found in Augustine, Hegel, or Marx. In fact, however, it has an ineradicable metaphysical dimension as well. All reflection on historical studies stems from what White called "metahistorical" assumptions. (This, of course, is also true of White's own work.)

#2   Even more disturbing was White's second attack, on the distinction between "proper" historical practice and (speculative) philosophy of history. Since the days of Leopold von Ranke, the alleged father of modern historical scholarship, historians had been taught to avoid all speculation and to stick to "facts" derived from primary source material. Indeed, Ranke himself already had explicitly contrasted his ethos of meticulous source criticism with the grand-scale narratives offered by Hegel.[8] But, again, White argued that the antithesis is misleading. For what is a historical fact? Do all events recorded in ancient documents classify as "historical"? If not, how then to justify the distinction between historical and other facts? Doesn't that distinction presuppose a substantive vision of what history is (a vision, perhaps, like Hegel's, who spoke about the "people without history" in Africa)? And what is a "fact" or an "event?" White was among the first to show that these categories cannot be defined without a metaphysics or substantive view of what reality is.

#3   Yet, the most provocative border incursion, so to speak, took place at the (supposed) boundary between history and fiction. White is known as a narrativist because of his claim that historians write stories, or produce narratives, much in the same way that authors of fictional novels do. As such, this is hardly a surprising insight: historians have often felt inspired by novelists. However, under the influence of positivist presuppositions, many of them considered the literary qualities of their writing a matter of form, more than of content. White, on the other hand, spoke about the "content of the form" or about the constraints that narratives put on how historians interpret the past. As long as historical writing is supposed to display the sort of coherence and plot development typical of the nineteenth-century realistic novel, said White, historians will view the past through the prisms of coherence and development. They will interpret the past in such a way that it fits their narrative model. Indeed, historians are often so accustomed to this narrative format that many of them would dismiss a history book following the stylistic example of, say, a modernist anti-novel or a Lacanian essay. White's point, then, was not that such an a-priori commitment to a particular (narrative) mode of representation must be avoided. He only wanted historians to realize that there are no obvious reasons why a history book needs to resemble a Sir Walter Scott novel more closely than a modernist work by Virginia Woolf. Whatever the genre they prefer, historians always adopt a (mode of representation.) They always construct a version of the past and cannot help but impose their own assumptions upon the reality of the past. In that respect, they resemble authors of fictional literature. Emphasizing this constructive element, White provocatively spoke about the "fictions" historians employ and even about the "the fictions of factual representation" (see chapter 4, this volume).

Conceivably, this was a recipe for controversy. "If the distinction between history and philosophy of history had been basic to historians, the most sacred boundary of all was that between history and fiction, and nothing outraged historians more than White's blurring of that dividing line," writes Peter Novick in his history of the American historical profession. Suspicious "of those who like Hayden White argue that historical narrative is just another form of fiction," at least a segment of the discipline began to treat White as a "symbolic embodiment" of "nihilistic relativism."[9] Of course, the accused could have objected that fiction is by no means identical to "say whatever you please." Doesn't the Latin word *fictum* mean "created" or "formed?" But such subtleties, like many others that will be addressed in this book, were lost in the turbulent reception history of White's philosophy of history. His blurring of three seemingly well-demarcated borders – all of which were supposed to distinguish good academic performance from the less good – turned White into a much-discussed and most controversial figure.

White's reputation

In a sense, controversy is what transforms important authors into "key contemporary thinkers." Without the polemics surrounding his work, White would not have acquired the status that justifies book-length treatment of his ideas in Polity's Key Contemporary Thinkers series. At the same time, this debate ranks high among the reasons why White is sometimes hard to understand. Indeed, there is no lack of misunderstandings stemming from stereotypes and prejudices about the nature and aims of his work. For example, if several polemical pieces assert that White does not offer any rational criteria for judging between competing interpretations of, say, the Russian Revolution, it is difficult to pick up *Metahistory* without the expectation that this issue of competing historical interpretations lies at the heart of the book. As soon, then, as one reads in the preface that White thinks there are only moral or aesthetic grounds for preferring one "perspective on history" over another, one may be forgiven for interpreting this as meaning that one can have only moral or aesthetic reasons for claiming that a certain study of the Russian Revolution is better than its competitors. In fact, however, White talks about "perspectives on history" or views on what counts as historical; not about interpretations of a particular historical event. This is not a minor difference. If White's phrase "perspectives on history" refers to cultural patterns of defining the mode called "history," rather than to a book shelf containing four or five different monographs on the Russian revolutionaries of 1917, the claims proposed in *Metahistory* turn out to be dramatically different than is suggested in much of the polemical literature. (I elaborate on this example in chapter 3.) One aim of the present book, then, is to offer a more sensitive interpretation of White's philosophy of history by explaining not what others have said about White, but what White himself might have wanted to say.[10]

The polemical reception history of White's publications is only one reason why new readers often find themselves struggling with these texts. There are at least two other reasons. One is that White's oeuvre displays a greater interest in originality than in consistency over time. In a sense, the author seems constantly on the move. The 27-year-old graduate student in the Vatican library who presented his doctoral dissertation as an "objective" account of the papal schism in 1130 represented a rather different type of historian than the flamboyant teacher at Rochester, in the mid-1960s, who captivated the freshmen in his classroom with amazing stories about nineteenth-century intellectuals.[11] The aged celebrity who gave, and still gives, skillfully improvised speeches to audiences varying from artists in Rome to young faculty in Oklahoma City reminds one only remotely of the structuralist-inspired pieces that White published as a mid-career scholar in the early 1970s. Also, White's first attempts to grasp the historians' work in terms of narrative – attempts still formulated in the language of analytical philosophy of history – emerged from concerns rather different from those that motivated his devastating critique of the historical discipline in *The Content of the Form*, or his perhaps surprising interest in ancient Christian Bible exegesis in the early 1990s. These examples do not intend to downplay the element of continuity in White's work or *modus operandi* – for instance, his frequent invoking of a theory of tropes and its application upon such diverse topics as texts, dreams, and music.[12] But even in this case, what White wanted his tropes to achieve, and how he employed them to gain maximum rhetorical effect, varied from context to context. Historian Richard T. Vann therefore rightly requires that any reflection on White must start with the question: "Which White?"[13] For this reason, the current book does not offer a systematic presentation of White's philosophy of history, but a chronological account of how his thoughts about history changed over time.

A third and final reason for the relative inaccessibility of White's work (despite, sometimes, the appearance of the contrary) is the author's preference for the genre of the essay.[14] When Vann calls White "perhaps the premier academic essayist of our times," he identifies a striking and important feature of much of White's writing.[15] White's favorite genre, indeed, was not the monograph, but the essay; not the 250-page answer to a single question, but the 25-page outburst of creativity. Guided by his fine intuition for what is original or exciting in the world of letters, White employed the essay-format to test new ideas and to provoke discussion. This should warn the reader not to expect from White a "position," in the sense of a well-grounded system of philosophical beliefs. The German critic Patrick Bahners certainly exaggerates when he claims that almost everything *Metahistory* asserts is refuted by other statements elsewhere in the book. But, admittedly, White's love of *inventio* – the style figure "related to concepts of creativity, productivity and progress" – always far exceeded his care for consistency.[16]

It therefore seems crucial for any interpretation of White not to focus too much on positions and answers. It is far more illuminating to examine the *questions* that motivated his work. White's oeuvre is better understood from its guiding concerns than from the variety of sometimes contradictory assertions it makes. It is more illuminating, for students of his work, to examine which questions captivated White in different phases of his career than to observe that, over the course of the years, the ideas, hypotheses, and theories proposed in response to these questions changed with the circumstances. In other words, the challenge is to treat White neither as a system builder nor as a constructor of theories, but as the author of a wide-ranging oeuvre that finds its coherence, not in answers, but in some deeply felt questions about history.[17]

Accordingly, when this study identifies White's work as a "philosophy of history," the word "philosophy" has not to be mistaken for rigid system thinking or for analytical thought in the tradition of Gottlob Frege and Bertrand Russell. Neither is it limited to what some authors call "historical theory," that is, philosophical reflection on the work of professional (academic) historians. As this study will make clear, White's interest was anything but confined to the historical discipline: his prime interest rather was historical imagination, in and (especially) outside the ivory tower of professional scholarship. "Philosophy of history," then, is better understood as indicating that the variety of issues White addressed in the course of his career were always informed and motivated by questions dealing with history.

White's questions

What, then, were these questions of history that guided White's work? On this issue, the literature on White – dozens of articles, in several languages, the most important of which are listed in the bibliography near the end of this book – is remarkably divided. Due, perhaps, to the ease with which White participated in a variety of scholarly debates, or to the fact that many commentators have taken up their pens in response to what appeared to be temporary positions, the answers White formulated at particular moments in time have sometimes been mistaken for the questions his oeuvre as a whole sought to address. In other words, the rhetorical and conceptual instruments White employed in particular phases of his career are often quickly identified with the principal concerns informing his work.

Take, for example, the figures of speech that almost every student first learns to associate with White: metaphor, metonymy, synecdoche, and irony (not to mention the four plot structures that White distinguished, or the ideological dimensions he detected, or the explanatory strategies he discerned, all of which can be neatly classified and presented in graphical diagrams). Given that White presented these rhetorical figures as "tropes," his analysis of historical writing in terms of these figures is often characterized as "tropological." For some authors, then, White is nothing but a tropologist, whose greatest pleasure consisted in analyzing the world of human affairs in terms of his fourfold rhetorical pattern. There is, of course, some truth in this observation. One of White's favorite rhetorical strategies, after all, was to show that an author, a tradition, or even an entire scholarly debate was locked within the confines of a single trope (in the mode of metonymy, for example) and then to suggest that other points of view were also available (in the metaphoric and synecdochic modes, for instance). But if White was a tropologist in his heart of hearts, then how to account for the almost complete absence of tropes in *The Content of the Form*? Or how to explain White's interest in "modernist events," "intransitive writing," and the "practical past," none of which can easily be encapsulated in a tropological theory (chapter 6)? It is no coincidence that the "tropological" interpretation of White was most forcefully suggested by reviewers of *Tropics of Discourse*. It may be less appropriate for White's later work, not to mention his pre-*Metahistory* writings. Moreover, interpretations of White focused on tropes run the risk of forgetting that, in White's hands, these rhetorical figures were never an end in themselves, but always an instrument for performing a specific type of analysis. And it remains to be seen whether this was an analysis of texts or discourse, as is usually assumed, or rather an analysis of patterns of thought metaphorically identified by rhetorical figures (chapter 3).

Others claim that White was first and foremost a narrativist. This usually refers to White's interest in how story-forms shape the way in which humans think about the world, and is an interpretation developed in the 1980s and 1990s in response to *The Content of the Form*. Those classifying White as a narrativist, or crediting him with a "theory of narrative explanation," usually do so in order to indicate a typical feature of White's mid-career work. White's philosophy of history, they say, is not focused on historical research, but on historical writing. Moreover, in so far as this writing is concerned, White is not interested in historical statements (in individual sentences such as "Nero was the fifth Roman emperor of the Julio-Claudian dynasty"), but in historical narratives (in book-length stories such as Edward Gibbon's *History of the Decline and Fall of the Roman Empire*). In particular, for White, such narratives are "autonomous linguistic entities," in the sense that they are underdetermined by the individual sentences they contain. Consequently, the argument goes, narratives such as Gibbon's *Decline and Fall* cannot be verified or falsified by empirical historical research: they fall into a category beyond truth and falsity. This, then, is the "anti-realist narrativism" that philosophers of history, in polemical manner, have ascribed to White (chapter 5).

Admittedly, this narrativist interpretation of White has some plausibility, too. For example, I will argue that White's understanding of narrative indeed relied heavily on arguments intended to challenge dominant forms of "realism." Also, it is appropriate to call White a narrativist as long as one deals with the work published in and around *The Content of the Form*, or when one refers to the effect that this part of his oeuvre has had, and still has, on the humanities. Yet, as an interpretative framework for understanding White's entire work, this narrativism is as limited as the tropological interpretation. For one thing, few commentators reading White through narrativist lenses have been able to explain *why* White was so eager to emphasize the artificial, fictive, and anti-realist nature of historical narrative. Few have realized that White – unlike his Dutch colleague Frank Ankersmit, for example[18] – has never tried to offer even the beginning of an argument as to why "truth" in a classic correspondence sense of the word is inapplicable to narratives like Gibbon's tragedy. More generally, few have recognized that White almost invariably approached narrative from rhetorical, ideological, and political angles, and almost never from an epistemological point of view. Besides, just like the tropological reading, the narrativist interpretation focuses on a specific phase in White's intellectual trajectory, thereby ignoring much of what White wrote prior to *Metahistory*. Finally, as chapter 3 will reveal, even *Metahistory*, often considered the flagship of narrativist philosophy of history, suffers if read through the lenses of White's later work.

Reinterpreting White

The alternative this book presents rests on three assumptions.[19] First, it supposes that White's philosophy of history can only be understood if it is read from the context of his entire oeuvre. Accordingly, this book does not start with *Metahistory*, but devotes two entire chapters to the "early White." Second, unlike some polemical pieces in *History and Theory* and other journals, this book does not merely treat White as a "philosopher of historiography," that is, as someone engaged in a philosophical examination of the knowledge that historians produce.[20] White's views on professional historiography were always part of a broader philosophy, in which existential attitudes towards the past, the uses and abuses of traditions, the paralyzing effects of bourgeois modes of realism, and the moral dimensions of historical knowledge were at least equally important themes. In other words, White was not primarily interested in the historical profession *per se*, but in what it means to live in a historical world, to orient oneself in the present, and to envision a morally responsible future. This is why historical imagination, as referred to in the subtitle of this book, served as a key concept in White's philosophy of history.

Finally, building on work done by Hans Kellner, David Harlan, Ewa Domańska, and Dirk Moses, this book argues that White's #3 desire to challenge the historical imagination of his contemporaries stemmed from his moral and political views, or more precisely, from his existentialist humanist idea that human beings ought to throw off their "burdens of history" if they are to contribute to "a better world for our children and their progeny."[21] More precisely, this book argues that at the heart of White's philosophy of history lies an existentialist-inspired understanding of human flourishing, which reveals itself, among other things, in White's unshakable confidence in the abilities of human beings to endow the "meaningless" realities of past and present with self-won meanings; in his imperative that human individuals must develop such meanings in order to free themselves from traditions, conventions, and other tyrannical powers; in his insistence that every historical interpretation entails a moral judgment, for which the author bears personal responsibility; and in what Novick calls White's "quasi obsession with the historian's liberty of choice."[22] White's philosophy of history is a series of reflections inspired by what one might call the first commandment in his moral universe: "thou shalt be responsible for thine own life." His rebellion against anti-utopian modes of realism and his recommendation of anti-narrative modes of representation were invariably motivated by the existentialist-inspired ideal of human individuals who take responsibility for their own existence and dare to plot the course of their own lives (as captured nicely in the image on the cover of this book).

Detecting such an existentialist-inspired program in White's philosophy of history is not the same as reducing his work again to a "position" or "system." In White's case, after all, it was part of his existentialist ethos to adapt his thoughts to changing circumstances. And although the influence of Jean-Paul Sartre and Albert Camus

– the French existentialists whose writings White absorbed in the 1950s and ever after invoked as uncrowned authorities in matters of moral decision-making – was more explicitly acknowledged in his early writings than in his later work, its traces can be found throughout his oeuvre. Indeed, this book will argue that without a proper appreciation of White's existentialist-inspired agenda, his reflections on language, imagination, discourse, and narrative remain hard to understand, and often difficult to relate to each other. White's thoughts on history and historical scholarship only come together and fall into place if they are traced back to his central question: how to live a morally responsible life in a thoroughly historical world?

Structure of the book

The structure of this book is relatively simple. As indicated above, the book starts with two full chapters on White's early work (1955–73). The first of these shows that White's earliest writings, from the 1950s, were heavily indebted to the German sociologist Max Weber. In applying Weber's leadership types to medieval Roman church leadership, White not only offered a new explanation of the papal schism of 1130, but also aimed at developing a sociological model describing the "rise and fall" of cultural powers. The opening chapter also shows that a similar theme can be found in the three textbooks White (co-)authored in the 1960s and early 1970s: *The Emergence of Liberal Humanism* (1966), *The Ordeal of Liberal Humanism* (1970), and *The Greco-Roman Tradition* (1973). Focusing on the rise of humanist ideals in Western thought, these volumes testify that White's Weberian views on ideology and human agency could be called "humanistic" if combined with a particular educational agenda. However, they also show that, by the end of the 1960s, Jean-Paul Sartre and Albert Camus had replaced Weber as White's main sources of inspiration.

   Chapter 2 shows how White blended existentialism, structuralism, and American Marxism into a philosophy of history that openly advocated "liberation historiography" (a term coined in analogy to liberation theology and liberation philosophy). In particular, this second chapter argues that White's fascination for the structuralist philosopher, Lucien Goldmann, strengthened his conviction that "visionary politics" in the Marxist manner were needed for realizing his existentialist ideal of moral freedom and responsibility.

Special attention is given to White's provocative piece "The Burden of History" (1966). With its vehement criticism of the historical discipline, this essay reads like a manifesto of modernist and existentialist philosophy of history. Although White would quickly dissociate himself from the hope that academic historiography could be liberated from its historicist presuppositions, the questions and concerns expressed in "The Burden of History" are crucial for understanding White's subsequent work.

Against this background, chapter 3 offers a new interpretation of White's *magnum opus, Metahistory*. Through a close reading of White's Ranke chapter, it argues that White understood his "tropes," "plots," "modes of argument," and "ideological implications" to mean something different than what is often assumed. It demonstrates that White's rhetorical terms do not primarily refer to qualities of historical narratives, but designate a number of different views on the relation between history and myth, or reason and imagination. Although both the introduction and the conclusion to *Metahistory* anticipated White's later ideas about the linguistic structuring of historical thought, the book itself did not offer anything like an analysis of historical narratives. Instead, the chapter argues, *Metahistory* is better read as a "moral text about freedom," in the sense that it tried to develop a notion of "historical realism" suitable for the liberation historiography discussed in the previous chapter.

If *Metahistory* dealt with myth and imagination, more than with narrative and discourse, how then did White become interested in the latter? In a careful analysis of articles later collected in *Tropics of Discourse*, chapter 4 argues that "discourse" was White's answer to the question of how to relate history and myth, or reason and imagination. Remarkably, however, White's reflections on discourse, figurative language, and "the fictions of factual representation" pulled him so deep into structuralist waters that his existentialist humanist concern for the human individual as meaning-producer almost seemed to disappear. The final sections of the chapter argue, though, that White was not prepared to accept the "anti-humanist" conclusions at which French thinkers such as Foucault and Derrida arrived – even though LaCapra not incorrectly argues that the sources of their attack on the humanist subject were latently present in White's thinking, too.

If White returned from his structuralist adventure with a renewed faith in the human subject, chapter 5 shows how he expected this subject to confront what he called the "sublime" meaninglessness of the past. Even more strongly than in his previous work, White positioned the human individual as a producer of meaning over against the chaos and arbitrariness that he attributed to the historical field. This existentialist-inspired understanding of meaning led White to endorse Louis O. Mink's dictum, "stories are not lived but told," as a starting-point for his theory of narrative. Special attention is devoted to some of the criticism White's work on narrative received, most notably from Carlo Ginzburg, whose charge that White was as helpless against fascism as Giovanni Gentile in 1930s Italy missed the humanism informing so much of White's work, but correctly pointed out that not knowledge but meaning is what White expected historical interpretations to offer.

Indeed, White's philosophy is not a "philosophy of historiography," but a series of reflections on how to throw off traditions, how to get rid of burdensome pasts, and how to liberate oneself from modes of realism that prevent one from imagining a world better than one's own. Chapter 6 argues that this is particularly apparent from White's experiments during the 1990s and early 2000s, which introduced such notions as "modernist event," "intransitive writing," "figural realism," and "practical past." In dialogue with authors reflecting on the horrors of Auschwitz, Hiroshima, and Nagasaki, White drew on modernist sources of the sort invoked in "The Burden of History" to advocate a non-narrative, non-totalizing sensibility towards the past. Only if we resist the coherence and continuity that narratives offer, and confront the ambiguities of what White, following Walter Benjamin, called "dialectical images," will we be able to rebel against the injustices of our time and imagine a future brighter than the dark age of late capitalism.

Finally, a brief epilogue presents White's view of the human subject as an appropriate starting-point for evaluation of his philosophy of history. It is supplemented with an extensive bibliography of White's works and a selective list of secondary titles.[23]

1

Humanist Historicism: The Italian White

Hayden White was a 25-year-old graduate student when he embarked on a journey that was to have a lasting impact on all of his work. Armed with a Fulbright fellowship, White left the University of Michigan, where he studied medieval history, to spend two years in Rome (1953–55). Judging by the work he produced there, the young scholar spent long hours in the Vatican library, that goldmine for historians of medieval Europe. However, perhaps more important was that he discovered some of the literature, the bookshops, and the museums that Rome had to offer. He learned the language and began to collect cheap editions of sixteenth-century Italian books.[1] At the university, he became acquainted with Mario Praz, the art critic and professor of English literature, who invited him to contribute to his journal, *English Miscellany*. White also paid regular visits to Carlo Antoni, the philosopher of history whose book on the decline of historicism and the rise of sociology he began to translate into English. Inspired by a sense of cultural urgency, the young White even started an overseas correspondence with Ezra Pound, the modernist poet who, in White's later recollection, "was the kind of person we had to come to terms with."[2] If anything, for White, the eternal city was a cultural eye-opener and a place to reflect on what it means to "do" history.

In a sense, White had had this experience before, back home, in the classrooms of Wayne University in Detroit. For a student with a working-class background – Hayden was born in 1928 in Martin, Tennessee, as the son of a worker who lost his job during the Great Depression, but found new employment on the assembly lines of

Detroit's automobile industry – a course in European or intellectual history was like an immersion in a hitherto unknown world of literature, philosophy, and art. White quickly fell under the tutelage of William J. Bossenbrook, a charismatic teacher with an amazing capacity to capture his students' imagination with beautiful stories and erudite philosophical discourse.[3] How different was this Republic of Letters from the smelly factories elsewhere in Detroit, or from the American Navy, where White, in the aftermath of World War II, had spent just enough time (in the V5 officer-training program) to secure admission to college through the G.I. Bill.[4] "For those of us who had grown up in the cultural and social wasteland of Detroit during the depression, he [Bossenbrook] was our introduction to the world of intellect; in fact, he *was* that world," White wrote in a *Festschrift* for his teacher. "More: he permitted us to believe that we could become a part of it on the basis of our intellectual abilities alone."[5] Encouraged by this example, the young White began to absorb Jean-Paul Sartre and Albert Camus ("very exciting for an 18/19 year old undergraduate") as well as other European existentialists, such as Karl Jaspers and Gabriel Marcel. He perused the *New Statesman and Nation*, Kingsley Martin's British Socialist magazine, and discovered Marxism, not in its political manifestations, but as a tradition of progressive, critical thought: "Existentialism, along with Marxism, seemed to me in my youth like the only possible way of looking at the human condition."[6]

One may wonder how these (reading) experiences shaped White's thoughts about history. So far, most of the secondary literature ignores White's 1955 Ph.D. dissertation and his contributions to Praz's *English Miscellany*. These are, however, indispensable for understanding White's later philosophy of history. This chapter is therefore devoted to "the early White." Starting with the dissertation White composed in the Vatican library, I argue that, during the 1950s, the German sociologist Max Weber served as White's most powerful source of influence. However, White's stay in Rome and his exposure to Italian historicism as represented by Antoni and his mentor, Benedetto Croce, stimulated a lasting fascination for more historical modes of thought. I argue that in this Italian period, White came to identify himself with a "humanist historicism," which combined a thoroughly historicized (and secularized) understanding of the human condition with an almost existentialist emphasis on the freedom and moral responsibility of the individual.

The papal schism of 1130

How did White, with his existentialist readings, come to specialize in medieval church history? In his own recollection, it was "because the world of a Catholic civilisation was so alien to my experience."

> The reason I was working on medieval history, and the church especially, was that the Roman Catholic Church was something I knew absolutely nothing about when I went to college. I found it amazing that an institution based upon a miracle, which by definition cannot be comprehended except through faith, could sustain itself and dominate even the monarchs and the political powers for over a thousand years.[7]

Obviously, such recollections say as much about an older White, looking back upon his youth, than about the young Hayden who eagerly began to explore a world dominated by popes, cardinals, and religious orders. Also, the passage just quoted illustrates a typical feature of what Allan Megill calls White's "rhetorical dialectic." It deliberately contrasts Rome with Detroit, church-life with college-life, faith with reason ("a dialectical opposition that he overstates for epideictic effect").[8] Nonetheless, for a working-class student whose cultural horizon was by and large still defined by the Navy and the auto industry – although both of his parents had Protestant affiliations, Hayden had not much religion to give up – the world of Bernard of Clairvaux, the French abbot and founder of the Cistercian order, may indeed have felt like a foreign country. Was it Bossenbrook, with his "fascination for apocalyptic and revolutionary social movements," who first stimulated White's interest in how Bernard and his reforming monastic order began to challenge the church administration in Rome?[9]

In graduate school in Ann Arbor, White channeled his interest into what he called a social-scientific study of the long-term causes of the papal schism of 1130. It may be helpful, at this point, to recall that this schism had erupted when Gregorio Papereschi (Innocentius II) and Pietro Pierleone (Anacletus II), each supported by large groups of Roman cardinals, had both presented themselves as the legitimate successor to Pope Honorius II (1124–30). Although the conflict had initially seemed to be won by Anacletus, Innocentius' claim had gained support at a council in Étampes, attended by Bernard of Clairvaux. In spite of this council's attempts to settle the conflict, peace had returned only after the death of Anacletus in 1138.

In the introduction to his dissertation, White declared that his study of this schism aimed, first of all, to be "objective," in the sense of undistorted by the apologetic tendencies that had characterized Roman Catholic and Protestant historiography (3).[10] Second, church quarrels were to be studied "in much the same way that a social scientist would analyze a political revolution" (15). This meant, among other things, that White aimed to study the papal schism in terms of group interests, power struggles and leadership competition, rather than in terms of lawfulness, legitimacy or theological appropriateness. He was especially interested in the "value systems" that had held competing groups together and suggested that these ideologies, in good sociological manner, could best be classified by means of Weberian ideal types.

This fascination for Weberian-inspired sociology antedated both the rapid growth of social history in the American historical profession, which would start in the late 1950s, and the large-scale entrance of Weberian concepts such as "legitimization," "class," "charisma," and "bureaucracy" into American sociology.[11] It is likely that at least part of White's interest in this Weberian sociological theory was stimulated by two of his supervisors, Palmer Throop and Frank Grace.[12] Bossenbrook may have been instrumental as well. As an undergraduate, White read with him Gerd Tellenbach's *Church, State, and Christian Society at the Time of the Investiture Contest* (1940), a Weberian-inspired book that served as a model for White's thesis.[13] And although I will argue below that his two-year stay in Rome decisively changed White's theoretical preferences, he may have encountered Weberian sociology in Italy, too. With its emphases on value-freedom and objectivity, it provided post-war Italian intellectuals with means for moving beyond the legacy of "neo-idealist" thought, which by that time was almost universally accused of "relativism" and soft-heartedness towards the Mussolini regime.[14]

Applied to the papal schism, White's sociological mode of inquiry resulted in a lengthy, massively documented narrative, which described the efforts of two competing schools of ecclesiastical thought trying to gain access to the Roman curia (the college of cardinals responsible for papal elections). Using a pair of ideal types from Weber's *Wirtschaft und Gesellschaft*, White characterized these schools as social movements adhering to "charismatic" and "bureaucratic" leadership ideals, respectively. The tenth-century moment of Cluny counted as an example of the former, whereas Pope Gregory

VIII, with his "purely legalistic view" of the papal office (49), was a typical representative of the latter. A great part of White's thesis, then, is an account of how both of these groups emerged, how their mutual tensions increased over time, and how the schism that eventually occurred in 1130 was "the institutional expression" of a long-existing "ideological split" (420). In the terminology of *Metahistory*, this narrative about competing leadership ideals could be characterized as a tragedy, especially insofar as, under the given circumstances, a bitter conflict in the curia was almost unavoidable.

White's Ph.D. thesis was never published, but supplied the material for two articles on Roman Gregorianism. Whereas in White's thesis the distinctions between charismatic and bureaucratic leadership ideals had already been schematic, the types were even more contrasted in these published essays. "Otherworldly" monasticism was put over against "purely material" interpretations of church power; moral reform against administration of *temporalia*; "the prophet-reformer" against institutionally defined church leadership. The moral ideal of a "return to the primitive Church" and the "administrative means envisaged for its realization" were portrayed as "fundamentally incompatible, if not directly opposed." With reference to Jesus' Sermon on the Mount – "It is written, but I say to you" – White even suggested that charismatic religious leaders typically legitimized themselves by criticizing bureaucratic practices. If such contrasts happened to coincide with generational differences, as had been the case in the monastery of Cluny, "the conditions for schism" had been created.[15]

Before examining what led White to this interpretation of twelfth-century church politics, it is worth noting that his schematic approach provoked the irritation of his colleagues no less than the tropological scheme in *Metahistory* would do in later decades. Critics pointed out that White's juxtaposition of Gregorianism and ascetic monasticism failed to acknowledge the extent to which both movements had been closely interwoven and, in some cases, represented by the same people. White was blamed, moreover, for using his Weberian ideal types not as heuristic instruments, but as descriptive labels – thereby suggesting that the conceptual distinctness of his ideal types was not, as Weber would have said, a provisional tool for ordering "irrational" historical realities, but a feature of ideologies and social groups themselves. At a more detailed level, White's interpretation of Bernard of Clairvaux and the *crise clunisienne* received ample amounts of criticism. Gerd Tellenbach, of all people, concluded that White asked relevant questions, but failed to give adequate answers.[16]

White's covering law model

What, then, was so controversial about White's approach? It was one thing that White assumed an "incompatibility" between what others saw as merely different aspects of Bernard's personality. But it was another that he superimposed a model upon a reality that had arguably been far less well ordered than the model could account for. According to this model, outlined in the introduction to White's thesis, all leaders face the challenge of convincing the people that their strategies, rather than others, are most effective in realizing the goals that "the masses" expect their leaders to attain. As soon as these "masses" become dissatisfied with the existing strategies or ask for different political goals, the leaders will have to revise their policies. But the longer these leader figures have been in power, the more rationalized and bureaucratic their institutions tend to be. In consequence, discontented voices from the people will not easily manage to realize political change. But if such changes fail to happen, people will inevitably look around for alternatives: "If the goals of the mass change or if the leadership seems to be foresaking the ideal goals of the institution in the eyes of the mass, a schism results" (17). New, charismatic leaders will make their appearance and promise the people that they can fulfill their demands. They will claim access to political positions and threaten violence, while old leaders, in order to strengthen their positions, will take refuge in bureaucratic strategies and blame their competitors for unlawful behavior. Whereas the old leaders will regard the new ones as rebels, the latter will consider the former usurpers of power. "A propaganda war will follow in which each party will attempt to sway the mass into believing that its own program is the right program," White assumed. "The success or failure of the revolutionary group hinges upon its ability to identify itself with the desires of the mass" (18). Once these new, charismatic leaders succeed in displacing the old ones, they in their turn, however, will become vulnerable to the danger of losing their charisma, too. If this happens, the cycle described by the model will start over again.

Influences of Karl Mannheim, Arnold J. Toynbee, and, particularly, Max Weber can be recognized in this model. Mannheim's analysis of increasing rationalization and bureaucratization in economic institutions functioned as a paradigm for how White explained the rise of "anti-charismatic" leadership ideals. A label for those characters in White's narrative who personified this anti-charismatic leadership style was provided by Mannheim's "manager type." In turn, Toynbee's "creative minorities," "challenges," and "responses" found their way into White's explanation of the resistance that these managers typically meet. But most importantly, White's thesis can be read as a lengthy attempt to apply Weber's "routinization of charisma" to the study of medieval church leadership. If there is one *Leitmotiv* in White's Ph.D. thesis, it is the notion that charismatic leadership will sooner or later be rationalized, mechanized, and institutionalized, thereby becoming as bureaucratic as the leadership forms it originally intended to challenge.[17]

To those associating White's name with strong resistance against Carl Hempel's "covering law model," it may come as a surprise that in White's dissertation, this scheme effectively functioned as a covering law. It perfectly fitted Hempel's definition of such a general law ("In every case where an event of a specified kind C occurs at a certain place and time, an event of a specified kind E will occur at a place and time which is related in a specified manner to the place and time of the occurrence of the first event"). Of course, not in every case did White precisely specify how event E was caused by factor C: Hempel would certainly have found White guilty of often providing only "explanation sketches." But when White explicitly discussed the causes of a leadership transition – "How had Hildebrand been able to launch his reform program?" or "Why had Bernard received so much support?" – the model outlined above served as his explanatory principle. Moreover, as a "universal empirical hypothesis," this model enabled White to write about papal attitudes "typical of the final stages in the development of a hierocracy" and to compare a certain stage in the development of the papacy with a similar phase in economic corporations (248, 249). In short, the model provided White with a framework that helped to reveal some patterns in the world of twelfth-century church politics.[18]

Although rejected by what Peter Novick calls an "overwhelming majority" of American historians, covering law models like this one made more than a one-time appearance in White's early work. For example, in Ibn Khaldūn, the fourteenth-century Arabic scholar, White discovered a "mechanism" or set of general principles describing the rise and fall of human civilizations. In Christopher Dawson, the twentieth-century Catholic historian, White also found a law-like phase theory of cultural transition. Although he recognized the "non-historical element" in every scheme that superimposes regularities or coherences upon the past, White in later years even defended Giambattista Vico's law of the *ricorsi* against its historicist critics and showed appreciation for Oswald Spengler's model of cultural decline. Also, one might argue that the tropological scheme outlined in *Metahistory* – especially the transition from metaphor via metonymy and synecdoche to irony – was nothing but a variation on the type of covering law models that so clearly fascinated White in the early days of his scholarly life.[19]

Returning once more to White's medievalist critics, it is clear that the use of a law-type of model *as such* did not elicit their disapproval. The issue, rather, was how White could believe that heuristic devices such as his self-assembled covering law model provided not merely ideal-typical principles of explanation, but adequate descriptions of how historical agents had thought and behaved. In other words, what led White to assume that a Bernard of Clairvaux or a Pons of Melgueil, abbot of Cluny, had defended his religious leadership ideals as consistently as White's model expected him to do?

"Ideology" or "value orientation"

To answer this question, we must examine White's concept of "ideology." In his thesis, White explained that this (by then increasingly fashionable) concept referred to the "value orientation" of a social group. Following the anthropologist Clyde Kluckhohn, White defined such a value orientation as "a conception, explicit or implicit, distinctive of an individual or characteristic of a group, of the desirable which influences the selection from available modes, means and ends of action" (15).[20] According to this definition, the value orientation of a social group, or "what the Germans might call the *Weltanschauung* or *Ideologie*" (15–16), identifies the normative principles according to which a social group tries to live. Like Kluckhohn, White assumed that every group of people is guided by some normative principles and therefore adhering to an ideology.

This is, indeed, a broad definition. For White, ideology did not have the pejorative meaning that Marx had assigned to the term when defining it as a distorted way of understanding reality. Nor did White accept Mannheim's conception of ideology as a "situationally transcendent" idea that cannot be realized in practice.

White's use of ideology rather followed the example of Vere Gordon Childe, the celebrated archaeologist, who had equated ideology with all ideals valued in a society. Like the interchangeable concepts of "value orientation" and *Weltanschauung*, White's notion of ideology included beliefs about the nature of reality and the nature of the good life. It encompassed ideas about what is and ought to be in a society. In short, it designated a wide range of basic beliefs that somehow guide an individual's moral life.[21]

How did White envision this to work? One reason why he paid so much attention to ideologies was his conviction that human behavior usually follows from the moral and metaphysical beliefs that individuals hold to be true. The reasons people have for acting in one way rather than in another can often be derived from their basic beliefs. Thus, if historians ask why religious leaders in eleventh-century Cluny or twelfth-century Rome came to favor "bureaucratic" ideas, the most plausible answer does not lie in social circumstances or unconscious drives, but in "the explanatory statements, norms of behavior, and ideals of the group" (16). To White, therefore, an ideology could serve as an *explanans* of how people act and think. Nothing in the methodology section of his thesis – written in that remarkably bold prose that would also characterize "The Burden of History" (1966) and the introduction to *Tropics of Discourse* (1978) – indicates that White reflected on the limits of this methodological individualism, on non-intentional backgrounds of human action, on willingly or unwillingly inconsistent behavior, or on the role of feelings and emotions in human decision-making. The author simply assumed that individuals normally act in accordance with the norms and values of their group.[22]

As I have shown elsewhere, this principle informed much of what White had to say about Pons, Bernard, and their allies. In his portrayal, none of these church leaders ever deviated from the ideologies that White had attributed to them. Confronted with an interpretational puzzle, about the consistency of Bernard's politics in 1122, White even rather chose to speculate than to accept that people can act irrationally or behave differently than how they themselves claim to prefer to act.[23] Accordingly, the amount of "means–ends rationality" (or *Zweckrationalität*, in Weber's vocabulary) that White attributed to human behavior was much larger than, for instance, his inclination to ponder "the crooked timber of humanity" (Immanuel Kant) or the conditions that so often cause human aims to miss their target. In Weberian terms, one might say that White's interpretation of these medieval churchmen – not to say his view of human nature in general – rested on the assumption of an unfailing commitment to ultimate values. Like Weber, White postulated the "essence" of a human person in "a constant and intrinsic relation to certain ultimate 'values' and 'meanings' of life." While resisting emotional weakness and distraction, the Weberian personality strictly regulates his life according to the values he regards as important. "[O]nly he who is devoted *solely* to the work at hand has 'personality,'" as Weber had famously stated. In his younger years, White likewise expected historical agents to be faithful to their beliefs.[24]

The disenchantment of the world

Weber's influence on the young White was considerable. As documented in a number of articles written back in Detroit, in the second half of the 1950s, traces of this influence are visible, not only in White's *reflections* on worldviews, but also in his *own* worldview. Unsurprisingly, perhaps, for a student who had experienced existentialism as a secular form of liberation theology,[25] Weber's thesis about the "disenchantment of the world" – the gradual disappearance of God, religion, and magic from the Western world – was convincing to the point of almost being a truism. His dissertation, on a world still dominated by religion, hardly allowed White to elaborate on this.[26] But his subsequent essays show that White, much like Weber, felt an urgency to insist on the "fundamental fact" that modern individuals are "destined to live in a godless and prophetless time."[27] The notion of the "secular" embraced in this argument is of crucial importance for understanding White's later philosophy of history. Three things must be noted.

First, White's essays on Collingwood, Toynbee, and Dawson, composed as wide-ranging introductions with critical comments, reflected the same fascination for worldviews and ultimate beliefs that characterized his medievalist studies. White paid attention to how these "anti-positivist" philosophers of history conceived of the relation between nature and culture, the goal of the historical process, and, in particular, the moral instruction that may (or may not) be derived from the study of history. Typically, whereas Toynbee was usually criticized on empirical grounds, White only objected to his views of culture and religion. Dawson's worldview was said to be indebted to a conservative Catholicism with an "anti-historical" and Western-European bias. And Collingwood, apart from being chastised for his metaphysical speculation, was accused of a "purely relativistic" understanding of truth.[28] So, both White's analysis of medieval thought and his study of modern historical theory focused on their underlying presuppositions.

Second, while not explicitly invoking covering laws, White vigorously argued that worldviews must be revised as circumstances change. In terms borrowed from the anthropologist Robert Redfield, White stated that Western civilization (a term then still in vogue) was characterized by a domination of a "technical order" over the "moral order." This means that scientific and technical control over nature determines how people order their life-environment and respond to risks and challenges. Because of this priority, science and technology set the limits for religion and morality, rather than vice versa. Concretely, White argued that Christians would do better not to protest against the modern "scientific worldview." They rather ought to follow the example of twentieth-century Hindus, who, in Sarvepalli Radhakrishnan's phrasing, can "find God in a test-tube":

> [I]f Christianity is to survive, it must abandon the older ritual order or at least modify it radically; this does not mean that the kernel of the Christian ethic, as contained in the Sermon on the Mount, will have to be abandoned, only its historical accretions. If it is argued that Christianity without its historical accretions is not Christianity, I can only say that such a view confirms the anti-Christian attitude which identifies that religion with a given culture. If in fact Christianity is so limited, then it deserves to pass with the culture which gave it birth.[29]

Third, White explained that the increase of scientific knowledge in the West, with its abandonment of a "geocentrically oriented cosmology," had disclosed nothing less than the true nature of human life. In a passage revealing his affinity with existentialist notions of fate and responsibility, White stated resolutely:

> Modern man must, whether he will or no, assume responsibilities for his own actions rather than have them exorcised by a priesthood claiming contact with the one, true God. If earlier societies seemed better adjusted or more harmonious than our own, it is because State and Church acted together to destroy individual responsibility rather than encourage it. For good or for evil, modern science has broken through these older compulsives and offered to man responsibility for everything he does. It is a terrifying gift but one eminently worthy of its recipient.[30]

Although this passage may raise questions, such as whether the sciences are as morally neutral as the argument seems to assume, it helps to explain why White considered Bernard an "anachronism" in his own time (595), why he rejected Collingwood's metaphysics, and why he insisted on the disenchanted nature of the modern world. White agreed with Weber, not only about the inappropriateness of moral beliefs that fail to correspond to the empirically known world, but also about the backwardness of "weak souls who cannot bear the face of today's life." In fact, whereas Weber was personally still afraid that the technical order might result in a "polar night of icy darkness and hardness," White's firm statement on freedom and responsibility reads like a consoling answer: "It is a terrifying gift but one eminently worthy of its recipient."[31]

From historicism to sociology

Although White continued to harp on this string for the rest of his career – freedom and responsibility became core elements in his thinking about history – his stay in Italy forced him to rethink at least part of his enthusiasm for Weber's typologies. This was mainly due to Carlo Antoni, the disciple of Croce who introduced White to the legacy of his then just-deceased mentor. Another American student in Rome in the mid-1950s, who also enjoyed Antoni's hospitality and direction, described the philosopher as someone "who knows Croce better than Croce knew himself and whose seasoned philosophical bearing was both sympathetic and critical towards Croce."[32] One reason for this identification with Italian historicism, as represented by Croce and Giovanni Gentile, was Antoni's distrust of German sociology. This put him at sharp odds with many of his Italian contemporaries, who used Weber, Georg Simmel, Ferdinand Tönnies, and Werner Sombart to dissociate themselves from "Fascist idealism." What got lost in this transition, Antoni feared, was a genuinely historical way of thinking. In his *Dallo storicismo alla sociologia* (1940), he had argued that this loss was already evident in Germany, where great historicists such as Ranke had been abandoned in favor of Weber and Ernst Troeltsch. Intrigued by this argument, and encouraged (again) by Bossenbrook, White decided to translate this book into English.[33]

From History to Sociology was a typically Crocean book, in the sense that it advocated a fully historicized understanding of human thought and rejected everything that aspired to be timeless or universally applicable. For Antoni, "ahistorical" approaches in the human sciences included in particular the typological fashions that had first threatened and later replaced the historicist tradition in nineteenth-century Germany. Speaking about Wilhelm Dilthey, for example, Antoni complained that this philosopher had explained the rise of *Weltanschauungen* by means of laws "analogous to those which described the formation of crystals." To Antoni, this could not but result in a concept of worldview that regarded the basic forms of human thought as "schematic and static entities," or as crystals, indeed, "which always remain the same in their type":

> This is the point of departure for that typology (*Typenlehre*) which is to be found everywhere in German intellectual life during the first quarter of the century: in the psychological typology (*Psychotypik*) of Spranger and Jaspers, in Wölfflin's forms of vision, and in German sociology. In fact, once the real movement and novelty of history were denied, it was inevitable that history be transformed into typology and sociology.

One wonders whether the word "inevitable" does not belong to the very discourse that Antoni intended to criticize. It illustrates, however, the anger with which Antoni observed the spread of typological modes of analysis. For Antoni, Weber's work in particular was an outstanding example of what happens when historians cease "to believe in history," that is, when they no longer adhere to Romantic-historicist notions of development, unfolding, and progress. A historiography modeled after Weberian sociology had "to confine itself to the construction of a gallery containing portraits of types of civilizations"; "There is lacking in this indifferent plurality of doctrines the negative moment, the insufficiency which translates itself into the painful need for and progression towards the new." In other words, how could these German thinkers have forgotten the basic historicist insight that history is always evolving and adapting itself to new situations, thereby displaying a creative vitality that can never be adequately captured in models and laws?[34]

In his introduction, White did not simply echo Antoni's "fairly desperate words," as Russell Jacoby argues,[35] but showed that he did not (yet) unreservedly share Antoni's fears. Ironically, he explained that German historical thought, which Antoni saw threatened by typologies, could be categorized into four ideal types. The first, called "objective history," was associated with the name of Ranke (who by then, especially in the United States, was often regarded as a forerunner of modern positivism).[36] In addition, White distinguished between three types of historicism: metaphysical historicism, as represented by Hegel; naturalistic historicism, associated with Weber; and aesthetic historicism, epitomized by Nietzsche and Burckhardt. In classifying these historicisms, White so rigidly defined his categories – asserting, for example, that in metaphysical historicism "action is subordinated to thought," while in naturalistic historicism the reverse is true – that he demonstrated more affinity with Weber's typologies than with Antoni's aversion to them.[37]

Still, White agreed with Antoni that Weber's naturalistic historicism put too little emphasis on how "history" differs from "nature" and that, consequently, it ran the risk of ignoring the freedom and responsibility that, above all other things, distinguish the human from the animal. For this reason, White began to lean more towards aesthetic historicism, which, in his own words, gave "individual human creativity (the demands of the will) and universal human responsibility (the demands of the reason) their proper place in a unified and total vision of reality." If this aesthetic historicism is indeed best represented by thinkers like Nietzsche, then did White's understanding of proper proportions leave room for what he would later praise as Nietzsche's "surgical operation on the historical thought of his own time" or the philosopher's "liberation of the creative imagination from restrictions placed on it by thought itself"? White, by then still far from the "ironic nihilism" that Eugene Golob would later detect in *Metahistory*, admitted that aesthetic historicism sometimes went too far, especially in aborting "the quest for any criterion of establishing historical truth" and thereby distorting the "unified and total vision of reality" that apparently had come to serve as White's ideal.[38] As we shall see in the next section, the need for such a balanced worldview – one that would acknowledge the relative truth in every modern "ism," but carefully avoid overemphasizing some aspects of human existence at the expense of others – soon became a central theme in White's appropriation of Croce.

A Croce partisan

In 1961–2, White spent another year in Italy, on a Social Science Research Council Fellowship awarded "for research in Italy on the relation between science and social thought in Italy, 1543–1643."[39] One may wonder: what led White to change his focus from church leaders in the Middle Ages to scientists in the post-Copernican Renaissance? Presumably, it was the Western Civilization course White taught at Rochester that stimulated his interest in what he called "the breakdown of medieval civilization and the beginnings of modern times." The typical goal of such courses, after all, was to trace, in a rather teleological manner, the origins and history of the modern, liberal, capitalist world.[40] As we shall see in the next chapter, Italian scholarship in the century after Copernicus' death – the subject of White's proposed research – figured rather prominently in the textbook that emerged from his "Western Civ" course. Apart from this, however, the second of his *italienische Reisen* yielded not a single publication in the field of Renaissance studies.[41] Instead, White returned to Croce and wrote a piece in which all his earlier hesitation seemed to have melted away.

"The Abiding Relevance of Croce's Idea of History" (1963) reads like a profession of faith or, in its American context, as the confession of an emerging heretic. Most American historians by that time associated Croce with "relativism" in matters of historical thought. Frequently, the philosopher was mentioned in one breath with Carl L. Becker and Charles A. Beard, two notorious "relativists" in the American historical discipline.[42] Maurice Mandelbaum, a philosopher with whom White had worked as a graduate student, had denounced Croce as a dangerous representative of "contemporary historical relativism." Richard Burks, though, instructor at White's *alma mater*, had been more sympathetic, writing with admiration about Croce's attempt to integrate Romantic and positivist conceptions of history.[43] White went even further: he molded Croce into a model for historians in troubled times.

Given White's later interest in historical narratives, one might expect that the author felt attracted by the early Croce, who had tried to subsume history "under the concept of art."[44] However, although White made some appreciative remarks on these directions in Croce's thought, he singled out three other aspects. What fascinated White in the first place was Croce's emphasis on the complexity of things and the impossibility of fitting reality into a single formula. Writing at a time when ideologies of various kinds claimed to have found a solution to economic decline, moral confusion, and political tension, Croce had warned against straightforward answers to difficult questions. In White's own words:

> Croce's historical works were a sustained warning to Europe against the dangers of simplicism in thought and fanaticism in action in their

constant repetition of the conviction that even the highest ideals become arid and oppressive when they are pushed to the outer limits of their potential development. Thus, both his *Theory and history of historiography* and his *History as thought and as action* were written as antidotes to the fascination of utopian programs, simplicist political theories, and monistic conceptions of man, society, and human history.[45]

White referred here to Croce's claim that modern ideologies such as Marxism erred, not in calling attention to a particular aspect of reality, but in overemphasizing such a singular aspect, thereby reducing the complexity of human life and overreacting against other ideologies.[46] As we saw above, White had followed a similar line of thought when he had argued that metaphysical, naturalistic, and aesthetic historicism were not so much wrong as rather one-sided. This anti-reductionism, White continued, also characterized Croce's understanding of the human self. Croce considered human nature as "a problem rather than a datum." Human nature is neither fixed nor settled; it is something which has to be realized again and again by human individuals. Human nature is what human beings, each in their unique historical particularities, want to be, rather than what they are told to be. White, then, approved of what José Ortega y Gasset had famously said: "Man has no nature, what he has is ... history." In other words, there are no universal or pre-existing models of human nature; there is only a freedom for human individuals to realize what they themselves regard as their human responsibilities.[47]

Not surprisingly, then, freedom emerged as a second key term in White's exegesis of Croce. In a rather anti-traditionalist mode, White put much weight on the freedom to act according to self-chosen values, rather than to values derived from the past. He did not deny, of course, that human action is in many ways constrained by limits imposed by the past. But the way in which individuals respond to their circumstances can never be derived from the past. In White's interpretation of Croce, human beings have a freedom to decide for themselves how to live:

> [H]istorical inquiry itself shows the impossibility of arriving at any *simple* formula for deciding where good and evil lie in any particular historical event or for predetermining choices in future existential situations ... History confirms our awareness of a moral sense in man but no particular moral code (except of the highest generality) can be derived from its study. If history teaches anything at all, it shows

us that moral decisions must be made with something less than complete knowledge of the situations in which they are called for and as little knowledge of the ultimate effects of those decisions upon the surrounding world.

Consequently, human beings always have to make up their own minds about how to act. They never enjoy full control over the situations in which they find themselves and, for this reason, always need a good dose of courage to decide what is right or wrong in a given situation. So, although history does not give any concrete indications as to how to live a responsible human life, it shows that, in every situation, it is the human individual who decides about good and evil. If, then, anything can be gained from the study of history, it is the insight that human beings are not spectators, but actors on the stage of history: "[H]istory alone ... provides us with *living* models of human beings willing to act within the limits thus given and teaches us that, potentially at least, we too possess a similar courage."[48]

This brings us, thirdly, to Croce's moral commitment. In White's view, the historian's moral responsibility did not consist in offering concrete suggestions as to how to solve unemployment in the 1930s, how to deal with the Versailles Treaty, or how to resist a Fascist regime. On the contrary, for White, Croce's greatness lay in *not* providing any answers, in *not* presenting "lessons from history." Croce's profound moral sensitivity was demonstrated by his *refusal* to draw straight lines from the past to the present and to leave his contemporaries the freedom to decide for themselves about good and evil. Take, for example, Croce's *Storia d'Europa nel secolo decimonono*. This controversial book on nineteenth-century liberalism – published in 1932, when Mussolini had been in office for a full decade – ended with the outbreak of World War I, thereby leaving the rise of fascism in the 1920s safely untouched. In an epilogue, the author had explained that the post-war crisis of Western liberalism asked for participation rather than for reflection. The rise of fascism was something that should be dealt with in the sphere of action, that is to say, in a sphere Croce was not allowed to discuss as a historian. White fully endorsed this argument:

His history of Europe ends in 1915, not because he was unable to "explain" fascism – that he could have done as easily as any of his contemporaries – but because for him the idea about which he was writing reached at that moment a point of critical decision. He knew that World War I constituted a failure of liberals, and from his own experience he knew that the challenge presented by the war had been too much for his own generation to cope with. It therefore remained for the next generation to choose between the ideal that had been betrayed and the easy faiths that claimed to transcend that ideal but were in reality merely manifestations of the betrayal. There was a great humility in Croce's willingness to forego the part of lawmaker or prophet even in the most critical situations and to content himself with the more difficult role of reminding his readers of their obligations in the definition of their own destinies.[49]

In later years, White never again wrote an essay as laudatory as this one. Read in the context of his early work, the article shows that, after a period of profound indebtedness to Weber, White found a second source of inspiration in Croce. Following David Roberts, one might even call the White of 1963 a "Croce partisan," as long as one does not forget that White's admiration of the Italian philosopher by no means implied a radical dissociation from the German sociologist.[50] As we shall see, White continued to employ "ahistorical" schemes and typologies, especially in his structuralist period. Moreover, Weber's "disenchantment of the world" and his observation that "precisely the ultimate and most sublime values have retreated from public life" led White to emphasize human freedom and responsibility in a manner totally consistent with Croce's moral philosophy. Likewise, in his understanding of the human self, Weber emphasized moral self-determination as much as Croce insisted on the self-realization of human nature through history. Both Weber and Croce, moreover, helped White conceive of history not as a result of impersonal powers or fortuitous circumstances, but "as a product of human intelligence and will."[51]

Interestingly, this is also where both Weber and Croce, in White's interpretation, shared common ground with some of the existentialist authors White had read with Bossenbrook. For example, Croce agreed with Camus that human beings "are without the heavenly searchlight," that they must always make their own decisions, that they have an inexhaustible creativity to do so, and that, last but not least, "there is a sense in which the individual risks his whole life with every decision." In Roberts's analysis, "Croce and Camus can even be considered colleagues in the attempt to build a post-Christian, non-Marxist humanism. Each sought to show how we could continue on our way, on the basis of the best of our humanity, even when we have abandoned all hope of deliverance or redemption – in another world or in this one."[52] What our discussion of

White's oeuvre so far has revealed is that White's first theoretical reflections took their point of departure precisely in this quasi-existentialist quest.

Questions in/about history

In many respects, the graduate student who, in 1955, completed his thesis on the papal schism of 1130 did not resemble the White most familiar to modern readers. Fascinated by the social sciences, committed to a form of "objectivity," and deeply involved in the exegesis of medieval text fragments, this student produced exactly the type of historical writing that White would later criticize for being overspecialized and culturally irrelevant. However, some striking continuities can be observed as well. A focus on worldviews and tacitly held presuppositions characterizes both White's dissertation and his *Metahistory*. The use of ahistorical typologies and grand-scale evolutionary models, so important in White's medievalist studies, would characterize a good many later publications as well – although White's growing attentiveness to what Jacoby calls the "specificity of history" would put such schemes in increasingly dialectical tension with the particularity of past events and the freedom ascribed to historical agents.[53] Even more important, perhaps, is that this freedom of the human self, especially in matters of moral decision-making, would come to play a key role in White's thinking. As subsequent chapters will demonstrate, the dream of a life lived according to self-chosen values – "a terrifying gift but one eminently worthy of its recipient" – became the driving vision for almost all of White's philosophy of history.

Whereas Hans Kellner traces this vision back to Kant, White's immersion in Antoni and Croce makes clear that these Italian philosophers were more immediate sources of inspiration for what one might call this "humanist historicism."[54] Speaking, therefore, about "the Italian White," this chapter has presented White's research periods in Italy, his encounter with Antoni, and his deep fascination for Croce as formative for his (future) thoughts on history and historical scholarship. Moreover, it was in Italy that White began to exchange the study of "questions *in* history" for that of "questions *about* history."[55] Although, for some years, he continued to write book reviews in medieval history – as late as 1964 he spoke about "we medievalists"[56] – his work became increasingly focused not on the solution of historiographical problems, but on questions of how the past should be studied, what benefits result from such a study, or how human beings can be liberated from a false sense of history. The next chapter will show how White, in an increasingly radical stance, addressed these questions in the years prior to *Metahistory*.

2

Liberation Historiography: The Politics of History

Another eulogy on Crocean liberalism, this time not in the form of a discursive essay, but along the lines of an enthusiastically written history of Western science and philosophy, appeared in 1966 as *The Emergence of Liberal Humanism*. Although this textbook, stemming from White's Western Civilization classes at Rochester, was rather conventional in its genre and style – the book chronologically told about great men and great ideas that helped bring about "the new idea of nature," "the new political outlook," and "the new religious outlook" in Renaissance and Enlightenment Europe – it openly sang the praises of Crocean ideas, such as those appropriated by White in the essay with which the previous chapter ended. Co-authored with Rochester colleague Willson H. Coates, *The Emergence of Liberal Humanism* was a rather Whiggish account of how freedom of thought and toleration had come to triumph over "dogmatism" and "fanaticism" in early-modern thought. Just like White's Ph.D. thesis, the book explained events from ideas rather than vice versa, presented secularization as a healthy liberation from metaphysical speculation, and embraced ideals such as individual self-determination and freedom of thought. "In its adventurous speculations and confident use of rational and empirical processes we recognize in the intellectual history of Western Europe a certain grandeur," White and Coates told their readers. And, quite frankly: "[F]reedom of conscience and liberty in all its aspects constitute the most important tradition of Western civilization."[1]

When, four years later, a sequel volume appeared, this optimistic tone had changed dramatically. Still subscribing to what the book called "liberal humanism," this second volume was much more defensive. The authors tried to explain that "liberal humanism is not yet ready for a Western European scrap heap" and explicitly addressed some "inherent weaknesses" in the humanist tradition, such as its tendency towards intellectual reflection at the cost of political commitment. Especially under totalitarian circumstances – in the mid-1960s, "fascism" and "totalitarianism" became hotly debated topics in the United States[2] – such a withdrawal to the realm of thought was not only dangerous, but immoral as well. Therefore, wouldn't humanism equal to the challenges of the twentieth century need to be more activist, more aggressive? These considerations changed White's appreciation of humanism in its Crocean version. Volume II concluded that Croce had been "irrelevant" during the Mussolini era: "Though Italians like Croce, Ruggiero, and Salvemini were among the most eloquent defenders of twentieth-century liberalism, theirs was a rhetorical liberalism not equal to the challenges of its most formidable twentieth-century antagonist, the totalitarianism of the Right."[3]

How is this to be explained? What happened to White and his thoughts about history after that exultant piece on Croce, written near the end of his Italian period? This chapter traces how White, faced by challenges of "mass society," "technological culture," and "fascism," came to emphasize the need for historians to become more activist and to commit themselves more actively to political ideals than Croce would have allowed them. More particularly, White wanted historians to engage with an avant-garde of the left, which not merely allowed individuals to live their lives according to self-chosen values, but actively contributed to the liberation of those whose social conditions had not yet allowed them to think and act on their own behalf. White, then, became an advocate of what this chapter calls a "liberation historiography" (a word coined in analogy to liberation philosophy and theology), which in White's case coupled an existentialist fascination for freedom with a Marxist-inspired political vision. Finally, this chapter shows how White, in a clear departure from his Italian period, also began to see his own task, as a philosopher of history, in thoroughly political terms.

Why history?

It all began, not long after White's return from Italy, with two reviews. In the first, White argued that history as written by historians is not necessarily the most adequate answer to history as experienced by individuals. What, if anything, White asked, have professional historians to offer to people trying to make sense of their passage through history? "The historical world-view is no more natural than any other world-view; and so, if such a world-view is to be justified, it must be justified by appeal to a more general human activity which encompasses both history and other forms of knowing – and shows that history provides us with meaningful insights into ourselves that no other discipline provides."[4]

A similar attempt to challenge the obvious – what is it that we call history and why do we devote a discipline to it? – appeared, ironically, at the apex of that discipline, in the newsletter of the American Historical Association. In a review of John Higham's *History*, White wondered aloud why history had become such a culturally irrelevant discipline. What had happened since the early nineteenth century, when historians like Alexis de Tocqueville and Jules Michelet had played major roles in European intellectual life as mediators "between past and future?" What had caused that enormous decline in the reputation of historical scholarship among novelists, philosophers, and politicians alike? In White's judgment, Higham had ignored the urgent question of whether history perhaps *deserved* to be marginalized, given its lack of interest in how other, more culturally up-to-date intellectuals perceived of the study of history:

> There is no mention of the radical a-historical views of N. O. Brown, of Marcuse's neo-Marxism, or ... of Camus, Sartre, Heidegger, and Merleau-Ponty, all of whom have advanced important arguments against history. ... The question for the historian today is not *how* history ought to be studied, but *if* it ought to be studied at all. This is the question posed in literature from Ibsen to Camus, in philosophy from Nietzsche to Sartre, in theology from Barth to Tillich, and in social theory from Weber to Popper.[5]

At stake in this question was not merely the adequacy of certain historiographical schools, but nothing less than "the worth of historical awareness" as such. Judging by the number of waking hours they spend in the study of the past, historians seem to assume that the past deserves attention. True as this may be from a scholarly point of view, what is it that average human beings, engaged in the struggles of everyday life, can learn from the past? Doesn't the mode of thought called history suggest that a solution to contemporary problems can somehow be found in the past? Doesn't it underestimate the extent to which present-day problems differ from previous ones, and discourage people from solving their problems by their own means?

Intrigued by these questions, the journal *History and Theory* invited White to expand his argument into what became his most daring and most provocative article ever: "The Burden of History" (1966).[6] Most striking, perhaps, to an audience interested in what White called "the Popper/Hempel/Dray/Donagan/Mandelbaum/ Gallie, etc., etc., controversy" (on matters of historical explanation),[7] was the author's invocation of literary characters, often from modernist novels and plays, as witnesses against a historical way of thinking. Among those were Dorothea Brooke, from George Eliot's *Middlemarch*, who broke off her relationship with a historian who had lost his interest in everyday life; Hedda Gabler, from Henrik Ibsen's play, who went literally crazy over a newly wed husband who appeared unable to see the difference between a honeymoon and a research trip; and the historian Antoine Roquentin, from Sartre's *La nausée*, who produced nothing because he lacked the courage and the will to live a life of his own. These examples intended to show, first of all, how much historians in twentieth-century fiction had come to be perceived as bats flittering in the shadows of times long gone: "In the world in which we daily live, anyone who studies the past 'as an end in itself' must appear as either an antiquarian, fleeing from the problems of the present into a purely personal past, or a kind of cultural necrophile, that is, one who finds in the dead and dying a value he can never find in the living."[8]

White's first (of four) points, then, was that historians, for reasons of cultural relevance, had better listen attentively to "the problems of the present" or the "problems peculiar to our own time" (a phrase recurring time and again in White's writings from this period). What these problems were, or how historians might respond to them, had not yet become entirely clear. White emphasized, though, that historians would do wrong to explain how present-day problems had emerged from the past. In an almost existentialist manner, he insisted on the incomparability of cultural epochs and on the urgent need to challenge perceived continuities between past and present: "[W]e require a history that will educate us to discontinuity more than ever before; for discontinuity, disruption, and chaos is our lot."[9]

This brought White to a second point, announced in the title of his essay. If human beings learn to see themselves as disconnected

from the past, and their lives as undetermined by the decisions of
earlier generations, they may come to realize what an enormous
amount of freedom they enjoy (that "terrifying gift but one eminently worthy of its recipient"). If human beings become aware of
the uniqueness of their situation and their liberty to follow their
own ideas, they might rise up and gather the courage to become
architects of their own lives, rather than products of traditions and
conventions. Not unlike Nietzsche, then, White hoped to rescue the
human self from its captivity by history. He wanted to prevent
history from undermining "that impulse to heroic exertion that
might give a peculiarly human, if only transient, meaning to an
absurd world."[10]

Against this background, the title of White's essay appears
ambiguous. On the one hand, there is the "substantive burden
imposed upon the present by the past in the form of outmoded
institutions, ideas, and values" – an echo of White's imperative that
the moral order ought to adapt itself to the technical order – "but
also *the way of looking at the world* which gives to these outmoded
forms their specious authority." On the other, there is the burden,
or responsibility, of historians to help their audiences overcome that
dictate of a historical worldview. In White's own words:

> [T]he *burden of the historian* in our time is to re-establish the dignity
> of historical studies on a basis that will make them consonant with
> the aims and purposes of the intellectual community at large, that is,
> transform historical studies in such a way as to allow the historian
> to participate positively in the liberation of the present from *the
> burden of history*.[11]

White's third point, therefore, was the responsibility of the historian
to engage in such liberating activities. Like (again) Nietzsche and
other nineteenth-century thinkers – Hegel and Tocqueville come to
mind – White stated "that the task of the historian was less to
remind men of their obligation to the past than to force upon them
an awareness of how the past could be used to effect an ethically
responsible transition from present to future." This could imply two
things. First, in a good Crocean manner, historians might want to
show that history is always, at least in part, a product of human
decisions. This might remind their audiences that the present is
also, partly, human-made and that, accordingly, it can "be changed
or altered by further human action in precisely that degree." Second,
like Ejlert Lövberg in Ibsen's play (and rather unlike Croce),

historians might want to get rid of the historicist idea that they are not entitled to say anything about the present or the future. Isn't Lövberg's grand-scale history of human civilization far more inspiring, at least in Hedda's eyes, than the dull archival research of Jörgen Tesman? Unlike Tesman, Lövberg writes not merely about the past, but also about the present. Unlike Tesman, Lövberg makes no attempt to extinguish himself, as Ranke put it, but writes right from his heart, with the full force of his personality. Whereas Tesman's imagination is confined to the past, Lövberg, said White, "inspires in Hedda the hope that his vision may afford a possible release from the narrow world circumscribed by Tesman's fractured imagination."[12]

At this stage, one might wonder whether White would go so far as to abandon the entire historical discipline which he himself had got to know as a medievalist. Doesn't the "revolt against history in modern writing" suggest that the historical discipline is *passé*? Or doesn't White's line of reasoning suggest that he had begun to dissociate himself from "scientific" history as practiced since Ranke? In his 1966 essay, White appeared not yet prepared to draw this radical conclusion. True, he went to considerable lengths explaining that traditional understandings of historical scholarship had become outdated: "[H]istorians of this generation ... must be prepared to entertain the notion that history, as currently conceived, is a kind of historical accident, a product of a specific historical situation, and that, with the passing of the misunderstandings that produced that situation, history itself may lose its status as an autonomous and self-authenticating mode of thought." But the passage continued with a passionate plea for innovation among historians – not for discontinuance of their discipline. Instead of rejecting scientific history, as he would do in later years, White argued that history suffered from old-fashioned ideas of science. When historians speak of science, they do not, in general, think of post-Einsteinian quantum physics, but of the natural sciences that Herbert Spencer practiced, back in the nineteenth century. Likewise, when they speak about the artistic aspect of history, they have in mind, not the work of "action painters, kinetic sculptors, existentialist novelists, imagist poets, or *nouvelle vague* cinematographers," but the Biedermeier novels of a Walter Scott: "If this is the case, then artists and scientists alike are justified in criticizing historians, *not because they study the past*, but because they are studying it with *bad* science and *bad* art."[13]

White's fourth and final point, then, was a plea for studying the past from a conceptually more adequate perspective. By the mid twentieth century, White argued, philosophy of science (Karl Popper) and philosophy of art (Ernst Gombrich) had both accepted the constructivist nature of representation. In both areas, the insight had been gained that representations are always shaped by the questions, language, concepts, and imagination of the artist or scientist. Accordingly, it is impossible to maintain that there is only a single "realist" mode of representation. For what counts as realistic – is Cézanne a realist painter, or Picasso, or Mondriaan? – depends on one's own conceptual framework. Therefore, White continued, Scott's narrative mode of representation cannot be said to be more realistic than the modernist anti-narratives of Joyce or Kafka. Consequently, historians have no good reason to favor the former over the latter. And if they want to reduce the burden of history, they might do well to employ more avant-garde modes of representation. What a liberation effect would occur, for instance, if historians followed the example of *Life against Death* by Norman O. Brown, White's colleague at Rochester – a book that among the 1960s New Left enjoyed something of a cult status because of its Freudian-inspired anti-establishment approach to the past.[14]

All this made "The Burden of History" an eloquent statement of White's 1960s ideal of a historiography that makes the past available to present-day individuals as a source of inspiration, a place of imagination, and a constant reminder that it is human choices that ultimately determine the course of history. Moreover, the essay illustrates how important it is to see White not as a philosopher of professional historiography, but as a politically engaged thinker concerned about the relations that people develop with their pasts. In comparison to White's earlier essays, this manifesto was more radical, especially in its anti-professionalism and anti-authoritarianism. Also, it was more fiercely presentist (and deliberately non-Crocean) in its insistence on the historian's responsibility to address present-day problems. As "the polestar that guided virtually everything [White] has written since then,"[15] the article reflects the position from which White, in the tumultuous decade of the 1960s, began to develop an argument presented most forcefully in *Metahistory*: that there are only moral and aesthetic grounds for objecting to a "liberation historiography" that fully allows individuals to "choose a past" in the same way as they "choose a future."

Choosing a past

What does it mean to choose a past? One day in 1967, White can-
celed his classes and traveled to Denver to address precisely this
question. At that time, one of his students remembers, White already
was a controversial figure:

> White was then, as now, the embodiment of the credo of the Sophist
> Gorgias, answering his opponent's seriousness with humor, his
> humor with seriousness. This drove some of his older colleagues
> crazy, and they worked hard to instill the graduate students with the
> notion that working with the faculty around White – scholars like
> Sidney Monas, Michael Cherniavsky, Harry Harootunian, R. J.
> Kaufmann, Loren Baritz – would lead to dead ends.[16]

Not that this helped much. Some graduate students became deeply
intrigued by White's eagerness to challenge conventional wisdoms
and by his ability to juggle with difficult ideas. As another student
recounts:

> From Calvin to Nietzsche, Rousseau to Camus, I became completely
> absorbed in the ideas and in White's presentation. ... Studying
> Nietzsche's *Genealogy of Morals* with White exerted a powerful impact
> on my thinking. ... Nietzsche, and White for that matter, seemed to
> call into question all previous assumptions about progress, Western
> values, religion, learning, and human nature. It may have been
> White's flamboyant and even belligerent style, his charisma which
> fed a witty sarcasm and urbane attitude toward the life of the mind
> that drew me in, stretching my own thinking into exciting and even
> fascinating realms.[17]

The paper White delivered in Denver was flamboyant and belliger-
ent, too. Following up on "The Burden of History," it argued that
(political, religious, intellectual) traditions are not given, but made.
Traditions, White claimed, only exist "in so far as individuals honor
them as appropriate systems for living a distinctively *human* life."
That is to say, traditions are always invented traditions, created by
individuals who choose to identify with certain practices or beliefs
from the past. Although White, faithful to his Weberian means–end
rationalism, understood such decisions to be conscious choices, the
argument also works with a less rationalist account of human decision-making. For even if people uncritically accept their society's

conventional wisdoms, they make an implicit choice of what counts as a good life, or of a tradition they want to continue. Moreover, White argued, such choices are typically justified by historical means. The past serves as a source of justification as soon as people appeal to ancient rites or customs, contrast their enlightened past with the dark times behind them, or revise their stories of descent in the light of changing situations. For White, then, every world-view has not only a vision of the future, but also a vision of the past. More precisely, such expectations of the future and visions of the past are mutually dependent: "In choosing our past, we choose a present; and vice versa. We use the one to *justify* the other."[18]

The rise of Christianity in Late Antiquity provided White with an example. When the Romans had converted to the Christian faith, they had to change their genealogies in such a way as to justify their conversion. To quote White at some length:

> What happened between the third and eighth centuries was that men *ceased to regard themselves as descendents of their Roman forebears and began to treat themselves as descendents of their Judaeo-Christian predecessors*. And it was the constitution of this *fictional* cultural ancestry which signalled the abandonment of the Roman socio-cultural system. When Western European men began to act *as if* they were descended from the Christian segment of the ancient world; when they began to structure their comportment *as if* they were *genetically* descended from their Christian predecessors; when, in short, they began to honor the Christian past as the most desirable model for creation of a future uniquely their own, and ceased to honor the Roman past as *their* past, the Roman socio-cultural system ceased to exist.

Note that such an invention of tradition presupposes a certain plasticity of the past, in the sense that different stories can be constructed out of what we know about the past. As White admitted: "The historical past is plastic in a way that the genetic past is not." Most important, however, is the distinction White made between the "historical" and the "genetic." Although human beings, whether they like it or not, are genetically connected to their biological ancestors, they always have the freedom to choose historical ancestors, or to invent a "fictional cultural ancestry." In later writings, White would invoke the Nietzschean and Foucauldian contrast between the "genealogical" and the "genetic" to make this same point (chapter 6). Unlike biological fatherhood, then, "social fatherhood is only bestowed by the sons." To that end, sons or daughters may want to "murder" their inherited fathers and engage in "retroactive ancestral substitution." For this reason, there is always a considerable amount of myth-making involved in traditions. As White had put it in "The Burden of History": "We choose our past in the same way that we choose our future. The historical past, therefore, is, like our various personal pasts, at best a myth, justifying our gamble on a specific future, and at worst a lie, a retrospective rationalization of what we have in fact become through our choices."[19]

Strong humanist father figures

It should come as no surprise that White insisted so heavily on the freedom to tell a personally relevant story about the past. For if it is true that people justify their dreams about the future with an appeal to the past, then the study of history is, among other things, an exercise in self-definition and a resource for shaping one's (political) imagination. Moreover, if people grow up with the idea of belonging to a "tradition" – if they are taught to consider themselves part of "Western civilization," for example – they can become truly autonomous individuals only if they, first, learn to see this tradition as a (political) construction and, second, create a "personal past" of their own. Accordingly, from the mid-1960s onwards, White invested considerable energy, first, in showing that the humanist tradition was also an invention and, second, in creating his own "personal past," consisting of historical figures whom White recognized as sources of inspiration for his existentialist-inspired political vision.

In a sense, the seven-volume series on "Major Traditions of World Civilization" that White edited between 1966 and 1973 was concerned with both of these tasks. Mostly written by (former) colleagues of White, the small paperbacks dealt with topics as broad as *The Judaeo-Christian Tradition*, *The Ancient Near Eastern Tradition*, and *The Enlightenment Tradition*.[20] White's own contribution, published with much delay in 1973,[21] dealt with *The Greco-Roman Tradition*. This may seem a remarkable choice for a medievalist turned into a modern intellectual historian, but makes perfect sense in the context of White's project. With heavy emphasis on the "fictional" character of the humanist tradition, White explained that the various humanisms of the modern age had all appealed "to Greco-Roman civilization as the *classical* model of their ideal values": "Whatever differences we perceive between their several perceptions of Greco-

Roman civilization, all of them honored that civilization as an exemplar of what a responsible humanity would aspire to. *They* made Greco-Roman civilization 'classical' by their choice of it as a matrix within which to articulate their successive visions of reality."[22]

The Greco-Roman Tradition offered a rather straightforward narrative of highlights in Greek and Roman history. It paid considerable attention to ancient philosophy, art, and rhetoric and was deeply indebted to a 1960s version of the secularization thesis. "We must never forget," White dared to write, for example, "that throughout the history of the ancient world the greater part of the Greek and Roman populace remained hopelessly bound up in the practices of magic, myth, and superstitious beliefs of the most archaic kind." Related to this was White's consistent emphasis on Greek and Roman ideals. "For it is the *ideals* of Greco-Roman civilization, rather than its realities, that must interest us as students of our own past seeking orientation in a distressed present."[23]

White was well aware, of course, that this approach resulted in what one reviewer called "a one-sided view of classical culture emphasizing those writers and artists who glorified man, his achievements, and his concerns," while suppressing evidence about the countless Greeks and Romans who "keenly felt man's impotence in a world ruled by the powers of nature."[24] White's goal, however, was not to offer a professionally acceptable narrative. His aim – corresponding to the second task identified above – was rather to stretch the imagination of his readers by offering them examples of ancient thinkers courageous enough to consider themselves the architects of their own lives. Referring to the "technical" challenges of the Cold War world, White agreed with Arnold Toynbee "that if we are to survive, we can do so only by nourishing our capacities to commitment to 'ideals' rather than to what appear to be the ineluctable 'realities' of our own time":

> To be sure, the ideals of a past age are not transmissible in their integrity to any future age as a living guide to the men of that age. But the story of how men frame ideals, articulate them, and hold fast to them in adversity is an education in a uniquely human power, the power that distinguishes man from other animals.[25]

It is worth noting that this view of history neatly corresponds to what Nietzsche, in the second of his *Untimely Meditations*, called "monumental history" (as distinguished from critical and antiquarian history). In Nietzsche's words, this monumental mode pertains "to the man of deeds and power, to him who fights a great fight, who needs models, teachers, comforters, and cannot find them among his contemporaries." However unlikely it may seem that White, with his iconoclastic reputation, ever operated in such a hero-worshipping mode, both here and elsewhere, White did exactly what Nietzsche believed the monumental historian to do: he searched for "models" and "teachers" in the past who could inspire people to "fight a great fight" in the present.[26]

As we shall see, the stimulating example provided by agents in the past who exercised their imagination and dreamt of a world better than their own would remain a central theme in White's thinking. Yet "The Burden of History" had also emphasized the need to address explicitly the "problems of the present." Judged by the introductions White wrote to most of the volumes in his series, he identified these problems in particular with "mass society," "technological culture," and "fascism" – three keywords that also figured prominently in Bossenbrook's writings from the mid-1960s.[27] Although White was more cautious than Bossenbrook in postulating causal relations between the three phenomena, he did not hesitate to suggest potential linkages: "[W]ithin the context of a rapidly industrializing, urbanizing, and democratizing social system, entrenched conservatives *may* opt for fascist methods – violence, thought control, terror, and even genocide – in the hope of saving whatever they can of their received way of life, privileges, and class values." Accordingly, what White appreciated in, for example, John Weiss's volume on the fascist tradition was that it explained how fascism remained "a distinct *possibility* for any society undergoing such processes," not only in so-called underdeveloped countries, but also in France, England, "and even the United States." "His study of fascism, therefore, leaves us precisely where any serious historical work ought to leave us: in the present, with our problems illuminated and our tasks clarified."[28]

Crucial, then, was that a solution to these problems required a "personal past," or canon of inspiring historical figures, equal to the challenges of the twentieth century. Could such figures be found in classical Antiquity? Or in the humanist tradition as portrayed in *The Emergence of Liberal Humanism*? The successor volume to this textbook, published in 1970, concluded with an epilogue in which White and Coates answered this question in gloomy terms:

> [I]t may be seriously questioned whether the fundamental convictions of liberal humanism still have the power to command assent in

the sense of providing programmatic direction for those Western Europeans born since 1925. The pace of technological and social change has been accelerating so greatly in the twentieth century that liberal ideals are becoming less relevant to those who were in no way responsible for the conflicts of the 1930s and 1940s. If, for them, the answers of communism seem too precipitate to be sound, those of liberal humanism seem too prone to mere tinkering with the social mechanism, too groping, too other-initiated, too little disposed to positive actions and firm convictions.[29]

If, in other words, "mass society" and "technological culture" required a stronger, more activist humanism than Croce's, who were the representatives of this new ethos, or the father figures of White's "adjusted" humanism? Among those selected as possible candidates, Albert Camus, the French existentialist, was perhaps the most important one. Although existentialism had influenced White from his days in college onwards, it was only in *The Ordeal of Liberal Humanism* that his admiration for the author of *L'homme révolté* became fully apparent. In a sense, White thoroughly identified with Camus's "rebel," the anti-authoritarian individualist. For White, the rebel "stands in opposition to the status quo, whether represented by a long-established social order or by a newly established revolutionary regime, for the rebel is the defender of humanity in all its variety and imperfection, and especially of that part of humanity which every system, because it is a system, must persecute." What makes the rebel a true humanist is that he (or she) always identifies with the individual rather than with a system or tradition. Suspicious of collectivities, the rebel is also a "strong" humanist – stronger than Croce – in actively opposing the powers that threaten the individual's freedom. He (or she) does so, however, not by simply substituting the "gods" or "fathers" of the repressive system with new, potentially equally suppressive ones. The only gods or fathers the rebel acknowledges are those committed to, or embodying, the capacity of individuals to live a life of their own, in accord with self-chosen values: "Translated into political terms, this means that the rebel will defend only a movement dedicated to the reduction of violence in the world and the increase of pragmatic freedom even at the expense of abstract perfect justice."[30]

Besides Camus, there were some other, older candidates. In the late 1960s, White developed a lasting fascination for Giambattista Vico, the eighteenth-century Neapolitan schoolmaster and philosopher of history whose *La scienza nuova* was as bold an exercise in creative imagination as White could think of. (As we shall see in chapter 3, Vico also provided White with the "tropes" employed in *Metahistory*.) Although not a political rebel, Vico's genius had been to challenge, intellectually, some of the most dominant modes of thought of his time, including in particular the Enlightenment dichotomy between reason and unreason or science and myth. It was not only because of his own attempt to overcome the nineteenth-century opposition between "proper" (realist) and "improper" (non-realist) history that White found an ally in Vico. He also appreciated the Italian critic of scientism for recognizing the significance of the human imagination as a faculty that is irreducible to reason, yet crucial for any attempt to understand the world differently than as taught by the authorities. "It is perhaps fitting," meditated White,

> that in an age that faces a barbarism more virulent than anything he could have imagined, this theorist of myth and unreason should finally come into his own as a culture-hero. Perhaps only the twentieth century has suffered sufficiently to match sensibility with the great Neapolitan thinker; he is certainly one of the few 'ancients' able to serve as a guide to our own uncertain future.[31]

Social conditions of freedom

So far, we have seen how White, in his attempt to develop a politically more relevant concept of history, simultaneously "deconstructed" the notion of tradition – thereby also demonstrating the "inventedness" of his own liberal humanist tradition – and searched for sources of inspiration for a more activist humanism than the historicist humanism he had subscribed to in his Italian period. Although, as far as the latter is concerned, Vico and Camus ranked highly among White's heroes, his strong humanist father figures ideally met one more requirement. For if the problems of "mass society," "technological culture," and "fascism" were not so much results of conscious decisions made by White's favorite species, the free and independent *Homo sapiens*, but rather caused by anonymous social processes, such as industrialization, urbanization, and democratization, what would be the benefit of presenting Vico and Camus as examples of creative, imaginative, self-thinking individuals? What would be the good of writing history in such a way as to encourage individual self-determination if the problems plaguing the present were far beyond the powers of the individual? Drawing from Marxist sources he had already encountered in Detroit, White came to see that the ideal of a morally autonomous life required a supportive social system. He therefore concluded that twentieth-century humanists needed to be committed not only to freedom of thought, but also to progressive politics aimed at creating social conditions under which people could actually exercise this freedom.

With this aim in mind, White began to immerse himself in philosophies – as diverse as Hegel's and Marx's – which tried to link the realm of thought – with which White so far had been almost exclusively preoccupied – to the realm of social affairs. Of course, White saw nothing in a Marxism which reduced the former to the latter. There were some more humanist Marxists, though, who seemed to share White's ideal of individual self-determination, while realizing that this ideal required a social constellation that, even in the modern West, was still more of a dream than a reality. White's 1969 essay, "The Tasks of Intellectual History," signaled the author's readiness to revise the straightforward humanist position he had defended so far in order to acknowledge the complex social realities that underlay the ideas and ideals of individual citizens.

In a grand-scale survey of twentieth-century historiography, the article examined the extent to which intellectual historians such as Ernst Cassirer, Johan Huizinga, and Arthur Lovejoy had been able "to deal with the great, cataclysmic shifts in world-view which are the main inspiration for undertaking intellectual history in the first place." The result was disappointing: "All three specialized in the study of great, global trends or epochs; but on the whole they avoided the problem of intellectual historical dynamics." Likewise, historically minded scholars in adjacent disciplines, such as Gombrich and Thomas Kuhn, could well explain changes within artistic or scientific practices, but had little to say about changing mentalities at larger scales, such as the decline of liberalism and the rise of fascism, White's prime example in these years.[32]

When White sought to provide intellectual history with a grounding in social reality, he might have turned to the history of mentalities, developed by the second generation of *Annales* historians. Indeed, White showed some interest in the concept of "mental apparatus" as employed by Lucien Febvre. Like Kuhn's "paradigms," White said, the notion of "mental apparatus" might enable historians to treat ideas and practices as expressions of broadly shared mentalities – so that a poem of Milton, a painting by Rembrandt, and a scientific tract by Leibniz can all be seen as manifestations of a single worldview. But, still, the question remained how such a worldview or conceptual apparatus could be related to its social context. Therefore, White searched for what he called "some theory of connection by which the various spiritual manifestations of an age can be brought into relationship with the institutional and customary comportment of the age" and professed to have found such a theory in the work of Lucien Goldmann.[33]

Although there is some exaggeration in Norman Cantor's claim that White was "an important disciple of Goldmann in the United States," it is true that, for some time, White heavily sympathized with this Romanian-French Marxist philosopher. Goldmann's work, wrote White, "offers the best suggestions for dealing with those cataclysmic transformations – those revolutions in sensibility – which the structuralism of Gombrich and Kuhn on the one side and of Foucault, Barthes and the *Annales* group on the other have avoided trying to analyze in any sociologically significant way." White even translated, together with Robert Anchor, Goldmann's *Sciences humaines et philosophie* (1952).[34]

In White's view, Goldmann's merit was to have grasped that changes of "mental apparatuses" cannot be explained without due reference to social infrastructures. To that end, historians must distinguish between a synchronic and a diachronic dimension of history. At the first level, they will find what White had called "ideologies" and Goldmann described as "world visions." Whereas White's notion of ideology had been strictly individual, Goldmann's world vision referred to a collectively shared mentality. For example, he understood Pascal and Kant to have a sufficient number of ideas in common – including a "tragic" understanding of human life – to share a world vision. Goldmann subsequently explained changes in such visions by changes in the social context. He thus read Racine's tragedies and Pascal's *Pensées* as responses to social and political transformation. More particularly, he took the tragic vision of French Jansenism to express the reservations felt by parts of the legal profession – the group from which Jansenism had originated – about the politics of their day. This feeling, in turn, had been caused by the rise of royal absolutism and the formation of a strong bureaucracy, which tended to reduce the social significance of lawyers associated with the parliament.[35] In a sense, Goldmann thus related mentalities to social conditions. Crucial for White, however, was that he did so without sacrificing individual freedom on the altar of social conditions:

> He does not pretend that class origin or allegiance explains everything in the texts, nor is he interested in "explaining away" that

genius of those who opposed the values for which Marxism militates. On the contrary, he explains the marvelous diversity of French thought and letters in the late seventeenth century by the fact that, for a while, the monarchy stood above, and mediated between, the various classes, representing no one of them exclusively; this, in Goldmann's view, provided the objective conditions within which thinkers and writers of all the different classes could give full and open expressions to the visions of the world, the "imaginary universes," aspired to individually by them.[36]

The key phrases in this quotation are "objective conditions" and "aspired to individually." White did not give up his passionate belief in the powers of human will and imagination. But what he derived from Goldmann was the insight that will and imagination need social conditions. White came to see that his dream of a world in which human beings decide for themselves how to live could only be realized if a "socio-economic infrastructure" enabling such moral self-determination would come into being. Therefore, rather than treating social conditions as *sufficient* causes for the emergence of certain ideas – or the social "base" as determining the intellectual "superstructure" – White called attention to *necessary* causes in the realm of social reality. Freedom of thought requires (but is not determined by) a supportive social system. Accordingly, a liberal humanist such as White, inspired by ideals of freedom and self-determination, must also be committed to a politics aiming at social conditions favorable to individual freedom. Goldmann's Marxist philosophy did not, therefore, compromise White's liberal humanism. It rather provided White with intellectual ammunition for pairing his existentialist dreams with a preference for socially progressive politics.[37]

This did not mean that White himself became politically active, although, in good 1960s fashion, he signed petitions against the Vietnam War and participated in campus demonstrations. (A telling anecdote comes from Claudio Veliz: "The last time I saw Hayden White he was sprawled on the bonnet of a police car, where he had jumped to express his opposition to the Vietnam War.") Also, in a letter demanding the release of Soviet dissident Vladimir Bukovsky, White and some colleagues described themselves as long-time activists "for the liberation of Angela Davis and other political prisoners in the United States." Although White's anti-authoritarianism seemed almost inborn, his strong suspicion of states and their bureaucracies – examples of which will follow in subsequent chapters – was fueled not least by these experiences.[38] More important, however, was that White's activism drew on the utopian dream that social conditions of individual freedom had come into reach, not only for the elite, but for middle and lower classes as well. In almost intoxicated language, White wrote that the promised land which Marx had seen from afar could now finally be entered:

> [T]he current avant-garde is able to take as a fact what every previous one had to regard finally as only a hope – that is, that the condition of material scarcity is no longer an inevitability and that we are at last ready to enter into a utopia in which neither myth, religion, nor elites of taste and sensibility will be able to claim the right to define what the "true" aims of either art or life must be.[39]

This is where Camus and Marx could meet and where the existentialist-inspired humanist that White was could embrace the Marxist ideal of social equality. If freedom of thought requires a certain standard of living or an equitable distribution of wealth, then liberal humanists ought to join the struggle for social equality and support campaigns for human rights and civil liberties. Likewise, in studying the past, humanist historians must be sensitive to conditions under which freedom became possible or, more often perhaps, to social constellations that prevented people from determining their own lives. If White called himself a Marxist, it was to express his commitment to this cause of social equality contributing to individual freedom.[40]

In defense of metahistory

Finally, how did this new insight modify White's plea for a monumental historiography aimed at showing how individuals in the past had taken command over their lives? As we have seen, White was interested not so much in social constellations *per se* – one youthful piece aside, he never wrote anything like social history[41] – but rather in social and political forces that sought to restrain the imagination and suppress the freedom for individuals to dream of a future better than the present. Yet, if imagination requires social freedom, then it is but a small step to notice how often conservative powers try to restrain the human imagination by condemning reformist or revolutionary thought as "unrealistic." White began to study, then, how the category of the "real" was employed, not only under extraordinary political circumstances, but also in that peaceful bourgeois context, back in the nineteenth century, that witnessed the rise of the "realist" novel and "realist" history.[42]

White's most illuminating article, in this regard, is "The Politics of Contemporary Philosophy of History" (1973), a keynote address delivered in Toronto, in April 1969, at a conference attended by some of the greatest names in philosophy of history: Frederick Olafson, Leon Goldstein, Louis O. Mink, and William Dray. All of these men had written extensively on historical explanation, the theme which at that time was still synonymous to philosophy of history as practiced in the pages of *History and Theory*.[43] But on that April evening in Toronto, White proposed a rather different agenda. In a manifesto-like style and vocabulary, he suggested that philosophers of history should reflect not on history as it is actually written, or on historical studies as they ought to be practiced from some philosophical point of view, but on the sort of history that might be welcomed from a progressively political perspective. Moreover, White told his audience, historians ought to be driven not by a Rankean desire to study the past as it "really" or "essentially" was, but by the aspiration to challenge what counts as "real" or "essential" in their societies.

White's argument proceeded in three steps. First, he observed that, in spite of the received wisdom that the kind of history historians produce depends on the kind of persons they are, few scholars are prepared to grant "that a *world-transforming* vision can appropriately be brought to the study of history." Whereas conservative historians are seldom charged with unprofessional conduct if they explicate their political preferences in their historical writing, colleagues with more politically radical views normally cannot do so without being perceived as violating the rules of professional practice. "This is," White claimed, "the true basis of the distinction drawn between 'straight' history and 'metahistory' by the current generation of Anglo-American philosophers of history, a distinction which, in its way, is as spurious as that drawn between 'straight' history and 'chronicle.'" In other words, philosophers of history – or historians themselves, for that matter – employ the term "metahistory" as a pejorative designation for histories that are deemed unwelcome because of their "socially innovative" agenda. The problem of metahistorians is that they hold "views threatening to the social establishments of their time, views which, to the conservative-liberal historiographical establishment appeared not so much mistaken as simply insane."[44]

If this is true, then, in the second place, the scholarly establishment – White must have been thinking of Rankean orthodoxy in nineteenth-century Europe – turns out to operate from political principles, too. Socially innovative historiography is threatening, not to historical studies as such, but to the conservative political agenda underlying the scholarship of Ranke and his followers. As White put it, "it seems to me that the objection to using a vision of a desirable future to give the form to one's account of past and present would bear weight only for those to whom the present is basically satisfactory as it is. And by the 'present' I mean the *social* status quo." White's aim, then, was to identify the "politics" of those who complained about a politicization of history in the hands of metahistorians. And what mattered most, to him, was not that this politics (unsurprisingly) turned out to be conservative; it was that *every* historian and *every* philosopher of history expresses political views in defining what "proper" history is. White's point was not – as one alarmed conference attendee thought – to obliterate "the distinction between history and propaganda," but rather to show that there is an inextinguishable dimension of politics or propaganda at work in *every* account of history and *every* reflection on the historian's work. This allowed White to redefine "metahistory" in such a way as to refer no longer exclusively to Toynbee or Brown, but rather, in a broader sense, to a political dimension underlying any conception of historical realism.[45]

What did this imply for the socially responsible, politically progressive philosopher of history that White himself wanted to be? "The question which ought to interest us, I think," answered White, "is which of the forms of metahistory now available to us bids fare to become the 'ordinary history' of the next age – and more importantly, what kind of vision of our past, present, and future do we need to permit us to make transition to a next age." Referring to both Sartre and Goldmann, White wanted discussions in philosophy of history to shift "from the dianoetic to the activist voice."[46] For only in this activist mode might philosophers of history perform the difficult task that White assigned them. If they wanted to contribute to a better world, that is, to a world in which more people enjoy the freedom to live their own lives, they should develop modes of historical realism that liberate people from conservative realisms, while offering them resources for developing realisms consistent with their own moral agenda.

A philosophy of liberation

Speaking about analytic philosopher Gilbert Ryle, Iris Murdoch once observed that the world of Ryle was "the world in which people play cricket, cook cakes, make simple decisions, remember their childhood and go to the circus; not the world in which they commit sins, fall in love, say prayers or join the Communist Party."[47] Likewise, in the late 1960s, White envisioned a world in which historians would not do their work "properly" – browsing through some newly discovered materials, adding some more footnotes to an overspecialized research article – but would stop in order to reflect on what is "proper" in the face of social unrest and political injustice. In White's world, philosophers of history would not dissipate their energy on how scholars like Roquentin and Tesman solve yet another problem of merely academic interest, but redefine the concept of history in such a way as to include those previously despised as "people without history." As this chapter has made clear, White felt that Crocean thought was not up to this challenge. Radicalizing his humanism into a more activist stance, while simultaneously adopting a Marxist-inspired concern for the social conditions of human freedom, White became a Camusian rebel who challenged his colleagues and students to rethink their discipline from a politically progressive point of view. His task, as he had come to see it, was to challenge conservative metahistories – realisms that confirm the social status quo – by developing resources for a more progressive, more liberating concept of historical realism.

For this reason, the ideal that White defended in these years may be described as a *liberation historiography* – a word I coin in analogy to the Latin-American liberation theology and liberation philosophy that swept Western academic circles in the very same period, around 1970. Under Marxist influences, liberation theologians such as Gustavo Gutiérrez and Leonardo Boff argued that Christian theology, often associated with abstruse dogmas, could gain political "relevance" by mobilizing Christian resources, such as Jesus' Sermon on the Mount, for the struggle against poverty and social exclusion. Likewise, liberation philosophers such as Arturo Andrés Roig and Ignacio Ellacuría developed concepts of agency aimed at enabling the poor and repressed to throw off their burdens.[48] There were, of course, important differences between these Latin-American thinkers and the Los Angeles-based history professor.

White did not work among the poor, never joined a revolution, focused on freedom of thought rather than on freedom from poverty, and never applied his scholarship entirely to the cause of liberation. Yet, as an unstoppable pulse in his work, there emerged a concern for freedom from conservative powers, for liberation from oppressive traditions, strikingly similar to that of the authors just mentioned. Just like them, White was primarily focused on negative freedom: a freedom from restraints imposed by institutions and intellectual traditions. But underlying this concern for negative freedom was, as we have seen, a positive affirmation of freedom in an existentialist sense: a freedom to shape one's own life, to realize one's own potentials.[49]

Written in an age of civil rights protests and antiwar demonstrations, White's plea for liberation historiography unavoidably bore the mark of its time. Especially, perhaps, the urgency that shouted from White's pages seems something of a 1960s phenomenon. Many of his later publications were far less explicitly political and written in a more reflective voice than the manifestos discussed in this chapter. However, as the next chapters will make clear, *Metahistory* and White's subsequent forays into tropology, discourse, and narrative theory were driven by very similar concerns. White's philosophy of history in the 1970s and 1980s was still a philosophy of liberation, committed to existentialist liberal values. Even if, at times, White's abstract analyses of historical representation seemed to move towards the world of Ryle more than to the world White hoped to conquer in the 1960s, the author never abandoned the program outlined in "The Burden of History." In fact, in White's hands, Vico's tropes and Northrop Frye's plot structures became the means for advocating metahistories, or modes of historical realism, inspired by an existentialist humanist vision. As David Harlan aptly remarks, "White is a humanist, a moralist, and a deeply religious thinker. He conceives of history as a quest for ultimate reality and an act of personal transcendence. He is a theorist of redemption in a[n] age of simulacra."[50] Only against this background can we begin to understand what *Metahistory*, White's ground-breaking book of 1973, sought to achieve.

3

The Historical Imagination: Four Modes of Realism

The book that made White most famous was *Metahistory* (1973).[1] In no fewer than 448 pages, this study synthesized almost everything that White had done so far. Following the program outlined in "The Burden of History" and the Toronto lecture of 1969, *Metahistory* examined how "liberating" or "constraining" the metahistories of some classic, nineteenth-century historians and philosophers of history had been. Simultaneously, it openly advocated a mode of realism able to accommodate the utopian political vision that White had embraced in the late 1960s. Yet, the book did even more than this. Most remarkably, it developed a "formal theory" (ix) about metahistories,[2] inspired not only by literary theory, but also by the then-booming field of structuralist linguistics. In a typological mode reminiscent of the Weberian typologies employed in White's dissertation (chapter 1), the book distinguished between arguments, ideologies, plots, and so-called "prefigurations" in the historian's work. Moreover, to the bewilderment of no small number of readers, the author sprinkled his text with technical and sometimes ill-defined terms such as "metonymy," "synecdoche," and "irony." These were the elements of what in due course became White's best-known contribution to philosophy of history: a theory of tropes. Accordingly, *Metahistory* was not merely a culmination of previous work, it was also the beginning of something new.

Given White's characteristic *modus operandi*, no reader should be surprised that old and new were anything but neatly integrated. *Metahistory* was an outburst of creativity. It presented the reader with a cheery eclecticism of models, examples, and exhortations. It mingled careful analysis of nineteenth-century metahistories with rigid criticism of Rankean professionalism and lyric identification with pre-professional "masters" such as Michelet and Tocqueville. Stimulating as all this may be, the variety of ideas and perspectives developed in the book might also cause confusion as to what to make of White's *magnum opus*. For example, many readers assume that the (famous) theoretical manifesto on the opening pages tells them what to expect from the rest of the book. The chapters following these opening pages, however, are far less indebted to structuralist theory than is the programmatic introduction.[3] Moreover, whereas the introduction promises an analysis of historical narratives, few of the chapters that follow pay more than cursory attention to the historical narratives written by the authors under consideration. Also, while *Metahistory* is known as a "manual of tropology,"[4] supposedly offering a set of technical instruments for analyzing the "poetic elements" (x) of historical writing, readers halfway through the book have already encountered a variety of other genres, including lengthy historiographical surveys and passionate discussions of what is morally objectionable in Ranke's version of historical realism.

One way to deal with these tensions is to differentiate between dimensions in the book. Hans Kellner, for example, speaks in the plural about *Metahistories*, indicating that White's study pursued various tasks at once.[5] Additionally, in a more diachronic mode, one may say that a decade of tumultuous reflection has found its expression in the book. This reading strategy is especially helpful if it also pays attention to such pieces as the draft chapter on Hegel, finished and published as early as 1966. A brief comparison with the Hegel chapter that eventually appeared in *Metahistory* suffices to show that White's main interests in this period remained constant – both texts focused in particular on the moral and political dimensions of Hegel's concept of history – but that the author greatly expanded his analytical armamentarium in the years between 1966 and 1973. Only the second version employed the "tropological" language for which *Metahistory* has become renowned (or notorious).[6] More important, however, is that such diachronic differences also appear between the body of the text – the ten main chapters – and the preface, introduction, and conclusion that set forth White's "formal theory." Whereas the author's fascination with structuralist linguistics, developed as late as the early 1970s, found its clearest expression in those programmatic texts, the historiographical chapters in between were mostly written before White made his "linguistic turn." The striking differences between the middle and the outer parts of the book can therefore be seen as indicators of how rapidly White developed new ideas, and how difficult it was to keep a lengthy manuscript in pace with that process.

Nonetheless, I will argue that the various parts of the book (the historiographical surveys, the complaints about "irony," the praise heaped on such figures as Tocqueville, and the tropological "system" outlined in the first dozens of pages) are best understood as closely related. Starting not with the tropes, but with what *Metahistory* most manifestly was – a history of nineteenth-century historiography – I show, in the first place, to what a large extent *Metahistory* continued the lines described in the previous chapters. Second, I explain some of the new terms that emerged in this history of historiography: irony, myth, and imagination. A careful reading of some selected passages then leads to an interpretation of the tropes that is remarkably different from how these four terms – metaphor, metonymy, synecdoche, and irony – are usually understood. More generally, I argue that *Metahistory* was not a book about narrativity, as is often said, but a study of metahistories or "prefigurations" of historical realism. Only against this background, the chapter concludes, is it possible to understand why White, in the early 1970s, adopted a structuralist linguistic vocabulary for describing the ways in which the human imagination thinks and dreams about what counts as "real" in history.

An inverted disciplinary history

Metahistory presents itself, in the first place, as a history of historiography. One popular way of writing such a history is to create a genealogy of the historical discipline. This genre traces the origins of the present-day discipline back to, for example, Ranke, and treats historians prior to Ranke as "precursors" of what scholars nowadays understand historical scholarship to be. Such a genealogy, then, offers "an account of the alleged historical development of an enterprise the identity of which is defined by the concerns of the current practitioners of a particular scientific field."[7] Stefan Collini calls it a disciplinary history: a triumphant story of how the present-day profession came into being. In White's terminology, it might be described as a myth of origin that serves the academic status quo.

Unsurprisingly, *Metahistory* avoided this self-congratulating genre. Remarkable, however, is that the alternative White provided was an almost exact inversion of what he rejected. White's history of nineteenth-century historiography also read like a pre-history of the historical discipline, focused on the emergence of a "professional" historical ethos, nourished in institutions such as Ranke's history seminar. In White's version, however, the narrative was not a story of progress, but a story of decline. The academic discipline that history had become was the culmination of a "professionalization process" that White regretted as much as others applauded it. For what professional historians did was to reject the wealth of historical reflection found in Romantic authors such as Chateaubriand, Carlyle, Froude, and Trevelyan. Moreover, with firmly drawn boundaries between in- and out-groups, or between "proper" and "improper" history, they also dismissed Marx's and Nietzsche's philosophies of history (269). Deaf to their message that professional history was "just as value laden and just as conceptually determined" as philosophy of history (276), they pretended to be "impartial," "objective," or even "value-neutral." For White, such pretensions could not but end in moral agnosticism: in a scientific view of history that forbids moral engagement and denies moral responsibility.

Like other disciplinary histories, White's book presented good guys and bad guys, or positive and negative examples, but in reversed order. Whereas "official professional orthodoxy" (277) as represented by Ranke served as White's *bête noire*,[8] his sources of inspiration were all pre-professionals. It was in the days of Tocqueville, a man who had paired historical writing with political and moral reflection, that history had experienced a "golden age" (xii, 434). White praised the French historian for the moral impulse that ran through his work. If Tocqueville had shown his readers anything, it was that historical events, such as the French Revolution, were in the end all caused by human decisions. Also, with his fine eye for ambiguities, Tocqueville had postponed any definitive conclusion on the "meaning" of the Revolution, thereby forcing the reader "to decide for himself 'what actually happened' in terms of what he desires to happen in his own future" (227). Most decisive, however, was that Tocqueville had not merely contemplated "how *this* grew out of *that*," but sought to link past and present by interpreting present-day problems in the light of the past experience *and* vice versa (226). This, as we have seen, was White's greatest dream. And it was precisely this ability that White, to his regret, saw disappear in such later historians as Ranke and Croce.

White saw no harm in drawing clear boundaries between his heroes and villains, or between the phases of decline that he believed them to represent. Schematic as these clear-cut distinctions were – critics often complained about this – they served the goal of highlighting discontinuities, rather than continuities, in historical thinking. Not unlike Michel Foucault, whose *Les mots et les choses* emerged in the first footnote, White hoped to lay bare a plurality of modes, or paradigms, of historical thought. According to White, Michelet, Tocqueville, Ranke, and Burckhardt had represented different *épistémès*, or "different conceptions of the historical process" (2). In other words, they had had different ideas about what history was, how it should be studied, and what the historian's responsibilities were. Like *Les mots et les choses*, then, White's multi-phase narrative sought to chart "fundamental changes in the deep structure of the historical imagination" (5).[9]

This also explains why *Metahistory* dwelt at length on great, dead, white, male historians, without paying any attention to women, non-elite authors, or more diverse genres of historical representation (such as painting and drama). White's aim was not – and would never be – to offer as careful and complete an account as possible of what had happened in the domain of historical representation. His goal was rather to sketch in broad strokes what sort of possibilities for historical thinking the nineteenth century contained. A handful of examples, of authors still known and recognized as classics, sufficed to alert his readers to modes of historical thinking that had once enjoyed a legitimate status, but that had been displaced by the successes of "professionalization." A 1972 essay that anticipated much of *Metahistory* even made the point with only three examples: Ranke's *Deutsche Geschichte im Zeitalter der Reformation*, Tocqueville's *De la démocratie en Amérique*, and Burckhardt's *Die Cultur der Renaissance in Italien*. "I do not have time to defend my 'readings' of these three examples," wrote White in characteristic prose, "but I hope that by my summary characterizations of their structures I have suggested the possibility of making two points about historical narrative in general."[10]

The general point, then, that White's story of discontinuities sought to convey was that "history" could be practiced in radically different ways, each of which, in principle, was equally legitimate. Just like Kuhn's paradigms or Foucault's *épistémès*, the models White distinguished in nineteenth-century historical thought all made an irreducible claim to "realism." Which of these "realisms" was most real cannot possibly be said – although, of course, historians may have their preferences. It is perfectly possible to prefer Ranke over Burckhardt, if only because Ranke's model comes closer to how history is often practiced at contemporary Western universities. However, argued White, we must then be so fair as to acknowledge that such a preference cannot be justified on theoretical grounds: "[T]here are no apodictically certain theoretical grounds on which one can legitimately claim an authority for any one of the modes over the others as being more 'realistic'" (xii). What sort of realism one prefers rather depends on reasons that are "ultimately aesthetic or moral rather than epistemological" (xii). Accordingly, if White preferred Tocqueville over Ranke, or Michelet over Croce, this choice was based on moral grounds, too. As the author made abundantly clear, it was not Ranke's archival ethos that irritated him, but his dangerous "moral self-certitude" (192). Likewise, it was "the essentially ethical bases" of Tocqueville's work (222) that made the French author White's favorite historian.

To be sure, in the 1970s, this was fairly revolutionary stuff. Although both the political dimension of historiography and the historian's narrative style began to receive attention,[11] no one before White had so radically distinguished between irreducible modes of historical thinking. As a Catholic teaching assistant in one of White's courses remembers:

> What I got from it all was that history had a history. Like everything else, historical consciousness was itself historically conditioned. Nowadays that may be second nature to all postmodernist graduate students, but then it was for me, just out of fifteen years of Catholic education, what illicit sex must have been for the Puritans: forbidden but so very interesting. Everything was open, this rather uptight Catholic discovered.[12]

In a sense, this was precisely the effect that White, the liberation historian, hoped to achieve. A Catholic who learns there is more than the Church has taught him, a conservative who dares to take a critical look at his tradition, a source-oriented historian who discovers that his approach is only one among many: these are fine examples of what White's "strong didactic agenda" sought to unleash.[13]

Escaping the ironist's cage

Familiar as all this may sound to readers of White's earlier work, new in *Metahistory* was the language of irony. In White's formulation of the problem, historical thinking near the end of the nine-teenth century had plunged into a "condition of Irony" and remained "locked" in this ironic perspective ever since (433). Although it is hard to say exactly what irony meant in *Metahistory* – one reviewer counted no less than twenty senses in which White used the word[14] – the Croce chapter offers a good illustration of what White found objectionable in it. His former hero was said to represent a final stage of nineteenth-century historical thought, or a mode of historical realism in which past and present were radi-cally separated. In a sense, past and present had already grown apart when historians, long before Croce, had subordinated moral judgment of the past to an attempt to understand history "in its own terms." Such an "Irony with respect to the past" (402) – regis-tering what had happened, without any attempt at evaluation from a present-day point of view – had not exactly characterized Croce's work. On the contrary, the Italian philosopher had felt no difficul-ties in tracing the development of the human spirit through the ages and distinguishing between what was "living" and "dead" in the achievements of former generations. However, because of his refusal to project such developments into the future – according to Croce, the future depended entirely on the choices future generations would make – the study of history could have no practical use for present-day deliberation. This, then, was what White condemned as "irony." By adopting a stance of "extreme Irony with respect to everything in his own social and cultural present" (402), Croce had put history "into quarantine as a guide to present activity and future aspiration" (415).

How could historians escape this "ironist's cage?"[15] What could be done to restore the study of history as a source of meaning and inspiration for people troubled by present-day problems? At first sight, White's answer looked surprisingly simple:

If it can be shown that Irony is only one of a *number* of possible perspectives on history, each of which has its own good reasons for existence on a poetic and moral level of awareness, the Ironic attitude will have begun to be deprived of its status as the *necessary* perspective from which to view the historical process. Historians and philosophers of history will then be freed to concep-tualize history, to perceive its contents, and to construct narrative accounts of its processes in whatever modality of consciousness is most consistent with their own moral and aesthetic aspirations. (434)

This seemed to imply that the paradigms of realism described in *Metahistory* were simply available for choice – as if there were no disciplinary conventions and discursive powers preventing historians from exchanging their Rankean or Crocean realism for a Tocquevillean or Marxist conception of the real. Of course, the liberation thinker that White was knew well that historians do not start from scratch. By the moment they are able to reflect on their work, they are already deeply socialized, or indoctrinated, into the irony of present-day historical studies. Historians must therefore be "freed" if they are ever to develop a non-ironic mode of realism.

Surprisingly, perhaps, White hoped to achieve such a liberation by turning the ironic paradigm against itself. As he declared in an often-quoted passage:

> It may not go unnoticed that this book is itself cast in an Ironic mode. But the Irony which informs it is a conscious one, and it therefore represents a turning of the Ironic consciousness against Irony itself. If it succeeds in establishing that the skepticism and pessimism of so much of contemporary historical thinking have their origins in an Ironic frame of mind, and that this frame of mind in turn is merely one of a number of possible postures that one may assume before the historical record, it will have provided some of the grounds for a rejection of Irony itself. (xii)

This passage has been the subject of much reflection,[16] but is arguably best understood against the background of White's Nietzsche chapter. In a sense, Nietzsche's meditation "Vom Nutzen und Nachteil der Historie für das Leben" had dealt with the same problem: how to rescue the past from the hands of those who treat it as essentially unrelated to the present? In White's reading, Nietzsche's remedy had consisted of two parts. First, historical knowledge needed to "turn its sting against itself," or to deconstruct itself by showing with historical means that history itself is historically conditioned and therefore unable to aspire to exclusive sovereignty in interpreting the past.[17] Subsequently, the space created by this "ground-clearing operation" (356) might be filled with the creative, artistic, and mythic perspectives that Nietzsche had offered in *Die Geburt der Tragödie*. In White's words: "When history itself shows the historical origins of a historical culture, the way will be open to the attainment of that 'unhistorical' or 'suprahistorical' vantage point from which the myth-making powers of art can do their work" (355).

Like Nietzsche, White believed that such a "liberation of the creative imagination from restrictions placed on it by thought itself" (372–3) required a strong "power of the will." Whereas a historicizing of history (step 1) results in "a consciousness of chaos," or in an awareness of the contingency of the ironic realism through which twentieth-century historians approach the past, one needs a vigorous "will to form" to embrace a non-ironic, "unhistorical," or "suprahistorical" perspective (step 2). Indeed, for White, just as for Nietzsche, life always moves back and forth between such a "consciousness of chaos" and "will to form" (346). Those who lack a strong will usually begin to panic when thinkers such as Nietzsche lay bare the "chaos" or contingency of their inherited modes of thinking. Like Weber's "weak souls who cannot bear the face of today's life" (chapter 1 of this volume), they complain about "relativism" and "nihilism." However, for those who possess a healthy will to form, a "turning of the Ironic consciousness against Irony itself" (xii) is not a recipe for relativism, but the actualization of a freedom to think about history "in whatever modality of consciousness is most consistent with their own moral and aesthetic aspirations" (434).

This insistence on the human will gave *Metahistory* a strong element of voluntarism.[18] Just as in his previous work, White drew on humanist, modernism, and existentialist resources in portraying human nature as guided by an essentially free will, and human thought, subsequently, as an expression of the sort of person one wants to be (433). White held that the way one approaches history eventually depends on the individual will: "That is to say, one can either adopt Marx's philosophy of history as providing the perspective from which one *wills* to view one's own place in the stream of historical becoming or one can reject it on similarly voluntaristic grounds" (283). As noted by several skeptical readers – does it suffice for a prisoner to will to be free? – White's strategy for escaping the ironist's cage was thus essentially a Pelagian one (named after the monk who had defended the free will against Saint Augustine). At the end of the day, liberation hinged on one's will to be free.[19] As White phrased his credo near the end of *Metahistory*:

[W]e are free to conceive "history" as we *please*, just as we are free to make of it what we *will*. And, if we *wish* to transcend the agnosticism which an Ironic perspective on history, passing as the sole possible "realism" and "objectivity" to which we can aspire in historical studies, foists upon us, we have only to reject this Ironic perspective

and to *will* to view history from another, anti-Ironic perspective.
(433–4, emphases added)

Although, shortly after *Metahistory*, White embarked on a structuralist adventure that came to threaten this humanist voluntarism
rather seriously (see chapter 4 of this volume), it is worth emphasizing how important this voluntarism was in *Metahistory*. As Kellner
aptly observes: "*Metahistory* undercuts all foundationalism, except
one, which it acknowledges as a mystery of great value. This foun-
dation is the human will."[20]

Imagination: thinking and dreaming

What, then, is the "mythic" alternative that this powerful human
will might envision for Crocean-style history? With reference to
thinkers already featured in "The Burden of History" – Yeats, Joyce,
Jaspers, Heidegger, Sartre, and others – *Metahistory* claimed that
such mythic modes of realism come in various forms. Over against
the irony of professional historiography, twentieth-century philosophers and novelists had suggested "conceptions of the historical
process which are cast in the modes of Metaphor, Metonymy, and
Synecdoche" (433). Just like irony, these three alternative "tropes"
were ancient figures of speech. They were names for various forms
of figurative language. Both metonymy and synecdoche, for
example, denoted forms of rhetorical substitution ("ten sails" for
"ten boats," or "Downing Street" for the office of the British Prime
Minister). But when White borrowed these tropes or figures of
speech from Vico, the Italian rhetorician, he used them for a different purpose. Just as he took irony – in most cases – to refer to a
mode of realism that had been favored in professional historiography since Croce, so metaphor, metonymy, and synecdoche also
referred to paradigms of realism.[21]

Take, for example, White's introductory chapter on eighteenth-
century historical studies, in which the author complained at length
about the antithetical manner in which Enlightenment philosophers
such as Voltaire had opposed reason to myth. The cause to which
the likes of Voltaire had devoted their lives was that of "truth
against untruth, reason against folly, and enlightenment against
superstition and ignorance" (50). Only Vico, said White, had recognized how naive such an opposition was. Only Vico had realized
that reason and unreason – or history and myth – are always inter-

twined. The question he had raised was how *mythos* can give birth to *logos*, or how reason can be detected in fantasy and myth: "The Enlighteners, because they viewed the relationship of reason to fantasy in terms of an opposition rather than as a part–whole relationship, were unable to formulate this question in a historiographically profitable way" (52). Crucial, then, is that *Metahistory* characterized the part–whole relationship suggested by Vico as synecdochic, whereas it labeled the opposition between reason and myth suggested by the French Enlighteners as metonymic (and as quickly sliding down into irony).

What was metonymic about the Enlightenment refusal to acknowledge interaction between reason and unreason was the effect this refusal had on Voltaire's conception of the real. His commitment to reason alone had led Voltaire to disregard dreams, myths, and fantasies as proper agents of change. Voltaire had seen the "historical field" – White's technical term for what we imagine history to be – as populated by chains of causes and effects, the interdependency of which can be rationally proven. Given that metonymies typically reduce phenomena to their underlying causes – in the "ten sails" example, it is the sail that drives the boat forward – White could say that Voltaire had conceived history "in the mode of Metonymy, or of cause-effect relationships" (67). Moreover, this metonymy had had an "Ironic consequence" (69), not so much because its focus on rational causes and effects had led to a pedantic condemnation of everything that seemed irrational, but rather because the strategy had been self-defeating:

> For, if I *begin* with an apprehension of the field of human history as an area of happening dominated by cause-effect relationships, then I am bound ultimately to regard anything in this field, any man, institution, value, or idea, as nothing but an "effect" of some causal nexus – that is to say, as a contingent (hence determined) reality, and thus as *irrational* in its essence. (66)

Regardless of how plausible this interpretation of Enlightenment historiography is, the example shows nicely what White's tropes were all about. As the foregoing makes clear, White did *not* claim that Voltaire's prose had been particularly rich in metonymic figures of speech, or that Enlightenment historians had increasingly come to favor the writing of ironic narratives. Rather than referring to the rhetoric of historical texts, the tropes, in White's hands, were metaphors for modes of realism or shorthand labels for presuppositions regarding the nature of the real that historians bring to the study of the past. Voltaire's thought had been metonymic because he had "precritically apprehended" (67) the historical field with the assumption that reason is incompatible with unreason. By contrast, White portrayed Vico and Herder as synecdochic historians because of their "precritical" belief that *logos* and *mythos* are mutually enriching aspects of the human mind, neither of which can exist without the other (52, 75).

All this explains what White had in mind when he suggested that the ironist's cage could be forced open with a Nietzschean deconstruction of "history," which in turn would offer the released prisoner the freedom to enter the realm of "myth." Despite the insinuations of some critics, this was not to say that historians, once they are liberated from irony, are justified to say about the past whatever they please.[22] White did not want to do away with such things as archival research or source criticism (even though he liked to challenge the authority historians often attribute to these practices). Neither did he deny that the writing of history fulfills different needs than the writing of fiction, or that there are criteria for distinguishing between good and bad historiography. Operating at a much higher level of abstraction, White's point was rather that the various forms of "realism" available to historians all presuppose a "precritically" conceived idea of how reason relates to unreason. His complaint about the irony pervading Croce's work – the rigid separation of historical studies and moral reflection – was an objection against a realism supporting such a separation by contrasting the "rationality" of historical inquiry with the "irrationalities" of moral reflection and political decision-making. In other words, the harsh treatment of White's former hero, Croce, in the book's last chapter did not merely reflect a desire for more explicit political commitment than Croce had displayed. The more fundamental point was that a productive relationship between the *logos* of historical scholarship and the *mythos* of morality and politics requires a realism in which both have a legitimate place. A "non-ironic" realism would allow *logos* and *mythos* to interact and reinforce each other. In short, White hoped for the oxymoron of a "mythistory."[23]

Against this background, the book's epigraph – "One can study only what one has first dreamed about" – begins to make sense. This Gaston Bachelard quotation not only says that every form of historical realism presupposes a "precritically accepted paradigm" of what history is (ix). More importantly, it reveals White's belief that *logos* cannot do without *mythos*, or that a "morally responsible human science" requires "a conjugation of thinking with dreaming."[24] Like Vico, the theorist of history and myth, White believed that *logos* and *mythos* are equally important aspects of the human imagination. Consequently, historical imagination – a keyword from the book's subtitle – must also be understood as a matter of both thinking and dreaming. It must be added, however, that if the imaginative mind begins to determine what is "real," it has the freedom to favor either *logos* (as is often the case in science) or *mythos* (as may happen among poets). In other words, it may prefigure the historical field in such a way that the belonging together of thinking and dreaming is destroyed or forgotten. White thus made two claims: that the "deep structural forms of the historical imagination" (31) are always simultaneously a matter of reason and myth – so that there are elements of thinking *and* dreaming even in the most rationalistic rejection of myth – and that these two elements each deserve a proper place in how the human imagination defines the real. Whereas the former was presented as an empirical claim, the latter was an unequivocal plea for modes of realism that would not reject the utopian dream of a socially progressive politics as "unrealistic."[25]

Strikingly, however, White declined to recommend one particular trope as most appropriate for this goal. Although his preference for the tropes of metaphor and synecdoche was more than evident, he refused to present one of these as the alternative that his audience ought to embrace. White rather consistently emphasized that there are possibilities from which human individuals may choose the option that best corresponds to their personal moral beliefs. Although this "pluralism" has been criticized as a rather inefficient strategy of attack against irony,[26] it gives clear evidence of how firmly White believed that any reader must decide for him- or herself what to make of history. Faithful to his existentialist-inspired humanism, White tried to practice what he preached: an uncompromising individualism in matters of the heart and will.[27]

A manual of tropology

In the meantime, the conclusion reached about the tropes – they refer to modes of realism, rather than to features of narrative texts – is not a particularly conventional one. Echoing White's introduction, most commentators suggest that the "deep structural content" that the tropes denote "is generally poetic, and specifically linguistic, in nature" (ix). One may wonder: doesn't this poetic or linguistic dimension pose a problem for the interpretation offered in the previous section? As long as one speaks about "a deep level of consciousness on which a historical thinker chooses conceptual strategies by which to explain or represent" (x) his or her data, the foregoing analysis makes perfect sense. But if one adds, with White, that on this level the historian performs "an essentially *poetic* act," the forms of which "are characterizable by the linguistic modes in which they are cast" (x), the question arises how Voltaire's or Vico's understanding of the relation between reason and myth can be "poetic" or "linguistic." Moreover, an attentive reader might ask: if it is true that tropes refer to modes of realism, then can the same be said about the three other dimensions that White distinguished in the historian's work: modes of emplotment, modes of argument, and modes of ideological implication?

In order to answer these questions, let us take an example and turn to the Ranke chapter. According to White,

> Ranke prefigured the historical field in the mode of Metaphor, which sanctioned a primary interest in events in their particularity and uniqueness, their vividness, color, and variety, and then suggested the Synecdochic comprehension of it as a field of formal coherences, the ultimate or final unity of which could be suggested by analogy to the nature of the parts. (167)

This was to say that the German historian had focused on "the particular for itself," or on the uniqueness of every historical phenomenon. At the same time, he had believed these "particulars" to participate in the "development" of the human spirit through the course of time. For White, the combination of these two beliefs could be characterized with the trope of metaphor. Just as a metaphor ("He is a wolf in sheep's clothing") describes one thing in terms of another, thereby highlighting both the similarities and the differences between them, so Ranke (in White's reading) had simultaneously emphasized the uniqueness of all historical phenomena and the process of development in which everything participated. If this explains why "Ranke prefigured the historical field in the mode of Metaphor," an additional feature of Ranke's historical work was that it had assumed a qualitative correspondence between singular and universal. The individual event and the grand-scale development of the human spirit had been supposed to share certain qualities. In White's understanding, Ranke had specified this relationship when he prefigured historical reality in terms of "micro" and "macro cosmoses," the latter of which had been related to the former in the same way that a man and his amiable character are related in the synecdoche "he is all heart" (36, 177). Accordingly, in White's terminology, Ranke's prefiguration of history had been not only metaphorical, but synecdochic as well.

Whatever one may think of White's exegesis of Ranke's world-view, it is clear that *Metahistory* used the tropes here (again) to refer to ways of defining what is "real" in the past, rather than to narra-tive structures or rhetorical devices. Whereas the metaphor denoted how Ranke had thought "the [historical] process as a whole was to be comprehended" (176), the synecdoche referred to his "tropologi-cal characterization" of the historical field (177). Just as in the cases of Voltaire and Vico, then, the tropes functioned as shorthand refer-ences to what Ranke had imagined history "essentially" to be. Therefore, following the book's subtitle, we may say that the tropes as used by White were labels for modes of realism devised by the historical imagination. Historical imagination, as we have seen, must be understood as that realm of thinking and dreaming in which people form their "precritical" ideas of what history is (their *Vorverständnis* or "pre-understanding," as the German philosopher Hans-Georg Gadamer would say). As labels for the modes of realism developed in the realm of imagination, the tropes then functioned as metaphors. Taken from the field of rhetoric, these figures of speech were transferred to the domain of imagination to classify the historian's prefigurations in terms of the analogies these prefigura-tions displayed with rhetorical figures of speech.[28]

What, then, about emplotment, argument, and ideology? To start with the latter: "ideological implications" were also more a matter of realisms than of narrative texts. Defined as "prescriptions for taking a position in the present world of social praxis and acting upon it," such ideological implications were said to stem from how the historian "precritically" approaches the domain of history, "attended by arguments that claim the authority of 'science' or 'realism'" (22). As, again, the Ranke chapter makes clear, such ideo-logical positions were supposed to stem from the historian's mode of prefiguration. Speaking about "the conservative implications of Ranke's idea of history" (173), White emphasized that the develop-mental process which Ranke had seen culminating in the nine-teenth-century nation-state naturally favored conservatism over radicalism. For if the Prussian nation-state had been "the goal toward which everything tends," the political reality of Ranke's own days had apparently counted as "the *ideal of all time*" (173). In other words, it was from Ranke's prefiguration of the real, rather than his historical writing, that White deduced his ideological position.

Much the same goes for the modes of formal argument. Without any reference to Ranke's collected works, White presented the man's "organicist" mode of argument as a "methodological projection" of his synecdochic prefiguration (177). Stemming from Ranke's belief in qualitative correspondences between micro and macro cosmoses, this "uniquely historical mode of comprehension" could be called organicist in so far as it treated historical events as organic parts of larger entities (179). As an organicist historian, Ranke had seen "individual entities as components of processes which aggregate into wholes that are greater than, or qualitatively different from, the sum of their parts" (15). The implications of this view can easily be traced in Ranke's historical writing. It is, in fact, not too difficult a task to find passages in which Ranke "explained" an event by portraying it as part of a larger whole. But this is not how White proceeded. Instead, he presented Ranke's organicism as a logical consequence of his synecdochic prefiguration. Strikingly, the only evidence White referred to was Wilhelm von Humboldt's essay "On the Task of the Historian," which he took as a reliable guide to the historicist worldview through which both Humboldt and Ranke had interpreted the past. White's modes of argument, then, also were modes of conceiving historical reality.

Unlike these modes of ideology and argument, the mode of "emplotment" – a neologism that led Richard Vann to wonder how such a linguistic "monstrosity" could make it into common parlance[29] – was somewhat ambiguous. When speaking about "the plot of Michelet's history of France" (176), in which *le peuple français* served as a collective hero, White unmistakably referred to the structuring of a story by means of a plot, which he declared to take place "in the course of narrating" a story (7). This seems to suggest that emplotments, unlike ideologies and argument, are first and foremost to be found in the historical narrative. Nonetheless, in his discussion of Michelet's *Histoire de la révolution*, White did not take the trouble to analyze the plot of Michelet's narrative. He did not investigate how different story-elements figured in Michelet's romance, or how this plot gave meaning to the story of the Revolution. Rather, the subject of White's analysis was Michelet's vision, his understanding of the historical role of the French people, and his view on the relationship between the various actors in the historical field. This is even clearer in Ranke's case. When White attributed Ranke with a comic plot, this was to say that Ranke had conceived of history as a process in which all tensions are gradually harmonized. Emplotment, then, referred to "the general framework, the mythic significance" (186) of history. So, again, White appeared not primarily interested in the historical text – in Michelet's or Ranke's plot-development or story-lines – but in the metahistorical vision that these historians had brought to the study of the past. As Fredric Jameson, responding to the White of 1973, correctly observes: "he is not interested in the narrativity of the historical discourse, thereby distinguishing himself from approaches like that of [Roland] Barthes. Nor can we look to his chapters for what I want to call ... a narrativist analysis proper of any of the histories that are his objects."[30]

Contrary to what is often asserted, then, the conceptual apparatus developed in *Metahistory* was not aimed at analyzing historical narratives. The four analytic categories employed in the book – tropes, plots, arguments, and ideologies – were not dimensions of the historian's written texts, but aspects of the "metahistorical" modes of realism underlying those textual forms of historical representation. Although, as we shall see in chapter 4, some of White's post-*Metahistory* publications would apply these categories to analyses of narrative discourse, this later usage should not be anachronistically read back into *Metahistory*. In fact, despite its reputation to the contrary (its alleged similarity to Erich Auerbach's *Mimesis*, for example),[31] *Metahistory* hardly dealt more than in passing with textual fragments from the historians and philosophers under discussion. White based his portrayal of Ranke as a "comic" historian not on such books as *Die römischen Päpste* or the *Deutsche Geschichte im Zeitalter der Reformation*, but on prefaces and lectures in which Ranke, often merely in passing, had informed his readers about his way of approaching the past. Likewise, the Burckhardt chapter rested, not on *Die Cultur der Renaissance in Italien* or *Die Zeit Constantins des Grossen*, but on lectures in which Burckhardt had explicitly invoked his metahistorical beliefs. Therefore, like Jameson, Dominick LaCapra hits the nail on its head: "What one ... misses in White is an analysis of the way in which the formalized schemata and patterns he elicits actually function in texts."[32]

Yet the absence of such narrative analyses should not surprise us. The foregoing suggests that White was primarily interested in the "modalities of conceptualization" (42) that historians bring to the study of the past. White's categories sought to classify the forms of realism that historians develop in the realm of "precritical" historical imagination. Therefore, trivial as it may sound, *Metahistory* was a book about metahistory. Tropes, plots, arguments, and ideologies were shorthand labels for the metahistorical prefigurations of the "real" that underlie the "narrative prose discourses" that White would examine in his later publications.

Structuralist linguistics

Yet why then did *Metahistory* employ rhetorical terms and claim to treat the historian's work "as what it most manifestly is: a verbal structure in the form of a narrative prose discourse" (ix)? A short answer is that White was in need of a vocabulary that could describe and classify those metahistorical modes of realism. A longer, more complicated one is that the author felt inspired by the possibilities that structuralist linguistics, coming into vogue in the late 1960s, seemed to offer for anyone in search of such a vocabulary. Obviously, the vocabulary presented in *Metahistory* was a hodgepodge of elements ("a *bricolage* that mistook itself for a system").[33] The plots were borrowed from Northrop Frye, the Canadian literary theorist whom White came to hold in increasingly high esteem; the ideological modes came from sociologist Karl Mannheim; the modes of argument were variations on a typology of "world hypotheses" developed by the American philosopher Stephen C. Pepper; and the tropes were derived not only from Vico, but also from literary theorist Kenneth Burke, who had suggested a fourfold typology of "master tropes" similar to Vico's in his *A Grammar of Motives* (14–15 n. 8). More importantly, however, White's use of the tropes was indebted to the structuralist theorists Roman Jakobson and Claude Lévi-Strauss.

In the 1960s, Jakobson, the Russian linguist, acquired fame for a theory of language based on the tropes of metaphor and metonymy. His suggestion was that metaphor and metonymy are irreducible aspects of linguistic behavior.[34] All meaningful language use requires a selection of words (metaphor) as well as a combination of words (metonymy). Metaphor and metonymy, then, are not only distinct, but also indispensable, dimensions of language use: disorders emerge as soon as one of them begins to malfunction. The French ethnologist Lévi-Strauss, in turn, applied these terms to the study of myth.[35] Metaphoric, in his sense of the word, is a mythic mapping of the human world onto a world of animals or supernatural beings:

gods and devils that behave like human beings or birds that are attributed with human emotions. Metonymic, by contrast, is the inclusion of the non-human in everyday life and the distinctions this inclusion requires between humans on the one hand and farm or domestic animals on the other.[36] Lévi-Strauss, then, imported a terminology originally devised by Jakobson for describing human *language* into the study of *myth*. But in this transfer, the distinction between language and myth was lost, or – better – deliberately given up. For Lévi-Strauss spoke not merely metaphorically, in linguistic terms, about myths; he went so far as to assert that "myth *is* language" ("to be known, myth has to be told; it is a part of human speech") and that, for this reason, Jakobson's distinction unconditionally applied to myths.[37]

In *Metahistory*, White came close to making a similar move. Admittedly, he rejected Jakobson's bipolar dyad in favor of a four-fold system of tropes, mainly because this allowed for a more subtle classification of historical realisms. Nonetheless, the way in which *Metahistory* presented these tropes approximated Lévi-Strauss's use of them. Whereas the ten chapters interposed between the introduction and the conclusion employed rhetorical terms as shorthand references for metahistorical prefigurations – thereby using the tropes metaphorically for modes of realism that display a structural analogy to the part–whole relationships reflected in the tropes – the introduction and conclusion to White's book took the further step of treating historical imagination *as* language. Although White still located the "precognitive and precritical" act of prefiguration in the historian's "consciousness," this consciousness was now, in Lévi-Straussian manner, equated with "poetic, or figurative, language" (31). Also, the modes of realism White had distinguished – metaphoric, metonymic, synecdochic, and ironic – were interchanged with "modalities of poetic language itself" (31). Accordingly, imagination, which we defined above as the realm where thinking and dreaming meet each other, came to be called a "linguistic ground" (431). Likewise, each of the tropes was said to represent a "linguistic paradigm" or "linguistic protocol" of how to conceive of history (37). Given this tendency to equate metahistory with language, the vocabulary that White developed became a metalanguage (a language about the language that is metahistory).

Yet it is hard to say what all these equations implied. Had White accepted the Lévi-Straussian wisdom that imagination is but another word for language, given that "to be known, imagination has to be expressed in language?" Had he come to believe that modes of realism were so dependent on modes of language that it made more sense to conceptualize the latter? Speaking about "the linguistic ground on which a given idea of history was constituted" (xi), White indeed seemed to imply that imagination is not identical to language, yet always confined by the possibilities it offers. But if this is the case – if "modes of historical thinking" crucially depend on "modalities of poetic language" – how then could White in one breath also speak about a "convention of discourse" (33 n. 13)? For although discourse always manifests itself in language, it is not identical to it. Discourses are sequences of sentences that employ the metaphoric and metonymic axes of language to the effect of producing a meaningful text or speech. Accordingly, to speak about the "linguistic grounds" of human imagination is not the same as to reflect on discourses in which that imagination expresses itself. In short, the question arises how White conceptualized the relationship between imagination, language, and discourse.

Although, in the course of the 1970s, White would reach a bit more clarity in these matters (see chapter 4 of this volume), *Metahistory* was still particularly unclear about it. Given White's *modus operandi* – he was a *bricoleur*, not a systematic philosopher – this was perhaps not altogether surprising. What fascinated White at this stage was rather that his "toolkit" allowed for a different sort of analysis than was usually conducted in studies of nineteenth-century historiography. It permitted him to abandon "the usual categories" employed in this field (427), including the often-made distinction between "proper" historical writing and "speculative" philosophy of history. Consequently, it enabled him to show that Ranke did not have a more realistic understanding of history than Hegel, Tocqueville, or Nietzsche. Besides, the toolkit made it possible to conceptualize historical studies in the same structuralist manner in which some leading theorists of the 1960s reflected on literature and art. Most important, then, about the "general theory" outlined in *Metahistory* was its methodological potential. Seen in this light, the author's sweeping statements about the "linguistic grounds" of historical thought are perhaps better interpreted as experiments in applying Lévi-Strauss to history than as indicators of a metaphysical position on consciousness or language. White was neither a systematic thinker nor a metaphysically oriented philosopher. "Language" and "discourse" entered his vocabulary only because of their potential in uncovering and naming the presuppositions underlying the various claims to realism in historical studies.

The freedom of imagination

Nonetheless, one question cannot but arise. Even if *Metahistory* should not be read too systematically, how did White's optimistic belief in the liberating powers of the human will relate to his interest in the modalities of language? If this book has shown anything so far, it is that White was an existentialist-inspired humanist. He was a twentieth-century Pelagius who expected the imaginative powers of the human individual to be sufficient to invent a new, rich, and meaningful way of relating past and present. But how could this new history be thought of if the human imagination is always limited to the modalities of poetic language? Doesn't the latter suggest a determinism incongruous with the freedom and creativity that White had emphasized so far? In short, doesn't *Metahistory* suffer from a tension between its "linguisticism" and its insistence on the freedom to devise a realism consistent with one's own moral agenda?

Recall that in his Toronto lecture, White had addressed the conservative powers that so often constrain the human imagination. The liberation historian that White was knew well that human thought is often imprisoned in conventions that confirm the status quo. Nonetheless, he saw it as the task of morally responsible thinkers to challenge such conventions by presenting socially progressive alternatives (chapter 2 in this volume). *Metahistory* addressed a similar tension. On the one hand, its tropes denoted modalities of language that determine how historians prefigure the historical field. On the other, White emphasized that a choice between these modes is always possible. Even if the number of possibilities is "not infinite" (31), alternatives to the ironic mode in which history is usually conceptualized are freely available. It may take a considerable amount of courage to break with powerful conventions. But the fact that conventions exist does not exclude the possibility of rebellion. On the contrary, White's insistence that such traditions rest on "aesthetic and moral rather than epistemological" grounds (xii) was meant to have an emperor-has-no-clothes effect. If the realism endorsed by the historical profession has no other justification than moral or aesthetic preference, why not write history in a way consistent with one's own moral convictions? Why not break out of the ironist's cage, inspired by the examples of Michelet and Tocqueville?

A similar tension characterized White's discussion of "historiographical styles," which he defined as combinations of tropes, plots, modes of argument, and ideologies. In the "quadruple tetrad" – Kellner's name for the diagram in which White organized his categories[38] – "elective affinities" exist between the four elements on each horizontal row (29):

Trope	Emplotment	Argument	Ideology
metaphor	Romantic	formalist	anarchist
metonymy	tragic	mechanistic	radical
synecdoche	comic	organicist	conservative
irony	satirical	contextualist	liberal

That is to say that certain "structural homologies" (29) exist between, say, a synecdochic prefiguration, a comic emplotment, an organicist mode of argument, and a conservative ideology. With its overarching interest in organic part–whole relations, a synecdochic prefiguration is, after all, most consistent with an organicist mode of argument. Also, emphasizing gradual transformation more than sudden change, this organicism is likely to have a conservative impact. Therefore, although the affinities are by no means inevitable combinations, they suggest, in rather ideal-typical manner, what sort of historiographical style is likely to follow once a historian has adopted a particular sort of realism. In passing, this illustrates that, for White, the tropes always precede the three other dimensions of historical representation. Prefiguration, or the conceptualization of what is real, takes places at "a deep level of consciousness" (x). Significantly, the relevant passages in *Metahistory* relied heavily on spatial metaphors. Since the "linguistic ground" of realism was said to "underlie" emplotment, argument, and ideology (xi), White needed "to penetrate to the deeper level" (x) to locate the modes of metahistorical prefiguration. The tropes, then, were the most decisive factors in what White understood the historian's work to be. Once a mode of realism is adopted, a historiographical style consonant with it follows, in many cases, almost automatically.

Powerful as the elective affinities between tropes and other dimensions may be, White, of course, believed it possible to break through them, if not by a sheer act of will, then at least through the sort of self-reflectiveness that *Metahistory* sought to encourage. None of the great figures discussed in the book fitted within a single row: they had all combined incongruous elements into unique blends of their own. Michelet, for example, had combined a Romantic plot type and a formalist mode of argument with a liberal ideology (29). Marx had even employed two modes of emplotment at the same time – tragedy for the bourgeoisie and comedy for the proletariat – while wedding them to both mechanistic and organicist modes of argument (286–7). These seemingly inconsonant combinations had caused "dialectical tensions" (29) that, according to White, accounted for much of the attractiveness of their work. The greatness of Michelet and Marx consisted precisely in their ability to challenge conventional patterns of representation. Yet, in doing so, they had not transcended the quadruple tetrad. So, the freedom in which they had developed a style of their own had lain not *outside*, but *within*, the modalities of language. More precisely, their originality and independence had manifested themselves in creative combinations of tropes with plots or arguments normally considered incongruous with them. The freedom applauded throughout White's book must therefore not be associated with something like a disregard for the modes of realism available in human language. It was not a freedom *from* possibilities, but a freedom *to use* existing possibilities in such a way as to encourage a socially progressive historiography.[39]

Consequently, the historian's freedom that *Metahistory* so eloquently praised was not an adolescent sort of freedom "to do whatever one pleases," but a freedom stemming from deep insight into the modes of realism that human language offers. In White's own words, the dialectic tension found in Tocqueville or Hegel was "nothing but a formalization of an insight into the tropological nature" of poetic language (428). In other words: these tensions were created by ingenious minds, thoroughly familiar with the rich but limited set of realisms available to human language-users. Accordingly, White's often-repeated insistence on the variety of available modes of realism aimed to alert historians to possibilities they need to be aware of in order to escape the ironist's cage. Rather than claiming naively or authoritatively that there is but a single correct mode of doing history, historians need to be "epistemologically self-conscious" or – which amounts to the same – "cognitively responsible" (23). In practical terms, this means that historians must not assume Rankean orthodoxy to be the final measure of things: they need to see that alternative realisms, such as discussed in "The Burden of History," are equally legitimate.

Yet an emerging tension between freedom and language cannot be denied. In particular, the introduction and conclusion to *Metahistory* reflected a shift of emphasis from an unqualified freedom of the imagination to linguistic modes through which that imagination defines what counts as real in history. Even if, as the foregoing makes clear, White felt not yet threatened by this tension, because he understood his quadruple tetrad, not as a restraint on the freedom of the imagining mind, but as a specification of how the imagination defines the real, it was but a small step to say, as White would do in later years, that not imagination but language is the real agent in the work of interpretation (see chapter 4 in this volume). Hans Kellner and David Harlan correctly detect the beginning of a "paradox" or "contradiction" between White's tendency towards linguistic determinism and his appeal to the historian's moral vocation.[40]

White's linguistic turn

In recapitulation, *Metahistory* was an end as much as a beginning. It was an end in so far as it brought together some of the lines described in the two previous chapters – White's existentalist humanism, his critique of Rankean professionalism, and his search for politically relevant alternatives – in a passionate plea for trans-formation of the historical discipline (or, in Vichian terms, for a *ricorso* from irony all the way back to metaphor). Influential as White's humanism would remain for his philosophy of history in later years, *Metahistory* was perhaps the last occasion on which White invited *professional* historians to change their mode of realism. In the 1980s, White came to the sobering insight that a non-ironic realism is more likely to be found outside the historical discipline. Encouraged also by the rather enthusiastic reception of his tropol-ogy among students of literature, White began to put his hope more in novelists and film directors than in historians. Whereas, as we shall see in the remaining chapters, he continued his battle against irony with undiminished zeal, White lost the "youthful idealism" that had made him believe historians would join his patricide on Ranke, the alleged father of their discipline.[41]

Simultaneously, *Metahistory* was a beginning, especially because of its proposal to speak about modes of historical realism in terms of languages. Not undeservedly, the book is often regarded as the initiator of a linguistic turn in the study of historiography.[42] Although, as we have seen, *Metahistory* was anything but clear about the exact status of language, especially in relation to imagina-tion and discourse, the book left no doubt that White wanted to treat historical imagination as language. Not discourse, but lan-guage – more particularly, poetic language – was what White postulated as the "ground" of any form of realism devised by the historian's imagination. This, I have argued, was not to deny the freedom of the historian to conceptualize history in his or her own way. Rather, White's "quadruple tetrad" intended to make historians aware of possibilities which they can freely combine. White's tropology did not compromise his individualist voluntarism; it tried to fuel it.

Metahistory's reception history confirms that the linguistic turn inaugurated by the book was the most important "beginning" White made in the early 1970s. Although a reviewer such as Michael Ermarth, writing in the *American Historical Review*, correctly observed that White distinguished "four different styles of realism," none of which was necessarily better than the other, he shared with many other readers a more substantive interest in the "arsenal" that White derived from structuralist linguistics ("a discipline that may become the *novum organon* of the twentieth century").[43] It was this linguistically inspired theory about historical writing that made *Metahistory* a turning point in postwar philosophy of history. Rather than clarifying theoretical issues arising *within* a scientific conception of history – such as the hotly debated covering law model of explanation – *Metahistory* raised questions *about* a scientific understanding of history. Even though its anti-ironic program turned out to be less than effective among historians, its attentiveness to questions of language, style, and representation would decisively change the agenda of (especially English-language) philosophy of history. From 1973 onwards, representation, language, discourse, and narrative became increasingly important key words. Yet, as the next chapter will show, it was only after *Metahistory* that White himself came to theorize discourse and narrative in their relations to historical studies, thereby making a discursive as well as a narrative turn in continuation of the linguistic turn epitomized in *Metahistory*.

4

The Power of Discourse: White's Structuralist Adventure

By the time *Metahistory* appeared, White had exchanged Los Angeles for Connecticut. At Wesleyan University, in Middletown, he took up the directorship of the Center for the Humanities (where he had previously, in 1969, spent a half-year fellowship). While the Center had a fresh interest in the cultural *avant garde* – it invited such experimental artists as John Cage to the campus – Wesleyan was also the place where White's good friend Louis O. Mink taught philosophy and where, together with Mink and others, Richard T. Vann edited *History and Theory*. In this intellectual atmosphere, White enjoyed a brief period of intense creativity. The years between 1973 and 1978 – when White moved back to California to start a History of Consciousness program at Santa Cruz – saw the publication of a great many articles. Some of them were devoted to an elaboration of the tropological model whose initial version we encountered in the previous chapter. During the 1970s, White adapted the model in such a way as to make it applicable not merely to metahistorical assumptions, but also to concrete specimens of historical narrative.

At the same time, White increasingly began to publish in literary theory, focusing especially on the most dazzling lights in that firmament: figures such as Roland Barthes, Michel Foucault, and Jacques Derrida. Also, under his guidance, the Center for the Humanities moved into areas that, at first sight, seemed far removed from White's prime interests. For example, when in 1973 the local press asked the newly appointed Director what his plans for the Center were, White answered: "I would . . . like to see the Center address itself to the problem of relating the so-called 'high' culture to its 'popular' counterpart, especially in American life." This was necessary, White explained – in what sounded like a remarkable dismissal of the liberal humanism defended in his previous work – because a "typical humanistic education prepares a person very well to live as a 19th century European gentleman rather than as a 20th century American. I think that the whole counter-culture movement has been a repudiation of this older, European high-culture. The problem of the humanities remains to link up the high culture with the popular one."[1] White did what he promised. In one of the first addresses delivered in his new capacity, he dared to regale his audience on a Barthes-kind of exposition on French fries, asserting that the French style of processing potatoes into fries is as informative about "the sustaining myths of France's national identity" as the novels of Gustave Flaubert and Marcel Proust.[2]

As this chapter will make clear, the structuralist fascination that we have already encountered in the preface, introduction, and conclusion to *Metahistory* became particularly important during the 1970s. In fact, White plunged into what is best described as a structuralist adventure with unanticipated consequences.[3] Inspired by Lévi-Strauss and Foucault, White began to examine the power of discourse, and discovered to his consternation that it could potentially destroy the humanist subject in which he had put his faith ever since his student days in Detroit. While examining, in some essays, how structuralism might contribute to a destabilization of "official" historical studies, he worried, on other occasions, whether Barthes, Foucault, and Derrida didn't go too far in their criticism of values cherished in the humanist tradition. These, then, are the themes I will discuss in this chapter. I will explain a number of concepts invariably associated with the name of White – narrative and figurative language in particular – and hope to add something new by contextualizing these concepts in White's struggle with the question of whether the voluntarism that *Metahistory* had vigorously defended could be maintained against the force of French structuralist thought.

Three modes of comprehension

Let us start with a less distant source of influence, on the Wesleyan campus: Louis O. Mink.[4] Arguably, White's interest in issues of narrative was greatly stimulated by a ground-breaking article Mink wrote in 1970 for the journal *New Literary History*. While this piece applauded the efforts of some recent philosophers of history – W. B. Gallie, Morton White, and A. R. Louch in particular – to argue that historians explain the past not by means of causal laws but by writing narratives, Mink took issue with Gallie's view that understanding a narrative means "following a story."[5] Although it may be true that historians construct stories for leading their readers through "possible routes towards the required but as yet undisclosed conclusion," most readers of Garrett Mattingly's *The Defeat of the Spanish Armada* do not follow Mattingly's story in the way they follow a detective story. They are not curious about the "outcome" of the story (the fate of the Spanish naval forces in their war against England), but about the "point of it all" (what constituted this defeat). In Mink's view, good historical scholarship allows the reader to "grasp together" a series of past events. It enables the reader to think together "in a single act, or in a cumulative series of acts, the complicated relationships of parts which can be experienced only *seriatim*."

Such an act of "grasping together" or "comprehension" can take different forms. Mink distinguished between theoretical, categoreal, and configurational types of comprehension. Whereas the first and second forms are typical for the natural sciences and philosophy, respectively, Mink considered the third type of comprehension ("the ability to hold together a number of elements in just balance") characteristic of historical studies. For what Mink believed historians to aim for is not a one-thing-after-another story, as Gallie's "phenomenology of following" suggests, but a view in which beginnings and endings are all encompassed in a *totum simul* view: "To comprehend temporal succession means to think of it in both directions at once, and then time is no longer the river which bears us along but the river in aerial view, upstream and downstream seen in a single survey."[6]

How much White welcomed this contribution by Mink is apparent from a letter he sent his friend in 1970: "I'd like to have a copy of your piece in New Lit. Hist., but I have really been studying it quite carefully."[7] Moreover, this study yielded immediate results. As early as 1971, White applied Mink's trichotomic distinction to the study of historical narratives. Yet, unlike Mink, White argued that historical writing is not only, or not predominantly, characterized by configurational comprehension, but simultaneously by all three modes of understanding.[8] Theoretical comprehension occurs in the *argumentative* dimension of historical discourse, categoreal comprehension in the *plot* of the narrative, and configurational comprehension in what White called the *story*.

White substantiated this argument with what one might call a four-level theory of historical interpretation. The first level is that of "atomic events." White did not yet explain what he considered such events to be, but seemed to think of them in a classic empiricist manner: as "raw data" that historians distill from their sources.[9] For White, interpretation starts only when historians, at a second level, order their events "in a rough chronicle." At this level, White emphasized, historians do not yet have a story. For, in order "to be transformed into a story, a set of events must be organized in such a way as to inspire a certain type of question in the reader, such questions as: 'What happened next?' or 'How did that come about?'" So, the chronicle – in White's ideal-typical definition, not to be confused with the medieval genre known by this name – is merely a selection of events, or, as White would say in later years, a description that transforms "events" (in the past) into "facts" (in historical discourse, that is to say, in any "verbal composition" longer than a sentence).[10]

Only when historians begin to organize this chronicle thematically, by "patterning events into motif-clusters," do stories emerge. Stories, then, are thematically ordered accounts of historical events. They organize a historical account by grouping events into thematic unities.[11] It is by means of story-telling that the death of Diocletian, for example, becomes part of an opening motif in a history of medieval Christianity, or part of a closing motif in a study of late antique Rome. Therefore, stories are forms of data organization that can be "followed" in the way suggested by Gallie. Moreover, at this story level, historians choose the characters figuring in their account (is it about an individual, about an idea, or about *le peuple français*?) and adopt a "narrative voice." Whereas a chronicle tells itself, so to say, a story is always told by a "knower" who orders the material in such a way as to answer a "What happened?" question.[12]

Finally, the story serves as the basis for either an "argument" or a "plot." Employing a classic distinction between analytic and narrative history, White argued that historians use their motif-units *either* as "components of an argument" *or* as "phases of recognizable, traditional story-models." In the first case, an "explanatory effect" is achieved through, for example, the use of a Hempelian covering-law model. In the second, a plot-structure is imposed upon the story to encode it in such a way that the reader recognizes the story as a romance, tragedy, comedy, or satire. Plots, then, are not identical to stories. Whereas stories can be followed, plots can only be grasped in a moment of insight. They are not understood until the reader sighs: "Oh, *now* I see what was *really* happening after all." Plots do not give answers to questions like "What happened next?" or "How did that come about?" but provide insight into "the point of it all." This happens only if the reader grasps how the motif-clusters of a story are interrelated: "Plot-structures charge the phases of a story with different affective valencies or weights, so that we can read the change in continuity (or the reverse) figured in the story as a consummation, a culmination, or a degeneration – that is to say, as a drama with Comic, Tragic, or Ironic significance, as the case may be."[13]

Armed with these distinctions, White suggested that the interpretative work done at the levels 2, 3, and 4 corresponds to Mink's three modes of comprehension: "On the story proper level, we might speak of 'configurational' comprehension of a set of events. On the level of argument we might speak of 'theoretical' comprehension of them. And on the level of plot we might speak of a 'categoreal' comprehension, though not of the events in the story so much as of the story itself."[14] Arguably, White was not wholly consistent when he contended that these three modes "can be simultaneously appealed to by historians," given that he had just made an either/or distinction between arguments and plots. Also, in spite of White's assertion to the contrary ("I am not saying that the Hempelian analysis is not useful"), he appeared far less interested in the argumentative dimension of historical studies than in their modes of emplotment.[15] If White emphasized anything, it was that historians always choose a plot and that this choice is dictated not by the materials under investigation (level 1), nor by the chains of events ordered in a story-form (level 2), but by what *Metahistory* called "ultimately aesthetic or moral rather than epistemological" grounds.

This, in turn, explains why White gave such a remarkable twist to Mink's modes of comprehension. Mink himself had suggested that configurational comprehension ("seeing things together") takes place when a reader grasps the point of a narrative. In other words, Mink had introduced the notion of configurational comprehension in order to account for what is typical about historical interpretation in a narrative mode. Although White agreed with this, he added that configurational comprehension comes in a limited number of forms. Whereas Mink, following Collingwood, had presented configurational understanding as a product of the historian's (and the reader's) individual imagination, so that, in principle, this configuration can take as many forms as there are historians or readers, White repeated a point encountered in the previous chapter: that the human imagination is not limitless, but bound to the four modes distinguished in *Metahistory*. In the end, White thus privileged the categoreal mode over the configurational mode. For him, an act of "seeing things together" (in the configurational mode) is always preceded by a choice (in the categoreal mode) from the plot-types available in modern Western culture.[16]

Figurative language

All this was written in November 1971, not long before White sent the manuscript of *Metahistory* to his editors at Johns Hopkins University Press. Interestingly, White still found a chance to incorporate these new ideas in his book. In the introduction, he outlined a "theory of the historical work" almost identical to the one just analyzed. One remarkable difference was that White replaced his two-class distinction between argument and plot with a three-class division between argument, ideology, and plot. Also, instead of treating these categories as mutually exclusive, he defined a historiographical style as a combination of some particular modes of argument, ideology, and emplotment (see chapter 3). Apart from this, both the model developed in response to Mink and the one that found its way into *Metahistory* were designed for application to written historical work. More specifically, both were developed for an analysis of historical narratives such as those produced by historians or historical novelists. Yet, because the larger part of *Metahistory* had already been written, it was impossible to bring the entire manuscript into accordance with this model. By consequence, in spite of the promises made in his introduction, White did not (yet) apply his model to actual historical narratives. As we have seen in chapter 3, the case-studies that followed White's programmatic introduction rather focused on modes of realism through which historians such as Tocqueville and Ranke had approached the historical field. In practical terms, this implied that White extended his model so as to make it applicable not merely to (written) historical narratives, but also to metahistorical ideas in the realm of the historian's imagination.

Yet, although *Metahistory* was sent off to the press without any example of the sort of narrative analysis advocated in the introduction, one of the first subsequent steps White took was to apply his model to concrete examples of historical writing. In a 1975 *History and Theory* article, he quoted a passage from *The Course of German History*, a book written by A. J. P. Taylor, and examined how this renowned British historian depicted the rise and fall of the Weimar Republic.[17] In what looked like a rather straightforward description of relevant facts and dates (level 1), White discerned, first of all, a chronicle (level 2) and, second, a story consisting of three units of time, corresponding to what Taylor called the emergence, stability, and crisis of the Weimar Republic (level 3). Moreover, this story turned out to be a particular kind of story, that is, to have a plot (level 4): it was a "pseudo or satirical tragedy." What made the decline of the Republic in Taylor's account not merely a tragedy but a satirical variant of that genre was Taylor's ironic assurance that it was a real tragedy only for those who believed that the Republic in its stable middle years had represented the "real" Germany. Taylor pretended to know better: a "deeper investigation" would reveal that the Weimar Republic had been anything but the "true" Germany.[18]

Crucial, then, is that this pseudo-tragic plot was a consequence of how Taylor had constituted or prefigured his object of study. Although, echoing *Metahistory*, we might say that modes of emplotment, argument, and ideology all stem from the act of prefiguration, White emphasized especially how emplotment follows from prefiguration. More particularly, he argued that the prefiguration on which emplotment depends is a matter of figurative language use. Figurative language is a collective term for the metaphors and other figures of speech that authors use in their texts. In the Taylor fragment White examined, these include such words as "created," "consumed," "reduced," and "overthrown." According to White, these verbs are important, first, for how Taylor constitutes his object of study (the Weimar Republic), but, second, also for the designation of his story as a pseudo-tragedy. The words just quoted "serve to characterize the *phases* of the archetypical literary fiction to which the Republic's life is being tacitly likened, namely, the pseudo-tragedy."[19] This implies that the plot of Taylor's story is an effect of the figurative language employed by the British historian. Innocent as such words as "created" and "consumed" may seem, they are, in fact, responsible for creating the conditions that allow Taylor's reader to exclaim at some point: "Oh, *now* I see what was *really* happening after all." In other words, it is the figurative language in the historian's narrative that endows a story with a plot. The "narrative technique" by which a historian moves from level 3 to level 4 is nothing other than "the techniques of *figurative* language": "All historical narratives presuppose figurative characterizations of the events they purport to represent and explain. And this means that historical narratives, considered purely as verbal artifacts, can be characterized by the mode of figurative discourse in which they are cast."[20]

In comparison to *Metahistory*, this focus on figurative language was relatively new. *Metahistory* did, of course, elaborate on the figures of speech known as the four "master tropes." Yet, in the 1973 book, these tropes had still been metaphoric labels for modes of imagination: White had not located them in the historian's written text. In the mid-1970s, however, the tropes became far more concrete. Signifying "modalities of representing relationships in words," these figures of speech, or figurative elements of language, became what they had been in ancient rhetoric: words and phrases through which rhetoricians create relationships – more particularly, part–whole or part–part relationships – between the elements in their discourse. In other words, White took figurative language to be a means for transforming "raw data" into "facts" that stand in some relation to each other:

> This means that the *shape* of the *relationships* which will appear to be inherent in the objects inhabiting the field will in reality have been imposed on the field by the investigator in the very *act of identifying and describing* the objects that he finds there. The implication is that historians *constitute* their subjects as possible objects of narrative representation by the very language they use to *describe* them.[21]

This argument had four interesting consequences. First, it undermined the old, empiricist distinction between description and interpretation. If facts are "events under description" – events described in such a way that they fit the form of the story the historian wants to tell – there is no description that is not, at the same time, interpretation. In historical discourse, interpretation goes all the way down. Thus, although White continued to speak about the "unprocessed historical record" from which historians derive their data – the archival sources they consult for their research projects – he developed a constructivist notion of facts. Facts are not found "out there"; they are constituted in the historian's language.[22]

Second, the argument undermined the classic (Aristotelian) distinction between history and poetry insofar as this distinction depended on an antithesis between the real and the imaginary. If works of history are "[v]iewed simply as verbal artifacts" – which is not the same as saying they are *nothing but* bodies of language – they resemble poems and novels in the use of figurative language for the purpose of constituting facts that suit a certain story-form:

> Novelists might be dealing only with imaginary events whereas historians are dealing with real ones, but the process of fusing events, whether imaginary or real, into a comprehensible totality capable of serving as the *object* of a representation, is a poetic process. Here the historian must utilize precisely the same tropological strategies, the same modalities of representing relationships in words, that the poet or novelist uses.[23]

As this quotation illustrates, White did not say (as some overly suspicious critics assumed) that there are no differences between history and poetry. As a matter of fact, White never denied that Taylor's *The Course of German History* belonged to a different genre than the *Iliad* or *A la recherche du temps perdu*. His point was only that none of these three works can avoid the use of figurative language in presenting its facts as objects of narrative representation. Just as it is impossible to write a history book without the use of language, so it is impossible to speak about the past (or the present) without the use of figurative language. Moreover, what historians and novelists have in common is that they can *choose* between various modes of figurative language, that is, between the four modalities of representing relationships available in language. Whereas some of the sciences (physics, chemistry, medicine) have become so disciplined that they have abolished this freedom by constructing "a formal technological system" for describing their objects, historians and novelists do not know such constraints: they can freely employ any of the modes of figurative language available to them.[24]

A third implication of the significance White began to attach to figurative language was an increasing interest in rhetorical analyses of historical work. Whereas *Metahistory* had signaled White's "linguistic turn," the author now made a "rhetorical turn" by shifting his attention to the narrative texture of what historians write. Although, in most cases, their books or articles simply present themselves as ordinary prose-texts, they always have, intentionally or not, a "poetical understructure" that can be uncovered by means of rhetorical analysis. Consequently, from the mid-1970s onwards,

White wrote a number of essays that sought to unravel the stylistic features of historical works. One of the most striking specimens of this genre was White's detailed comparison of Marx's *Der achtzehnte Brumaire des Louis Bonaparte* with Flaubert's *L'éducation sentimentale*. If such articles showed anything, it was that White no longer consulted prefaces, letters, and lecture notes to reconstruct the modes of realism underlying a historiographical oeuvre (as he had done in *Metahistory*). He rather treated realism as an effect of the historian's style, that is, of a particular combination of prefiguration, emplotment, argument, and ideology. Following Roland Barthes, then, he considered the historian's style responsible for the production of a "reality effect." In other words, the realism that historians seek to achieve is not only *imagined*, in that realm of the historian's mind where dream and reason meet; it is also *made* by means of figurative language.[25] In passing, I note that this type of rhetorical analysis ranks high among the most influential parts of White's oeuvre. Whereas White himself felt inspired by Lionel Gossman's study of Augustin Thierry, to which he wrote a brief introduction, his own work was admired and imitated by younger students of nineteenth-century historiography, such as Stephen Bann and Lynn Orr, both of whom explicitly drew on White's essays of the mid-1970s.[26]

Less influential, but equally important to White, was a fourth and final implication of his interest in figurative discourse. Although, as I shall show in the next section, White continued to explore the relationship between historical and fictional discourse, repacking his message concerning their structural affinity in the language of myth and fiction, he also raised a question that was of particular significance in the light of his previous work: to what extent was a structuralist analysis of the historian's language compatible with a humanist understanding of human selfhood? As we shall see in the final sections of this chapter, the tension that had emerged in *Metahistory* developed into a serious confrontation between White's "linguistic determinism" and the humanist subject whose "death" was celebrated by authors such as Foucault.

Fictions of factual representation

In White's mid-1970s writings, the similarity between historical and fictional discourse remained a prevalent theme. With real *Entdeckersfreude*, White played with his new insight, applying it to various classic texts (Charles Darwin's *The Origin of Species*, for example),

reformulating it in different vocabularies, and pushing it to its fur-
thest limits – much to the concern of Mink, who was always careful
not to obscure the distinction between history and fiction.[27] Whereas
more cautious authors than White might have done their best to
avoid misunderstanding, especially on the part of those historians
who tended to emphasize the differences rather than the similarities
between history and fiction, White deliberately formulated his
point in the boldest possible terms. Historical interpretation, he
claimed, was not only a matter of using figurative language; it also
involved myth-making and fiction-making.

Readers familiar with *Metahistory* know that White had described
the historian's imagination as a realm where myth has its legitimate
place. As we have seen in chapter 3, *Metahistory* had depicted the
human imagination as a field where *mythos* and *logos* are engaged
in creative interplay. Accordingly, whether historians like it or not,
the "deep structural forms of the historical imagination" are always
a matter of both reason and myth. In his post-*Metahistory* essays,
White emphasized the myth-making operations of the historian
even more aggressively. He eagerly quoted Lévi-Strauss as saying
that the "coherency" history seeks to achieve is nothing but "the
coherence of myth." This was not to imply that coherence is illusory.
On the contrary, what Lévi-Strauss and White had in mind was that
the coherence created by means of a plot-structure depends on
modes of emplotment – the four modes distinguished in *Metahistory*
– "which the myths of the Western literary tradition sanction as
appropriate ways of endowing human processes with meaning." In
other words, the reason why historians have four plots at their
disposal – no more, no less – is that these are the plots provided by
"our generally cultural and specifically literary heritage." Accordingly, White felt no hesitation in using the words "plot-structure"
and "myth" interchangeably.[28]

If this is true, then historical discourse can be said to have a
double referent: while *dealing* with the past, it *employs* the myths or
story-forms available in Western culture. Therefore, following
Barthes, White claimed that historical discourse simultaneously
points at the past under investigation (what White would later call
the *referent* of the discourse) and at the repertoire of mythic story-
forms available in the present (what he would call the *content*):[29]

> The facts and their formal explanation or interpretation appear as the
> manifest or literal "surface" of the discourse, while the figurative
> language used to characterize the facts points to a deep-structural

meaning. This latent meaning of an historical discourse consists of the generic story-type of which the facts themselves, arranged in a specific order and endowed with different weights, are the manifest form. We understand the specific story being told about the facts when we identify the generic story-type of which the particular story is an instantiation.[30]

If poetry, in Samuel Coleridge's famous definition, is the art of "making the familiar strange, and the strange familiar," history, according to White, typically aims for the latter. History writing is a form of making the "foreign country" of past experience familiar to modern readers "by endowing what originally appears as problematical and mysterious with the aspect of a recognizable, because it is a familiar, form."[31] Obviously, this is not the same as allowing historians to smooth away the strangeness of the past. On the contrary, White was always among the first to insist on the otherness of the past. His point was rather that historians reflecting on this otherness necessarily do so in the language of their own time. They unavoidably employ story-forms or plot-structures familiar to themselves and their audience.

In fact, as we shall see in chapter 5, White so much emphasized the qualitative difference between the past "out there" and the stories that historians write about it that he came to consider historical narratives as "masks of meaning," whose mythic coherence can never be found in the past itself and is therefore a product of the historian's imagination. Although White developed this sharp contrast between meaningful narratives and a past that is meaningless in itself only as late as the early 1980s, White hinted in that same direction when he spoke, in the mid-1970s, about "the fictions of factual representation." Of course, the word "fiction" carries some perilous connotations. When historians, in agreement with the ethos of their discipline, try to justify their accounts with evidence from the past, it is quite conceivable they are not too amused to find the results of their efforts described as "verbal fictions, the contents of which are as much *invented* as *found* and the forms of which have more in common with their counterparts in literature than they have with those in the sciences."[32] But what this meant was simply that historians cannot write history without the plot-structures that are available in their society. Indeed, in White's vocabulary, "fictive" came close to being synonymous with "mythic." The "fictions of factual representation" were the story-forms that historians employ when they transform their raw data into facts that fit a narrative (or when they translate their "facts" into "fictions," as White liked to say). In other words, the interpretation of past events is a "literary, that is to say fiction-making, operation" insofar as it casts these events in a literary form derived from the historian's own culture.[33]

Yet, as any rhetorician knows, words say more than they say. To introduce the language of myth and fiction in an analysis of historical interpretation is more than offering a vocabulary for speaking about the historian's narrative techniques. It also reveals an enthusiastic willingness to challenge the self-images of the historical discipline. In particular, White's article "The Fictions of Factual Representation" was characterized by a marked hostility to Rankean-style historiography, which the author (here as in *Metahistory*) interpreted as having succumbed to the illusion of scientism. In a rather patronizing tone, White complained that historians in the early nineteenth century had sacrificed the wisdom of the rhetorical tradition to the dreams of factual accuracy and scientific objectivity. "Typically," White wrote, "the nineteenth-century historian's aim was to expunge every hint of the fictive, or merely imaginable, from his discourse, to eschew the techniques of the poet and the orator, and to forego what were regarded as the intuitive procedures of the maker of fictions in his apprehension of reality." "They did not realize that the facts do not speak for themselves, but that the historian speaks for them, speaks on their behalf, and fashions the fragments of the past into a whole whose integrity is – in its *re*presentation – a purely discursive one."[34]

White's own vocabulary – words like myth and fiction in particular – reveals his readiness to take issue with those "naive" nineteenth-century historians, especially in so far as they were still regarded as fathers of the historical discipline. Moreover, the stereotypes he created of Ranke's generation indicate how strongly he dissociated himself from their understanding of the historian's craft.[35] On White's part, "myth" and "fiction" were declarations of war against historians who denied that they employed the story-forms of a Scott, Austen, or Balzac. Allergic to historians pretending to be absent from their own writing, White lost no opportunity of reminding them that they unavoidably engage in the same act of fiction-making they rejected in Scott or Balzac.

In short, in deliberate contrast to any scientific conception of historical studies, White developed a "poetics of history."[36] His emphasis was not on the logic, but on the tropics of historical discourse. Over against those insisting that the historian's knowledge must *match* historical reality, White claimed that knowledge *makes* reality, or rather, that what counts as historical reality is a product of the historian's language. White's interest in rhetoric, language, and discourse stemmed from a desire to change the terms in which we speak about historical scholarship. Trying to put aside the modern preoccupation with how our knowledge corresponds to the past, White raised a much older question (central to philosophy and religion in ancient and medieval times): "Which account of reality best orients our living?"[37] This more practical concern explains why White kept returning to pre-professional historians such as Tocqueville and to ancient rhetoricians such as Vico. It explains why White regarded the scientification of history as a modern deviation from a respectable historiographical tradition, if not an outright attempt to break that tradition. Ironically, perhaps, it was precisely this time-honored concern for "what orients our living" that inspired White to explore the newest, most revolutionary theories available in the 1970s. It was his aim to develop a non-scientific, rhetorically oriented alternative to the scientism permeating the twentieth-century discipline that drove White deep into structuralist waters.

Objectivism and relativism

Although White's rhetorically oriented philosophy of history challenged a number of conventional demarcations – for example, those between history and fiction, history and metahistory, dream and reason – its sharp critique of the "noble dream" called objectivity nonetheless seemed to reinforce another old dichotomy: the one between objectivism and relativism. In philosopher Richard Bernstein's definition, objectivism is the view that knowledge, truth, and reality exist independent of human cultures, frameworks, or paradigms. Relativism, in turn, is an exact inversion of objectivism: it is the view that knowledge, truth, and reality are relative to human cultures, frameworks, or paradigms. By criticizing the former and embracing the latter, observes Chris Lorenz, White tended to strengthen rather than to weaken this either/or dichotomy. Moreover, given that this mutual exclusivity between objectivism and relativism is itself a product of objectivist thought, allowing for no shades of grey between absolute certainty and absolute uncertainty, Lorenz detects in White an "inverted positivism" (better perhaps: an "inverted objectivism"), or an implicit acceptance of the objectivist view that myth and fiction are the only

alternatives to reason and logic. Could it be that White, in his
attempt to offer an alternative to scientism, continued to depend
on scientist presuppositions?[38]

Although some of White's provocations, including especially
those formulated in the language of myth and fiction, seem to
confirm Lorenz's argument, it is instructive to see why it is mislead-
ing to think of White's philosophy of history in terms of objectivism
versus relativism. For one thing, we have seen in chapter 3 that
Metahistory had explicitly sought to overcome this very distinction.
In White's view in 1973, an escape from the ironist's cage requires
the insight that *logos* and *mythos* are not as mutually exclusive as
they have long been considered. Since "one can study only what
one has first dreamed about," *Metahistory* had proposed to treat
reason and unreason as mutually enriching aspects of the human
imagination. Five years later, in the introduction to a collection of
essays entitled *Tropics of Discourse*, White was still on this same
track. Moreover, in the meantime, he had discovered discourse as
the place where that much-desired interaction between *logos* and
mythos takes place:

> The tropological theory of discourse gives us understanding of the
> existential continuity between error and truth, ignorance and under-
> standing, or to put it another way, imagination and thought. . . . The
> tropological theory of discourse helps us understand how speech
> mediates between these supposed oppositions, just as discourse itself
> mediates between our apprehension of those aspects of experience
> still "strange" to us and those aspects of it which we "understand"
> because we have found an order of words adequate to its
> domestication.[39]

More especially, in White's understanding, discourse (as derived
from the Latin *discurrere*) is a movement backwards and forwards
between *logos* and *mythos*, between reason and dream, or between
"alternative modes of encoding" reality. Accordingly, for White,
discourse was not an alternative to the concerns of the objectivists,
but rather the place where the *logos* cherished by the objectivists
and the *mythos* emphasized by the relativists are in constant,
dynamic interaction.[40]

But what, then, to make of White's sweeping statement, in 1975,
that "there can be no such thing as a non-relativistic representation
of historical reality?" And didn't White, on various occasions,
openly declare that "I am a relativist?"[41] Admittedly, this rhetoric

achieved its intended provocative effect only as long as its audience saw relativism as the terrifying other of objectivism. Nonetheless, White never embraced the "anything goes" that Bernstein defines as characteristic of relativism. Remember that the opposition between objectivism and relativism is so powerful because the two hold each other in critical tension. Both positions represent what the other rejects. Both presuppose their mutual exclusivity. Both deny the possibility of a third way between absolute certainty and absolute uncertainty. As Lorenz nicely paraphrases Dostoevsky: if "the God of the 'single authoritative story' of history is dead the historian is engulfed by chaos and arbitrariness."[42] However, although White, in "The Burden of History," had claimed that "discontinuity, disruption, and chaos is our lot" in the realm of human affairs, he did not believe that, in matters of historical interpretation, chaos and arbitrariness are all there is once the god of objectivism has died. In fact, the whole point of the quadruple tetrad was to *deny* that historians can say about the past whatever they wish. For, as White did not stop repeating, *what* historians say about the past is inseparable from *how* they say it. And the *how* of historical interpretation is limited to the repertoire of available forms. Rather than asserting that "anything goes," White claimed: only four things go. Historical interpretation is limited to the four archetypical modes of prefiguration, emplotment, argument, and ideological implication.

Interestingly, whereas Bernstein seeks to *transcend* the objectivist–relativist dichotomy (by emphasizing, in good Gadamerian fashion, that knowledge is too rich and too subtle to be fixed in the either-or categories of both objectivists and relativists), White took what can be described as a *middle position* between the two camps. While agreeing with the objectivists that there cannot be an infinite number of interpretations of, say, the French Revolution, he granted the relativists that there is no single authoritative story about this Revolution either:

> If, as Lévi-Strauss correctly observes, one can *tell* a host of different stories about the single set of events conventionally designated as "the French Revolution," this does not mean that the *type* of stories that can be told about the set are infinite in number. The types of stories that can be told about the French Revolution are limited to the number of modes of emplotment which the myths of the Western literary tradition sanction as appropriate ways of endowing human processes with meaning.[43]

Moreover, with the relativists, White held that choices out of the
available number of story-forms are made on grounds that are
"ultimately aesthetic or moral rather than epistemological": "All
the historian needs to do to transform a tragic into a comic situation
is to shift his point of view or change the scope of his perceptions."[44] Thus, an event like the storming of the Bastille on July 14,
1789, can be part of an ironic tragedy as well as of a romance, as
the writings of Tocqueville and Michelet illustrate. Even though
White frankly acknowledged that there are criteria for distinguishing between good and bad historiography (such as "responsibility
to the rules of evidence," the "relative fullness of the narrative
detail," and "logical consistency"), he considered it impossible to
choose on grounds other than moral or aesthetic preferences
between two equally skilled and equally sensitive historians
working from different metahistorical assumptions, as was the
case with Michelet and Tocqueville. Indeed, on the level of metahistorical prefiguration, White accepted an irreducible plurality of
options.[45]

Yet, peculiar to White's position was that he saw this plurality as
limited to four. In his own assessment, this fourfold pattern offered
"a way out of an absolute relativism." For if historical interpretations are mediated through "the language-mode in which the historian casts his original description of the historical field prior to
any analysis, explanation, or interpretation he may offer of it," and
if these language modes come in four archetypical forms, then there
are four modes of realism in historical studies – that is, more than
any objectivist would accept, but less than the relativists assume.[46]
Of course, White did not deny that variations on this fourfold
pattern can exist. As we saw in chapter 3, *Metahistory* employed the
quadruple tetrad rather flexibly. The "pseudo or satirical tragedy"
detected in Taylor also may count as a mutated version of White's
archetypical tragedy. This made his position more subtle than is
acknowledged by those who reduce White to his structuralist grid.[47]
Nonetheless, with these nuances, White offered what is best
described as a *limited pluralism*.[48] Despite some charges to the contrary, he did not advocate a simple "tell whatever you like."[49]
Because one can only tell something in language, the plurality of
historical discourse is limited to the four principal modes of language. It was this limited pluralism that prevented White from
succumbing to a Dostoevskian "everything is permitted," or to relativism as defined by Bernstein.

The prison-house of language

Yet, granted that White was not a relativist, wouldn't it be fair to describe him as a linguistic determinist? After all, his middle position between objectivism and relativism depended on the determining influence of the language-modes described by the tropes of metaphor, metonymy, synecdoche, and irony. Whereas *Metahistory*, with its emphatic insistence on the voluntarist subject, seemed to offer the historian a free choice out of these four tropes, the essays produced in White's structuralist period almost seemed to forget this freedom. For example, in "Historicism, History, and the Figurative Imagination" (1975), White frankly characterized his tropology as a "theory of linguistic determinism." Elsewhere, he stated that language "has its own forms of terminological determinism, represented by the figures of speech without which discourse itself is impossible." This seemed to imply that the historian's originality or creativity does not play a major role in historical interpretation. It suggested that interpretation is nothing more than "the formalization of the phenomenal field originally constituted by language itself on the basis of a dominant tropological wager."[50] Strikingly, the subject in these sentences is language, not the historian. But if language itself is the acting subject in historical interpretation, then hadn't White arrived at a position incompatible with the voluntarism of *Metahistory*? Had White lost his faith in the liberating powers of the human individual?

Judging by a long review essay on Foucault, published in *History and Theory*, White was not insensitive to how, in the 1960s and 1970s, the humanist subject was deconstructed in the name of language, most notably in Foucault's *Les mots et les choses*. What made Foucault such a noteworthy thinker, in White's judgment, was that he tried to expose "the linguistic bases of such concepts as 'man,' 'society,' and 'culture.'" This was to say that, for Foucault, words like "man" or "human" did not correspond to specific things in the world, let alone to the existence of a privileged species called *Homo sapiens*. According to the French philosopher, "man" and "human" were just words or "linguistic formulae that have no specific referents in reality." If some people, most notably in the humanist tradition, had erroneously become convinced of the reality of something specifically "human," this was because they had taken their figurative language too seriously. The humanists had been captivated by their own language or, more precisely, become captive of "the *figurative* modes of discourse in which they constituted (rather than simply signified) the objects with which they pretend to deal." Consequently, Foucault did not hesitate to announce the "death of man." As he put it in a famous line near the end of *Les mots et les choses*, such words as "man" and "human" will one day be erased "like a face drawn in sand at the edge of the sea."[51]

Obviously, this threatened to undermine much of what White had argued for in the 1960s. Although *The Ordeal of Liberal Humanism* (1970) had extensively reflected on various attacks launched against the humanist tradition in the twentieth century, White had sought to fend them off with a more aggressive humanism grounded in that same individual will-power that *Metahistory* admired in Tocqueville or Nietzsche. Foucault, however, taught White that, from a linguistic point of view, this strategy was hopelessly naive. For the assumption that the human will is qualitatively different from the rest of the universe, and in a position to judge the world of human affairs, originates in a linguistic prioritizing of the human. It depends on a linguistic "order of things" in which the human is given a privileged place. But such ascriptions are ultimately arbitrary, because they cannot be said to correspond to an order "out there." For what counts as order is precisely what is at stake.[52]

To what extent White was inclined to accept this Foucauldian argument ("In my view, the principal contention of *Les mots et les choses* is correct and illuminating") became apparent at the 1974 meeting of the Popular Culture Association in Milwaukee, where White unreservedly presented himself as spokesman of the structuralist movement. In front of a 700-person audience, he made short work of his old humanist convictions:

> For the Structuralists, . . . the culture-system *lives* the individuals and groups caught within its mazes rather than the reverse. *We* do not dispose the elements of culture as a set of instruments for realizing specific personal goals; rather, culture disposes *us* for the purpose of realizing its potential for imposing order on a world. . . . The only true subject of history is culture itself. *It* lives *its life* through us; it is the sole agent of history and we its agencies, even though we do not recognize ourselves as such but persist, at least in the West, in thinking it is *we* who live *it*.[53]

Does this imply that White, in the mid-1970s, gave up his faith in the human will? Did he reject his voluntarist commitments as "youthful idealism" (a phrase he used in a 2010 retrospection)?[54] However much this seemed to be the case, and however eagerly

White, in Milwaukee and elsewhere, experimented with structuralist lines of thought, there were, nonetheless, several moments at which White made a halt, looked back, and decided that it was worth trying to liberate the old, humanist subject from what Fredric Jameson, in his critical account of structuralism, called "the prison-house of language."[55]

First of all, in the introduction to his essay collection *Tropics of Discourse* (1978), White chose to present prefiguration, not as a function of language or culture, as Foucault would have done, but as an operation performed by *consciousness*. Following Ernst Cassirer rather than Foucault, White said he conceived of language as a structure mediating between consciousness ("words") and the world ("things"). Even though, again, he did not explain how exactly he saw language relate to consciousness – was the former a product of the latter or did it merely, metaphorically, serve as a model of how consciousness seeks to grasp the world? – it is worth noting that he did not *reduce* consciousness to language. Also, in his speculations about the "tropological structure of consciousness," White refused to say that, as an analytical category, consciousness could easily be replaced by language. Instead, he presented "the fourfold scheme of tropes as a model of the modes of mental association characteristic of human consciousness." So, whereas *Metahistory* had been rather vague about the relation between language and consciousness, *Tropics of Discourse* at least made clear that White did not identify the two. Also, he dared to speak about "human nature," of which scientific knowledge was perhaps impossible, but which can be known through literature and art in general. Most significant, however, was that White, in his very last sentences, articulated the decidedly unstructuralist hope "to continue to speak about culture as against nature – and, moreover, speak about it in ways that are responsible for all the various dimensions of our specifically *human* being."[56] Whereas some readers have been startled by the rather structuralist message of this introduction – most notably by its daring suggestion that the Vichian tropes, Freud's mechanisms of dream-work, and the four phases of child development distinguished by Jean Piaget, the French psychologist, are all versions of the same mechanism – it is perhaps more appropriate to emphasize how remarkable it is that White, in spite of the structuralist gospel he had preached to the crowds in Milwaukee, appeared prepared to defend such an un-Foucauldian idea as that there is a specifically human nature for which "we" bear responsibility.

Second, although White agreed with Foucault that "things have no order," in the sense that order is nothing but a linguistic construction, White abhorred "the self-doubt and irrationalism which this realization engenders." For this reason, perhaps, he searched Foucault's oeuvre for glimmers of hope, that is, for clues that the French author, like Nietzsche, considered his "ground-clearing operation" a preparatory stage for "the rebirth of the gods," or a renewed apprehension of the human imagination.[57] When this search yielded only few results, White appealed to another of his favorite theorists, Vico, to rescue the human imagination from the potentially annihilatory powers of structuralist linguisticism. Wouldn't the human imagination, or, more particularly, the human will to imagine a world different from our own, have the capacity "to 'begin again' in the face of the realization that things have no order?" Cannot the human will serve as our anchor when the gods of culture, civilization, and tradition are dead? This focus on the will was what White appreciated not only in Vico, but also in such Vichian authors as Edward Said, whose *Beginnings* White enthusiastically endorsed:

> Like Nietzsche, Said takes the health of the modern will as his problem. In the midst of the current "Hellenistic" condition of culture, he asks: how is it possible to *begin again*? ... Said suggests that answers to these questions or solutions to the problems which inspire them lie less in the further cultivation of our rational faculties (as neo-Positivists of the last generation hoped) or the release of the emotions (as the current, infantile brand of "left-wing anarchism" teaches), than in a steeling of the will and a renewed faith in our power to *impose* meaning on the world.[58]

A steeling of the will in times of crisis: that sounded, indeed, like the muscular language of *The Ordeal of Liberal Humanism*. Even if White, compared to his 1970 book, had increasingly come to acknowledge the inventedness of his humanist tradition, he had anything but lost his voluntarist view of human nature.

A remarkable third indication of White's unwillingness to sacrifice his humanist conception of selfhood appeared in a 1976 article solicited by Murray Krieger for the journal *Contemporary Literature*, "The Absurdist Moment in Contemporary Literary Theory." In this wide-ranging essay, which surveyed the current state of literary theory, White used his usual typological method to distinguish between four types of literary critics (illustrating his adage that "the beginning of all understanding is classification").[59] At this point, readers familiar with White's earlier work might have expected the author to identify these four types with the archetypical modes of tropological prefiguration. Also, they might have expected White to argue that the succession of these four types was a matter of rhetorical elaboration of tropological possibilities contained in the initial, metaphoric phase. However, this was not how White proceeded. Instead, he drew a sharp contrast between what he called "normal" and "absurdist" critics. Moreover, without denying the "historical significance" of the absurdist movement, as represented by Foucault, Barthes, and Derrida, White complained at length about the excesses of absurdism. For one thing, absurdist criticism "is more about criticism than it is about literature." Also, "in a culture that no longer believes in God, in tradition, in culture, civilization, or even 'literature,'" these absurdist critics treated the text (a novel, a poem, a historical monograph) as a mere collection of signs, utterly unrelated to, for example, human ideas. Consequently, they no longer considered themselves contributing to human culture or civilization:

> For the Absurdist, criticism's role is to take the side of "nature" against "culture." ... Absurdist criticism achieves its critical distance on modern culture, art, and literature by reversing the hitherto unquestioned assumption that "civilization" is worth the price paid in human suffering, anxiety, and pain by the "uncivilized" of the world (primitive peoples, traditional cultures, women, children, the outcasts or pariahs of world history) and asserting the rights of the "uncivilized" against the "civilizers."

Laudatory as it may be to identify with the marginalized, the problem of the absurdist's anti-cultural stance is that the purpose of this identification remains unclear in the absence of any substantive vision of culture or civilization. If Derrida describes his aim as to put himself "at a point so that I do not know any longer where I am going," the critical "I," said White, is hypostatized at the cost of precisely such a shared human project. Absurdism dissociates the critic "from any collective human enterprise."[60]

Unsurprisingly, this critique was not particularly welcomed by White's comrades in structuralist and post-structuralist circles. Krieger, the soliciting editor, was not sure what to make of it, while Dominick LaCapra wondered aloud "how a writer of White's intelligence and perspicacity" could possibly come up with such caricatures of, for example, Derrida.

There is, of course, a point at which everyone feels inclined to become Horatius at the bridge. The question is where one locates that point. I would suggest that one way to see White's reaction is as a turn toward secure "sanity" and conventional irony in the face of the "other," who actually articulates things that are "inside" White himself – but an "other" whose articulation is perhaps too disconcerting or at least too alien in formulation to be recognizable.[61]

In plain English: didn't Derrida point out the implications of what, among others, White himself had been saying? Why did White demur from these consequences, given that he, in other essays, had traveled so far in the very same direction? And wasn't this rejection, apart from disappointing in LaCapra's eyes, remarkably inconsistent with the general tenor of White's work in the 1970s?[62] Indeed, if White's work was ever fraught with tensions, it was in the years following *Metahistory*. His structuralist adventure inspired White to explore how language molds the ways in which humans perceive the world. Combining Lévi-Strauss and Foucault, the godfathers of French structuralism, with Vico, the ancient theorist of tropes, White was among the first philosophers of history to acknowledge how, in the study of history, discourse is not merely an instrument in the hands of sovereign individuals, but a power in its own right, capable of shaping the historian's thoughts and texts. Yet such an autonomy of language was hard to reconcile with an autonomy of the human subject. At this point, then, White drew back. Although, on the one hand, speaking about alternative descriptions of reality that are mediated in the historian's discourse, he had become enough of a structuralist to reject the notion of a "transcendental subject or narrative ego which stands above the contending interpretations of reality and arbitrates between them," he could not possibly, on the other, accept the idea of a discourse operating independently of human subjects.[63]

In a sense, it was impossible for White to extricate himself from this dilemma. The discursive power of language and the will-power of the individual could not but remain in tension. Yet, if his encounter with Lévi-Strauss and Foucault had let the pendulum swing far towards linguistic determinism, White tried to move in the opposite direction by reflecting upon the notion of translation (his third attempt to rescue the human subject). Even if language is the determining power in how historians prefigure the historical field, argued White, it is not impossible to get acquainted with various languages. It suffices to study the history of historical writing, which, as *Metahistory* had shown, is a storehouse of examples of histories written in various modes of prefiguration. Besides, what had distinguished Tocqueville or Marx from their less talented contemporaries was their ability to recognize the existence of multiple languages and their efforts to mediate between two or more of them in their own historical work (see chapter 3). For this reason, White said he dreamt of "a means of translating from one mode of discourse to another, in the same way that we translate from one language to another."[64]

Obviously, translation is impossible without a competent translator. However profoundly language may determine the mode in which an individual perceives historical reality, it takes a human subject to express what is said in one language in words belonging to another language. If this already indicates the need for a human subject capable of reflecting upon language, White's rebellion against the prison-house of language spoke even more strongly from his proposal to define progress in historical studies in terms of multi-language competence:

> [I]f the tropes of language are limited, if the types of figuration are finite, then it is possible to imagine how our representations of the historical world aggregate into a comprehensive total vision of that world, and how progress in our understanding of it is possible. Each new representation of the past represents a further testing and refinement of our capacities to figure the world in language, so that each new generation is heir, not only of more information about the past, but also of more adequate knowledge of our capacities to comprehend it.[65]

So, while *Metahistory* had advocated "cognitive responsibility" and "epistemological self-consciousness" – two criteria stipulating that historians need to be aware of their own prefigurations and of the legitimate existence of alternatives to their preferred mode – White now reformulated his demands in terms of "linguistic self-consciousness." If there was a path of escape from the linguistic determinism that structuralist thought seemed to suggest, it consisted in acquiring proficiency in various languages, or more precisely, in the ability to translate "the perceptions of an historian who has cast his discourse in the mode of metaphor into those of one who has cast his in the mode of synecdoche, or those of one who sees the world ironically into those of one who views it in the mode of metonymy."[66] In short, the power of discourse may be large, but not so all-embracing as to lock the human subject in a single mode of discourse, said the humanist *redivivus* in White. Like the ironist's cage, the prison-house of language has an escape route for those able to find it.

Getting out of history

If the structuralist project had such potentially disturbing implications for the human subject, why then did White become intrigued by it in the first place? And if it appeared so difficult to maintain a humanist view on the distinctiveness of human nature in the light of Lévi-Strauss's and Foucault's critique, why did White present himself as a structuralist, in the mid-1970s, and remain indebted to structuralist insights for the rest of his career? These questions allow us to draw together the threads discussed in this chapter and to contextualize them within the larger project of White's anti-scientist philosophy of history. For even though White, as the director of Wesleyan's Center for the Humanities, increasingly began to operate outside the bounds of the historical discipline – publishing in such journals as *Contemporary Literature* and *New Literary History* – the question guiding his work in this period was still identical to the question *Metahistory* had sought to answer: how to conceive of history in such terms as to contribute to forms of realism that do not condemn a socially progressive utopia as unrealistic?

In his structuralist period, White basically used the same strategy as he had adopted in *Metahistory*. This strategy consisted of a consistent relativizing of the claims to superiority made on behalf of the reigning paradigm of realism by drawing attention to the existence of alternative, equally justifiable, and equally meritorious conceptions of the real. The prime function, then, of the key terms discussed in this chapter – narrative, figurative discourse, rhetoric, myth, and fiction – was to support White's case for the equality of these alternative modes of realism. Regardless of whether White spoke about the mythic aspects of emplotment or about the "fictions of factual discourse," his point was that these mythic and fictional dimensions are characteristic of *all* versions of history, "orthodox" and "heterodox" alike, so that there are no compelling intellectual reasons for sanctioning one of these at the cost of others. Accordingly, the only grounds for favoring one mode of realism over others are moral, political, and aesthetic – which is to say that only moral concerns, political leanings, and aesthetic conventions justify the standards upheld by the historical discipline. So, rather than committing himself *directly* to a political cause – as not a small number of American historians in the early 1970s did[67] – White opted for the *indirect* approach of undermining the hegemonic discourse by "revealing both the wholly arbitrary nature of its classificatory systems and methodologies and the ultimately mythical nature of its presumed object of study."[68]

For this project, both Lévi-Strauss and Foucault offered valuable ammunition. Indeed, when White reflected on the implications of their insights for the study of history, as he did in Milwaukee, the greater part of his exposition was devoted to how the two Frenchmen could inspire a deconstruction of present-day historical studies. He explained they were not only "anti-scientist," but also "anti-historic." The logical corollary of their questioning of such dichotomies as culture versus barbarism and legality versus illegality was that both the "myth of the historical continuity of civilizational experience" and the distinction between high and low culture – both of which had been crucial to the project of liberal humanism – could be dissolved. And the same goes for the foundational myth of historical studies. As White declared, "the very idea of historical analysis," as distinguished from present experience, is "a product of a misconception":

> What this does is shift the interest of cultural history from the study of a culture's evolution in time to the study of present cultures' different conceptions of their evolution in time and, more importantly for historians, to the study of Western culture's obsession with the idea of learning something new from the study of history. In other words, sciences of culture should be *present-oriented*, concerned to explicate the relations between the various spheres of cultural activity *currently distinguished* in present societies, but without any presumption that one sphere is any more noble or any more reflective of the presumed shared humanity than any other.[69]

Hence White's suggestion, in a less than ironic twist, that the production process of French fries may be as interesting for a student of contemporary France as the celebrated novels of Flaubert and Proust.

This, to be sure, was an effective way to "get out" of history, if the latter is understood as the hegemonic discourse White sought to challenge.[70] But as we have seen in the previous section, the structuralist approach appeared *too* effective in that it undermined the very goal it was supposed to serve. Instead of preparing the ground for a rehabilitation of heterodox modes of realism, it threatened the human subject that White expected to profit from these alternative modes. It was of decisive importance, then, that White concluded his structuralist adventure (as well as his time at Wesleyan University) with the assurance that he still aimed "to speak about culture as against nature – and, moreover, speak about it in ways that are responsible for all the various dimensions of our specifically *human* being." As chapter 5 will show, in the years around 1980, White found new ways of doing so, especially in conversation with philosophers of the sublime.

5

Masks of Meaning: Facing the Sublime

If his structuralist adventure yielded White "a renewed faith in our power to *impose* meaning on the world," as he phrased it in his essay on Said, it is worth investigating to what extent his humanist affinities informed his so-called "narrativism" – the not altogether felicitous name by which the body of work produced in the 1980s on the theme of historical narrative has become known. Did White hold on to his voluntarist conception of the human subject when he declared that "stories are not lived but told"? To what extent were his forays into the sublime – a Romantic notion that White famously applied to issues of historical representation – indebted to the existentialist humanist vision we encountered in White's work of the 1960s and early 1970s?

Most of the texts discussed in this chapter were written at the University of California at Santa Cruz, where White moved in 1978 to direct a History of Consciousness program that contributed in no small degree to his growing reputation among literary scholars and cultural theorists.[1] Moreover, in his Californian years, both *Metahistory* and *Tropics of Discourse* increasingly began to receive critical attention. Some of the first articles about White found their way into print, while his "position" was increasingly one that others felt a need to relate to. In this chapter, then, more than in previous ones, I will pay attention to some of the better-known criticism White's work received (most notably from Roger Chartier, Carlo Ginzburg, and Dirk Moses) and compare his "narrativism" with that of two philosophers who are often mentioned in one breath with White: Louis O. Mink and Frank Ankersmit. As this chapter will make clear, White's work of the 1980s was still greatly indebted to the modernist and existentialist sources we encountered in the preceding chapters.

The content of the form

In the previous chapter, we saw how White treated the historian's plot-structure as an index of underlying metahistorical beliefs. He examined the kind of stories historians tell – do they opt for a romance or comedy or rather prefer a tragic or satirical mode? – in order to find out through what sort of lenses they prefigure the historical field. In other words, what counted was not that historians write stories *as such*; White's interest was rather focused on the *sort* of stories historians produce. Nonetheless, the fact that historians write stories cannot be taken for granted. For one thing, in the post-World War II decades, French historians associated with the *Annales* school (not to mention various schools of social, economic, and quantitative history, in both Europe and the United States) argued polemically that narrative history was greatly inferior to the more scientific, analytic sort of prose they admired in the social sciences.[2] Also, for rather different reasons, White himself had reflected on the possibilities of non-narrative historical representation when, in his manifesto of 1966, he had speculated about historiographies following the example of Norman Brown, the psychoanalytic historian, or drawing on the artistic styles developed by "action painters, kinetic sculptors, existentialist novelists, imagist poets, or *nouvelle vague* cinematographers" (chapter 2 in this volume). It is no surprise, then, to find White continuing his analysis of historical narrative with an investigation of why historians write narratives in the first place.

Again, White used the history of historiography as a repository of examples. In what became one of his most anthologized papers, "The Value of Narrativity in the Representation of Reality," delivered in October 1979 in Chicago at a conference on narrative, White returned to his original field of study, that of medieval Europe, and chose the annals of Saint Gall as his case-study. Reproducing the entries for the years 709 to 734, White allowed his readers to observe, first of all, that in this 26-year period, the monks of Saint Gall had deemed it necessary to record only twelve occurrences. Moreover, although it was not entirely impossible to detect a pattern in these events – it seemed that most of them were liminal events, or at least extreme by the annalist's standard – they were listed without any attempt at explanation or coherence. The entry for 731 ("Blessed Bede, the presbyter, died") seemed wholly unrelated to the event recorded in the year thereafter ("Charles fought against the Saracens at Poitiers on Saturday"). There is no recognizable story, let alone an explanation or a plot. Although the annals designated the years as *anno domini* (years of the Lord), thereby tacitly invoking a Christian master narrative, they made no attempt to interpret the battle at Poitiers or the death of Bede in the light of Christian theology. All this, said White, "is frustrating, if not disturbing, to the modern reader's story expectations." The modern reader, after all, "seeks fullness and continuity in an order of events" and feels uncomfortable about "gaps" and "discontinuities." A history of Saint Gall meets modern standards only if it shows how extreme weather, bad agrarian yields, and plundering raids by hostile neighbors were *related* to each other, or what these events *meant* to the monks.[3]

Obviously, White's question was what this reveals about the modern sense of realism. Why does a bare list of years and events not classify as proper history? Why do "we moderns" prefer coherence, continuity, and closure? Or, in White's own words: "[W]hat kind of notion of reality authorizes construction of a narrative account of reality in which continuity rather than discontinuity governs the articulation of the discourse?" Although a desire for coherence and continuity in historical representation does not necessarily reflect the belief that reality *itself* is coherent and continuous, at least it suggests that coherence and continuity are more *meaningful* than disjunctions and disruptions. Given that narratives typically offer meaning in terms of closure – "that summing up of the 'meaning' of the chain of events with which it deals that we normally expect from the well-made story" – the question becomes what our modern preference for narrative in historical representation says about our view of realism. Do we experience only a coherent story as "really real?" But, then, isn't the realism of the friars at Saint Gall at least equally plausible?[4]

For White, it seemed plausible to say that reality itself was not in a position to arbitrate in a conflict between such alternative realisms. For what was at stake was precisely the question of what counts as reality. Therefore, one might expect White to remain agnostic in matters of metaphysics and to focus on how narratives reinforce those forms of realism that cling to coherence of the sort that narratives offer. White indeed made much of this second task.

Following Hegel, he suggested that historical narratives are typically written within stable socio-political orders, with well-established bodies of law, since only such orders provide "some notion of the legal subject which can serve as the agent, agency, and subject of historical narrative." More generally, one might say that people's behavior can only be interpreted against the background of moral codes and legal standards that define what counts as good or evil. White even went so far as to accept Hegel's claim that the state typically provides such a legal system, so that, without a state, human individuals cannot be identified as wrongdoers or law-abiding citizens. As often in White, this hyperbolic statement should not be taken too literally, as if a state (the Prussian nation-state that Hegel had in mind?) is in all circumstances a *sine qua non* for narrative prose. White rather seemed to suggest, in positive terms, a causal relation between narrative as the preferred genre of most nineteenth-century historians and the political agendas set by nineteenth-century nation-states in Europe. In White's reading, historical narratives socialize citizens into a moral order: "And this suggests that narrativity, certainly in factual storytelling and probably in fictional storytelling as well, is intimately related to, if not a function of, the impulse to moralize reality, that is, to identify it with the social system that is the source of any morality that we can imagine."[5]

Yet, however important he considered this socialization function of historical narratives, White remained anything but agnostic in matters of metaphysics. Just as he denied that events are inherently tragic or comic – the historian rather imposes a tragic or comic plot-structure on the events under discussion – so he denied, in a series of long rhetorical questions, that narrative order exists in reality:

> Does the world really present itself to perception in the form of well-made stories, with central subjects, proper beginnings, middles, and ends, and a coherence that permits us to see "the end" in every beginning? Or does it present itself more in the forms that the annals and chronicle suggest, either as mere sequence without beginning or end or as sequences of beginnings that only terminate and never conclude? And does the world, even the social world, ever really come to us as already narrativized, already "speaking itself" from beyond the horizon of our capacity to make scientific sense of it? Or is the fiction of such a world, a world capable of speaking itself and of displaying itself as a form of a story, necessary for the establishment of that moral authority without which the notion of a specifically social reality would be unthinkable?[6]

If narrative cohesion is not to be found in the past, White argued, the implication of this is hard to miss. Narratives are, then, just as mythic and fictitious as the plot-structures discussed in the previous chapter. In White's firm prose, narrative, "far from being a neutral medium for the representation of historical events and processes, is the very stuff of a mythical view of reality, a conceptual or pseudo-conceptual 'content' which, when used to represent real events, endows them with an illusory coherence." Instead of revealing the true essence of past reality, historical narrative imposes a mythic structure on the events it purports to describe. As soon as historians embed "hard winter," "deficient in crops," and "flood everywhere" in a narrative with beginnings, middle, and ends, they superimpose coherence on the past (the coherence of a romance, comedy, tragedy, or satire, as the case may be). The realism of narrative, then, is that of a mask. A mask may be beautifully decorated, serve important purposes in ritual contexts, and provide a *persona* or distinct identity for its wearer – but that identity is always different from the mask-wearer's real self. A mask conceals as much as it reveals and is therefore anything but "real."[7]

This explains what White had in mind when he coined, in the title of his second collection of essays (1987), that by now notorious expression, "the content of the form." If narrative discourse, irrespective of its specific plot-structure, creates an illusion of coherence and, in doing so, imposes meaning on the past, the ostensibly innocent "form" of narrative can be said to have a "content" of its own. Moreover, that content is not merely mythical, in the sense of being derived from the mythic repertoire of Western civilization; it also entails "ontological and epistemic choices with distinct ideological and even specifically political implications." For if narrative creates coherence and tends to proceed along lines of gradual development rather than through ruptures and breaks, it favors conservatism more than the socially progressive politics White felt committed to. As Nancy Partner aptly summarizes, "the narrative impulse carries us into the arms of social stability and naturalizes bourgeois desires for coherence, harmony, intelligibility, and order" – precisely the sort of things that White, for moral and political reasons, hoped historians would dare to challenge. White's so-called "narrativism" is therefore *not* to be understood as an endorsement of narrative history writing, let alone as an encouragement to imitate narrative historians such as Macaulay. His narrativism was rather a critical reflection on the "moralizing impulse" characteristic of narrative discourse.[8]

Stories are not lived but told

If White treated narratives as "masks of meaning," made instead of found, and imposed upon the past rather than characteristic of the "real" past, does that make him an anti-realist?[9] This is an important question, because White is frequently lumped together with Louis O. Mink and Frank Ankersmit as "anti-realist narrativists," a category usually contrasted with the "realist narrativism" represented by authors such as David Carr. Whereas the latter claim that reality itself has a narrative structure, the former challenge this claim by emphasizing the extent to which historical narratives are constructed by historians.[10] But how useful is it to call White an anti-realist, or to group him together with Mink and Ankersmit?

Mink coined the key phrase for the debate when he famously argued that "stories are not lived but told." Mink's point was that stories have beginnings, middles and endings, whereas everyday life has not. "There are hopes, plans, battles, and ideas," Mink said, "but only in retrospective stories are hopes unfulfilled, plans miscarried, battles decisive, and ideas seminal." This means, first, that the significance of a particular event or occurrence can only be determined from a hindsight point of view (as Arthur Danto, a few years earlier, had argued in his *Analytical Philosophy of History*). Second, Mink assumes that historians are typically interested in such "outcomes." This was already implied in Mink's claim that "configurational comprehension" (looking at a river from an aerial point of view) is most characteristic of historical scholarship (see chapter 4 of this volume). Third, Mink's argument implied that, in writing narratives, historians cannot find support in what historical actors themselves thought about their lives. For although these actors figure in the narratives, it is not their experiences or their life-stories, but the (unforeseeable) significance of their actions that makes up the subject of the narratives. For Mink, therefore, an unbridgeable gap exists between the life of historical actors and the narratives written by historians.[11]

For rather similar reasons, Ankersmit, the Dutch philosopher of history, insists on a qualitative difference between how people in the past experienced their own time and how historians write about those times. For what historians typically do, says Ankersmit, is to reflect on the past in such terms as "late Middle Ages," "radical Enlightenment," and "French Revolution." These are colligatory concepts, or examples of configurational comprehension, insofar as they group a host of different events (the storming of the Bastille, the women's march on Versailles, the royal flight to Varennes, etc.) under a single heading (French Revolution). Given that such headings are constructed by historians – or, if the term in question was already in vogue, defined in such a way as to serve a specific configurational purpose – they do not have a referent in the past in the same way that factual statements have. Whereas a sentence like "the storming of the Bastille took place on July 14, 1789" corresponds with a real occurrence in the past, which could in principle be observed by any contemporary, a colligatory concept lacks such a referent in the past. Likewise, for Ankersmit, the coherence offered by a narrative is a linguistic construction, the aim of which is not to say something about a single event in the past, but to synthesize our knowledge of such events into a larger whole.[12]

Although White could easily agree with these arguments – he always treated Mink and Ankersmit as allies in his struggle against scientism in history[13] – he had reasons of his own for asserting that "stories are not lived but told." Instead of presenting an epistemological argument, as did Mink and Ankersmit, White made a metaphysical claim that stemmed from moral and political convictions. The claim was that completeness and fullness are properties of a narrative, not of real life. They are, said White, impossible to experience and only to be imagined in stories, dreams, and poems.[14] Further justification for this claim was not offered. Instead, White explained why he considered it important to drive a wedge, or to acknowledge a real existing difference, between life and narrative cohesion. For him, to think of life itself as narratively structured would "deprive history of the kind of meaninglessness which alone can goad the moral sense of living human beings to make their lives different for themselves and their children, which is to say, to endow their lives with a meaning for which they alone are fully responsible."[15]

If White's previous work had gone a long way to marginalize the human subject, this passage clearly illustrates how seriously White took his "renewed faith in our power to *impose* meaning on the world." For his refusal to see real life as narratively structured stemmed from nothing other than White's moral conviction that life is lived better without "given" or "prefabricated" meanings. White considered human dignity and freedom incompatible with meanings that were "received" or "found" instead of personally "made." In other words, the anti-realism ascribed to White stemmed from moral beliefs. The humanist virtues that White had come to rediscover after his structuralist adventure – taking responsibility for one's own life, defining one's own moral standards, plotting the course of one's own life – required the contrast of a meaningless past.

Does it make sense, then, to classify White as an anti-realist narrativist? This classification is justified as long as one focuses exclusively on the question of whether life as experienced by people, past or present, displays the structure of a narrative. On this issue, Carr took a diametrically opposed position. The philosopher argued that persons or communities cannot exist without conceiving themselves as part of a narrative. Even the simplest action is impossible without intentions, that is, without a narratively structured anticipation of the desired effect.[16] Although White, as we have seen, strongly disagreed with this, the foregoing suggests that, even if Carr were proven right, White would still maintain his "discontinuity thesis."[17] That is to say that White was not really interested in the arguments put forward by Carr. Moreover, although he tended to accept Mink's and Ankersmit's epistemological anti-realism, his own reason for treating the past as meaningless in itself was a moral consideration. Accordingly, those who treat White as a contributor to a debate on realist/anti-realist narrative run the risk of missing the point. As always with White, that point was moral and, by implication, political rather than epistemological. Again and again, he stressed "there is no such thing as politically innocent historiography."[18]

Sublime historical reality

These words also applied with regard to a theme White began to address in 1982: the "sublime." The notion of the sublime originated from the decades around 1800, when such thinkers as Edmund Burke, Immanuel Kant, and Friedrich von Schiller reached for words to express the awe and confusion they sometimes experienced. They referred to moments in which individuals experience something truly overwhelming – say, the Swiss Alps or a thunderstorm at sea – and feel imbued with a sense of fear and fascination. This experience is what they called sublime. To be clear, the idea was not that mountains and thunderstorms *as such* were sublime, but rather that the human *experience* of these things, resulting in feelings of enchantment and defenselessness, could be named sublime. (In passing, I note that contemporary theories of the sublime tend to emphasize this element of experience, too.)[19]

White, however, showed his talent for what Harold Bloom calls "clinamen" – "creative correction that is actually and necessarily a misinterpretation"[20] – by re-interpreting the sublime in such a way that it was stripped of its experience-character and reconfigured into an ontological predicate. In White's version, the sublime was not an experience-related concept, but a feature of historical reality. It did not refer to the impossibility of making sense of particular experiences, but to the impossibility, in White's view, of saying that reality has any meaning at all. Reformulating his long-held idea that meaning is made rather than found, White ascribed to the eighteenth-century theorists of the sublime the view that history is "meaningless 'in itself.'" Schiller, for example, was said to be so impressed by the "moral anarchy" that he perceived in history that he called historical reality a "sublime object." Not the fear and fascination felt by a human observer, but the "anarchy" and "confusion" characteristic of the past itself were labeled "sublime." Therefore, as Donald Pease correctly notes, White identified the sublime, not with the sort of experience the eighteenth-century theorists tried to describe, but with the "utter confusion and chaos of events in history" or with "the sheer arbitrariness of the historical field."[21] This, of course, recalls the *fortissimo* chords near the end of "The Burden of History," in which White had exclaimed that "discontinuity, disruption, and chaos is our lot." In fact, White's comments on the sublime can be seen as a radicalization of his statement, back in 1966, that life will be lived better if reality "has no single meaning but many different ones." More frankly than "The Burden," White's essay on the sublime located the plurality of meanings that can be assigned to the past, not in historical reality itself, but in human attempts to render "the meaningless meaningful" (as Theodor Lessing had put it).[22]

Saying that the past is thoroughly meaningless in itself implies that all meanings associated with historical events or persons are imposed upon the past. Given White's firm belief that individuals should have the freedom to devise such meanings for their own purposes, it is no surprise that he responded with a special sort of disapproval to ideological attempts to deny the sublime nature of historical reality, and thereby the freedom to conceive of history in individual terms. Ideologies, in White's analysis, "impute a meaning to history that renders its manifest confusion comprehensible to either reason, understanding, or aesthetic sensibility."[23] In former days – especially during the early 1960s, when White had fought in Crocean spirit against ideologically driven attempts at obscuring the "complexity" of history – he had complained that such forms of historical interpretation ignore the multiplicity of the past, for example by reducing historical causality to a single factor (class struggle, in the Marxist case). But by accepting the view that reality does not have any meaning at all, White could no longer maintain this criticism. For what exactly can be said to be reduced or ignored if there is no meaningful reality to which historical accounts can be compared? The charge of reductionism presupposes a standard in comparison to which ideological distortions can be identified as reductionisms. If, however, such a standard is not to be found in the past itself, it no longer makes sense to accuse ideological histories of reductionism with regard to the "complexity" of historical reality. White himself was the first to accept this consequence:

> The totalitarian, not to say fascist, aspects of Israeli treatment of the Palestinians on the West Bank may be attributable primarily to a Zionist ideology that is detestable to anti-Zionists, Jewish and non-Jewish alike. But who is to say that this ideology is a product of a *distorted* conception of history in general and of the history of Jews in the Diaspora specifically? It is, in fact, fully comprehensible as a morally responsible response to the meaninglessness of a certain history, that spectacle of "moral anarchy" which Schiller perceived in "world history" and which he specified as a "sublime object." The Israeli political response to this spectacle is fully consonant with the aspiration to human freedom and dignity which Schiller took to be the necessary consequence of sustained reflection on it.

What White believed Palestinians on the West Bank could do, in response, was not to criticize the Zionist ideology for its reductionism (as a "soft" humanist would do), but to develop an alternative to it (as the "strong" humanists praised in *The Ordeal of Liberal Humanism* supposedly did). In other words, a "politically effective response" to Israeli Zionism would require "a similarly effective ideology, complete with an interpretation of their [Palestinians'] history capable of endowing it with a meaning that it has hitherto lacked."[24]

This, then, is what White, the liberation historian, had in mind when he argued that the sublime enabled people to dream and to plot the course of their own life. White's reflections on the sublime resulted in the (unsolicited) advice to Palestinians on the West Bank to use their historical imagination, to think of alternative emplotments of history, to interpret their past from a different set of metahistorical assumptions. More particularly, White believed they needed to see history "as a spectacle of crimes, superstitions, errors, duplicities, and terrorisms that justified visionary recommendations for a politics that would place social processes on a new ground." This, of course, would lead to a break with the past as known so far: "One can never move with any politically effective confidence from an apprehension of 'the way things actually are or have been' to the kind of moral insistence that they 'should be otherwise' without passing through a feeling of repugnance for and negative judgment of the condition that is to be superseded."[25] Therefore, what White derived from (or, better, attributed to) Burke, Kant, and Schiller was anything but politically innocuous. In White's hands, the sublime served as an aggressive argument in favor of self-determination: "In my view, the theorists of the sublime had correctly divined that whatever dignity and freedom human beings could lay claim to could come only by way of what Freud called a 'reaction-formation' to an apperception of history's meaninglessness."[26]

Finally, it is worth nothing that, just as in *Metahistory*, White substantiated his argument with an inverted disciplinary history. He emplotted the history of historical thought as a tragic story of "de-sublimation" and "domestication," especially in the nineteenth century. Time and again, he lamented how history, enjoying a status comparable to nature in the eighteenth century and theology in the Middle Ages, had been granted the power to define the real, thereby excluding everything (the miraculous, the grotesque, the utopian) that did not fit the narrative mode favored by historians of the time. White therefore invoked the "pre-professional" category of the sublime as an alternative that historians, or Palestinians on the West Bank, might find worth embracing. Rather than disciplining the historical imagination, with all the Foucauldian associations of that term, the sublime would allow individuals to project their own meanings upon the past. Keith Jenkins therefore correctly speaks about "the utopian sublime" in White.[27] The sublime repeated in a new register White's old utopian dream of human self-assertion in the face of political oppression, conservative traditions, and religious intolerance.

The specter of fascism

The notion of the sublime, however, convinced a number of critics that White steadily went down the path of what they called "relativism." More particularly, they feared that this relativism might have unwelcome political consequences. For although White claimed that ideological regimes typically express their visions of the past in grand-scale historical narratives, hadn't figures such as Giovanni Gentile, the Italian philosopher of history (and colleague of Croce), on similar grounds provided support to Mussolini's fascism? And if White encouraged Palestinians to develop an anti-Zionist interpretation of history, would he also stimulate Irish Catholics and Protestants or Serbs and Croats in Bosnia to subordinate the past to their own political agendas?

As early as 1982, White admitted that the sublime was more likely to be embraced in right-wing political circles than by Western social democrats:

> Something like Schiller's notion of the historical sublime or Nietzsche's version of it is certainly present in the thought of such philosophers as Heidegger and Gentile and in the intuitions of Hitler and Mussolini. But having granted as much, we must guard against a sentimentalism that would lead us to write off such a conception of history simply because it has been associated with fascist ideologies.[28]

This was a characteristically Whitean move. Although freedom can be misused, it is better than slavery. Although utopian politics are dangerous, they are certainly to be preferred to a "piecemeal planning" that sets "a Scandinavian sharing of the wealth as the outer limits of its oneiric aspirations."[29] And although a view of history based on the sublime may, in principle, open the door to all sorts of historical dreams, including those of a Hitler or a Mussolini, it is better than not dreaming at all.

A number of critics, though, more concerned with criticizing political abuses of the past than with stimulating people's historical imagination, took offense at White's words, including especially his belittling comment on the "sentimentalism" of those who saw the fasces or the swastika looming behind the sublime. Among these was Roger Chartier, the French historian, who asked how White could possibly provide a barrier against revisionist histories of the Holocaust. White felt not particularly impressed by that question. As he explained in a rejoinder, revisionists typically employ the same methods and techniques that "ordinary" historians use. Moreover, both have roughly the same empiricist idea of what constitutes a fact. In other words, there are hardly any metahistorical issues at stake in the dispute between revisionists and their opponents.[30]

More notorious was Carlo Ginzburg's attack, launched in 1990 at a conference organized by Saul Friedlander, a Jewish historian of the Holocaust. Tracing White's philosophy of history back to his Italian period, Ginzburg not only called attention to the major role that Croce had played in White's early thought, but also detected a "quasi-Gentilian flavor" in White's writings, especially since "The Burden of History."[31] Although Ginzburg did not straightaway assert that White was a Gentilian fascist, as the accused said lapidarily,[32] he rejected what he saw as a common element in Gentile and White: their unqualified approval of attempts at developing morally and politically desirable alternatives to "official," academic historiography. Following these lines, he especially abhorred White's advice to the Palestinians with its suggestion that the effectiveness of a historical account matters more than, or is identical to, its truth-value. In Ginzburg's own words, "White's argument connecting truth and effectiveness inevitably reminds us not of tolerance but of its opposite – Gentile's evaluation of a blackjack as a moral force."[33]

Obviously, the most ponderous question Ginzburg put on the table was not whether White was a crypto-fascist. No one familiar with White's deeply humanist work can possibly take that charge seriously. Neither, though, was it how closely White's philosophy of history resembled Gentile's. As the surprisingly intensive debate evoked by Ginzburg's comments made clear, a number of contiguities and discrepancies between the two philosophers could easily be detected.[34] For example, both Gentile and White believed that historical scholarship ought to serve moral and political ends. Also, both consistently emphasized elements of choice in matters of historical interpretation. If Gentile considered knowledge to be "the product of a conscious *choice* on the part of active consciousness for which we individually and collectively [are] *responsible*," White had nothing to object.[35] Moreover, Gentile and White shared an almost existentialist sensitivity to the historicity of human morality, emphasizing that moral choices can only be made in the here and now, without recourse to time-transcending principles. A major difference, though, was that Gentile considered the state the prime moral agent, whereas White could not possibly conceive of legitimate agents other than the human individual. Arguably, this made White's "quasi-Gentilian flavor" almost too elusive to taste.

The important question Ginzburg's criticism raised, then, was rather how easily White's defense of the freedom to interpret the past for moral or political purposes could be misused for goals diametrically opposed to White's own. This was, basically, the same question A. Dirk Moses later raised in *History and Theory*: can White's work "be used to provide the theoretical arguments that justify the instrumentalization of historical memory by nationalist elites in their sometimes genocidal struggles with their opponents?"[36] Unlike many other criticisms leveled against White, this was a question that went to the heart of his philosophy of history. However unfortunate Ginzburg's quest for Gentilian traces in White, the Italian historian understood more accurately than many others that, at the end of the day, White's work served a moral end. Likewise, Moses correctly identified White's "hypergood" as the "radical autonomy of human agency," and the agenda underlying his work as an attempt to make history available as a resource for moral orientation: "It cannot be stressed too strongly that for White the business of the historical profession is meaning rather than knowledge because it is always written *for* a certain group, society, or culture that draws on the past for its praxis in the present and future."[37] The question is: can White's argument in favor of such meaning-production be hijacked by less humanistically inclined people? Can it be misused for totalitarian ends?

Although White did not straightforwardly respond to Ginzburg – his paper on the middle voice (to be discussed in chapter 6), which he delivered at the same conference in Los Angeles, was written before he learned about Ginzburg's attack – the obvious answer was: of course it can. Freedom of the kind that White consistently advocated can always be used for various purposes. As long as White's liberation discourse was focused on negative freedom (freedom *from* prison-houses of various sorts), it did not say anything about positive freedom (the goals *for* which freedom might be used). Moreover, White was too much of an existentialist to be willing to stipulate for others how they should use their freedom. Although White's own humanist goals were hard to miss, his liberation work could in principle also be employed for anti-humanist purposes. The only problem would be his ingrained commitment to skepticism. As White defended himself in a reply to Moses: "The Nazis were anything but relativists. And I do not think that Hamas and the Zionists or for that matter the Neo Cons in Washington are relativists either. Would that they were. As for skepticism, I had always thought it was a necessary component of any scientific worldview and a necessary counter to dogmatism."[38]

But, then, relativism or skepticism was not exactly what White advocated when, in his musings on the sublime, he encouraged

Palestinians to develop an ideology equal to the Zionist one. Arguably, even less relativistic was the "Promethean" left-wing politics that White envisioned. As he wrote in 1972: "'Promethean politics' may be dangerous, and doubly dangerous in an age of atomic weaponry, but it may be the only alternative to the 'logistical politics' which that weaponry generates."[39] In a sense, therefore, White was willing to take the risks that Ginzburg and Moses pointed out. In his assessment, it was better to dream than not to dream, even if a dream could turn into a nightmare. Besides, White never pretended to offer a position valid for all times and places. He wrote for Americans who worried (or ought to worry) about a latent totalitarianism in the United States government, not for Muslim Albanians in Kosovo.

Why White insisted on the Palestinians' need to dream becomes even clearer if we recall his 1960s preoccupation with the theme of totalitarianism. As we have seen in chapter 2, totalitarianism was one of the three contemporary problems that White at that time urged historians to examine. Moreover, in a number of subsequent writings (all ignored by Chartier, Ginzburg, and Moses), White had continued to reflect on the historian's responsibility vis-à-vis the threats of totalitarianism. For White, this threat was anything but over in an age of Cold War and the nuclear arms race. Like Ginzburg, then, White considered intellectuals to have a responsibility to help prevent the rise of new totalitarian regimes. Ironically, like Ginzburg, he also responded critically to thinkers whom he believed took this responsibility too lightly.

In a 1978 piece on René Girard, for example, White argued rather bitingly that Nazi Germany perfectly met the criteria for a "healthy" society outlined in Girard's *La violence et le sacré*: "Is Nazi Germany then to be taken as a model solution for the problem of 'modernity'? It certainly envisioned itself as such a solution."[40] Some years later, he responded with equal involvement to the Italian philosopher Mario Perniola, who, for an American audience, had portrayed Italian philosophical culture as fascinated by ambiguities, mixtures, and compromises, and therefore as a postmodernism *avant la lettre*.[41] In his reply, White skeptically asked how this Italian "postmodernism" related to the Mussolini regime: "Repetition as an end in itself, transmission of a message without a content, mixture which 'does not gain anything and ... does not take away anything,' and the body without identity – all of these could be listed as components of that purely theatrical and specular 'politic' we associate with the Italian forms of fascism." Moreover, well aware that fascist types of totalitarianisms had not died out since Mussolini, White wondered whether Perniola's playful postmodernism was sufficiently strong to resist the totalitarian temptation:

> Is there any reason to believe that the culture that permitted its growth [that of Italian fascism] can stand as a barrier to an even more powerful and pernicious brand of totalitarianism in this age of nuclear warfare and of a manipulation of culture? Against these threats *sprezzatura*, or what I take to be much of the same thing, "ritual and opportunity," are very weak defenses indeed.

And again: Perniola's philosophy may have "the undeniable appeal of its inherent *civility*," but "it seems a weak base on which to erect a defense against technological nihilism or the various totalitarianisms with which we are confronted today."[42]

Therefore, just as in the late 1960s White had dissociated himself from Croce because he had perceived the latter's armchair humanism as unable to put a halt to fascism in Italy, he considered Perniola's philosophy too weak to counter a future totalitarianism. Just as in *The Ordeal of Liberal Humanism*, then, White opted for a stronger humanism. The threat of totalitarianism was an important factor in leading White to emphasize the need to dream, the importance of stretching the human imagination, and the necessity of developing a "utopian" mode of realism. Liberation from a hegemonic discourse requires more than bourgeois decency; it takes a full-fledged master narrative. This explains why, in White's judgment, Palestinians on the West Bank needed an ideology equal to the Zionist worldview in order to escape from the "totalitarian, not to say fascist," treatment they received from the Israeli government. Accordingly, White's recommendation related rather differently to totalitarianism than Ginzburg believed. Whatever one thinks of White's encouragement, his advice to create a powerful historical ideology was explicitly targeted *against* a totalitarian regime.

Modernist anti-narrativism

The advice remained problematic, though. Earlier in this chapter, we reconstructed White's conviction that "stories are not lived but told" as stemming from a humanist commitment to values of individual self-determination. However, it is hard to think of Palestinian ideologies in other than collectivist terms. Also, although White's belief in the inherent meaninglessness of historical reality rendered, in principle, all narratives imposed upon it equally plausible, it might be more accurate, on White's view, to say that the sublime made them all equally *implausible*. Wasn't White's insistence on the sublimity of the past targeted against the illusory cohesions created in narrative? Didn't he, the existentialist-inspired humanist, believe that life is best lived in the face of a yawning abyss of meaninglessness? And, then, didn't White see the sublime as belonging to the stylistic repertoire of those modernist writers he had called upon in "The Burden of History?"[43] Wouldn't any of these modernist authors reject political ideologies? More generally, wouldn't any modernist worthy of that designation cultivate an awareness of gaps, breaks, and inconsistencies in history impossible to reconcile with fully fletched ideologies?

In an article on Fredric Jameson, published almost simultaneously with his piece on the sublime (1982), White indeed appeared to sympathize more fully with a modernist critique of narrative than with attempts, however ingenious, to devise new *grands récits*. Although White greatly admired Jameson's intellectual powers, he was rather critical of his Marxist master narrative. Jameson still dared to emplot history as a story of redemption. Moreover, unlike White (or Mink and Ankersmit, for that matter), Jameson understood the narrative structure of his redemptive story to correspond to "the 'narrativity' of the historical process itself." And, unlike White, he believed his Marxist story to provide an adequate basis for distinguishing between true and false consciousness.[44]

Now, whereas White conceded the Palestinians their ideology, he responded with defiance to the Jamesonian narrative. The differences between Jameson and White focused not least on their attitudes towards literary modernism. Whereas Jameson, from his Marxist perspective, equated modernism with "decadence" – "the form of literature and art which reflects the crisis in which late capitalism has entered"[45] – White took it upon himself to defend the modernists against Jameson and, moreover, to criticize Jameson's conception of history from a modernist point of view. Over against Jameson's "insistence that historical knowledge can serve as a secure baseline from which the ideological dimensions of any representation of social reality can be measured,"[46] White wanted to problematize the notion of history itself:

Is it not possible that the doctrine of "History," so arduously culti-
vated by the Western tradition of thought since the Greeks as an
instrument for releasing human consciousness from the constraints
of the Archaic age, is ready for retirement along with the "politics"
that it helped to enable? And could not the death of "History," politics, and narrative be all aspects of another great transformation,
similar in scope and effect to that which marked the break with
Archaism begun by the Greeks?[47]

The modernists featured in "The Burden of History" had certainly
thought so. They had sought to replace a nineteenth-century sense
of history as the story of "universal human experience" with a less
sanguine, more gloomy understanding of history as the recapitulation of "finite parts." They had no place for History with a capital
H or, by analogy, for Politics with capital P, based on those noble
ideals that, back in the nineteenth century, had secured History its
position as arbiter of the real. This analogy explains why White,
with unequivocal sympathy for this modernist line of thought,
could simultaneously reject Jameson's grand narrative and accept
that West Bank Palestinians have no other "realistic" option than
ideological counteraction. For when politics can no longer be measured against history, or conceptualized from within a grand narrative of one kind or another, "the crucial problem, from the
perspective of political struggle, is not whose story is the best or
truest, but who has the _power_ to make his story stick as one that
others will choose to live by or in." In other words, if the modernists
were right to record the death of History as an arbiter of the real,
then not truth but effectiveness is what counts. Yet White's own
preference unmistakably rested with those who rejected narrative
in favor of sublime realities that unremittingly remind them of the
arbitrariness and provisional nature of their "masks of meaning."
Rejecting Jameson's consoling narrative of history as redemption,
White believed that redemption could only be achieved by "getting
out of history."[48]

In sum, then, this chapter shows us a thinker deeply suspicious
of narrative. With even greater force than in his previous work, the
White of the early 1980s denied that history is narratively structured. The category of the sublime enabled him to repeat, with a
louder voice than before, his message that reality is meaningless,
that meaning is always a work of human hands, and that life is lived
better if people remain lucidly aware of these insights. If anything,
this threefold message showed that the existentialist humanism we

encountered in previous chapters had not yet left White.[49] Nor would it leave him in the years to come, as chapter 6 will illustrate. Arnaldo Momigliano's question, "Where does White find the evidence he will need either to live in chaos or to save himself from chaos?," appears to have a rather simple answer: in his modernist existentialism.[50]

6

Figuring History: The Modernist White

How decisive were the modernist affinities that White's response to Jameson displayed? Although White is often seen as a representative of postmodernism in the study of history, the aim of this final chapter, devoted to White's work since the early 1990s, is to argue that it is more appropriate to see White as indebted to modernist and existentialist sources than as a forerunner of postmodernism. Of course, given the plasticity of the word "postmodernism," it is not totally impossible to conceive of postmodernism in such a way that White stands out as its "most magisterial spokesman."[1] However, problematic about this move is not merely that it threatens to lump White together with some of the figures he most vocally rejected – Derrida is the most obvious example – but also that it tends to downplay, or even forget, the distinctively modernist sources of inspiration that informed White's work, not least in the 1990s and early 2000s.

Throughout the preceding chapters, we have encountered White's fascination with modernist authors such as Proust and Woolf. The revolt unleashed in "The Burden of History" was clearly inspired by a modernist sense of anti-historicism (chapter 2, this volume). Likewise, the desire to get beyond any realism that rules out the "dream" as delusory had evident affinity with modernist critiques of tradition (chapter 3). Remember also that White, in his Italian period, corresponded with Pound in St. Elizabeth's Hospital because "Pound was the kind of person we had to come to terms with" (chapter 1). Most important, however, is the insight reached near the end of the previous chapter: that White's "sublime" attack on narratives had a clear affinity with the modernism that had served as White's source of inspiration in "The Burden of History." As I shall argue in this final chapter, modernism became nothing less than a key word in White's essays written during his final years in Santa Cruz and after his subsequent appointment as Professor of Comparative Literature at Stanford (1995). In particular, this chapter will unpack five crucial notions figuring in White's writings of this period: "modernist events," "intransitive writing" (or "middle voice"), "figural realism" (or "figure" and "fulfillment"), "practical past," and "dialectical images." Rather than a postmodernist, the White that will emerge from this discussion is an "arch-modernist,"[2] as deeply committed as always to the cause of liberation from realisms that obstruct the dream of a better life by excluding the utopian from the real.

Modernist events

Back in the 1960s, in his Major Traditions series, White had identified "fascism," "mass society," and "technological culture" as the greatest challenges of the twentieth century (chapter 2 of this volume). In the 1990s, White again addressed these issues, not with the aim of contributing to a solution to the problems they posed, but with the question of how to represent them in language or images. Among students of Holocaust studies, a field that had emerged in the early 1970s, the issue how to represent the horrors of the Nazi death camps had become fiercely contested. Some had even come to see "representation of the Holocaust" as something close to a contradiction in terms. Doesn't the world of Auschwitz lie "outside speech as it lies outside reason," as George Steiner had famously stated?[3] Isn't the Holocaust such a unique event, or conglomerate of events, that it renders "normal" representational practices inadequate? What exactly made the Holocaust so vastly different from other catastrophes – the unprecedented number of victims, the industrialized killing-machines in Eastern Europe, or the deliberate attempt to extinguish an entire people? – was not always plainly articulated. After some attempts at demarcation, White also concluded that "we cannot establish on the basis of any strictly factual account, whether the Holocaust was a new event, a new kind of event, or simply an old kind of event with a different face."[4] Yet, beyond doubt was that many considered it a priori inappropriate to treat the Holocaust as standing on equal footing with other events.[5]

At Saul Friedlander's invitation, White joined this rather delicate conversation at the very same conference that provided Ginzburg a platform for his attack on White (see chapter 5 of this volume). Even though White did not know in advance about Ginzburg's criticisms, it took little imagination to see that his reputation as a "relativist" was the main reason for him being invited to Los Angeles. Could the Holocaust be emplotted in any of the four modes *Metahistory* had distinguished? Would White, confronted with the horrors enacted at Auschwitz and other concentration camps, continue his pleas to break away from conventional styles of interpretation? "Or do Nazism and the Final Solution belong to a special class of events, such that, unlike even the French Revolution, the American Civil War, the Russian Revolution, or the Chinese Great Leap Forward, they must be viewed as manifesting only one story, as being emplottable in one way only, and as signifying only one kind of meaning?"[6]

Characteristically, while endorsing the widely held conviction that the Holocaust was qualitatively different from earlier pogroms, wars, and crimes against humanity, White did not believe that a "special class of events" would be exclusively populated by the Nazi attempt to exterminate the Jews. For him, the Holocaust belonged to a category that also included "World War I, the Great Depression, the invention of a new kind of warfare made possible by nuclear weapons and communication technology, the population explosion, the imminent destruction of the zoosphere, famine on a scale hitherto inconceivable, the advent of genocide as a policy consciously undertaken by 'modernized' regimes," "the assassination of a leader such as Kennedy, of Martin Luther King, of Ghandi," "Hiroshima and Nagasaki," and even such abstract things as "boom and bust economic cycles."[7] Diverse as this list of events may seem, White presented them, at later occasions, as *modernist events*. In the early 1990s, he used many an occasion to reflect on how to represent such modernist events. Before examining what sort of representational practices White judged befitting for this type of occurrence, let us investigate what White understood such modernist events to be.

Lectures from the 1990s suggest three definitional components. First, not unlike Zygmunt Bauman, the sociologist who linked the Holocaust to a typically modern desire for control and manipulation, White emphasized that such events as the Holocaust could not take place without modern technologies. Modernist events presupposed an advanced level of industrialization or what White called a "monstrous growth and expansion of technological 'modernity.'"[8] Although, of course, modern technology has borne rich fruits, it takes on a Faustian dimension as soon as it transcends the human scale and, because of a lack of control, begins to cause effects utterly unimaginable to earlier generations. Auschwitz, Hiroshima, the climate crisis: White holds them to be "events of a scope, scale, and intensity unimaginable by earlier centuries."[9] This was not to deny that all sorts of catastrophes – think only of the sacking of Rome, the eternal city, in 410 – have been experienced as defying human imagination. White's point was that, in the case of modern events, this unimaginability was an effect of uncontrolled technological development.

Of course, such an incapacity to come to terms with an unanticipated event says as much about our expectations and assumptions as it does about the event in question. More specifically, though, the question is what sort of presuppositions are challenged by modernist events. The answer was provided in White's second definition. As unintended consequences of technological innovation in the twentieth-century West, modernist events do not, in general terms, resist all "inherited categories and conventions for assigning meanings to events," but, more specifically, call into question the inherited categories and conventions that the twentieth-century West is most familiar with.[10] As always, White was quick to identify these traditionally sanctioned modes of thinking with the sort of realism represented by the nineteenth-century realistic novel:

> When you take the traditional realist novel, Balzac, or Dickens, the kinds of problems that he is dealing with may be painful and may arouse our sympathy, and we may be able to identify with the people. But for example it is very difficult, it is virtually impossible for me to identify with these pilots that were flying these flights over Kosovo at fifteen thousand feet in order to drop these electronic bombs – they seem like aliens to me. The CIA, they seem like monsters to me. I can't identify them with the traditional spy of the nineteenth or early twentieth century, or James Bond, or someone like that. They seem utterly inhuman, alien. The same thing is true for people like Stalin, or Mao for that matter, Hitler ... These people do not fall within the categories that I recognize as defining the human.[11]

In passing, this argument reveals that modernist events not only challenge nineteenth-century modes of representation, but also pose a problem to White's own humanist approach to human behavior. As White admitted, modernist events defy "the categories underwritten by traditional humanism" insofar as the latter presuppose "the activity of rational or irrational but at any rate 'agents' conceived in some way to be *responsible* for their actions."[12] Accordingly, his inability to identify with Stalin, Mao, or Hitler can be said to stem first and foremost from the unfeasibility of applying such categories as means–end rationality (discussed in chapter 1 of this volume) and individual responsibility (chapter 2) to the suffering, persecution, and mass murder carried out under the dictators' regimes. Not these cruelties as such, but the challenge they posed to nineteenth-century realism and traditional liberal humanism was what distinguished modernist events from earlier catastrophes.

Third, more specifically, modernist events challenge the realism of a Balzac or Dickens (or Ranke, for that matter) by resisting historicization. That is to say, these events do not simply belong to a past, distinct from the present, that historians may reconstruct by means of documentary evidence. For one thing, in the case of modernist events, the very distinction between past and evidence is often unclear. Think of such media events as the explosion of the *Challenger* space shuttle on January 28, 1986, or the attack on the Twin Towers in New York on September 11, 2001. Live television images of 9/11 or the explosion of the space shuttle quickly became "icons," drawing more attention to themselves than to the reality they were supposed to represent. "The networks played the tapes of the *Challenger* explosion over and over," explained White. But these images did not answer the question of what had happened, or why: "All that the 'morphing' technology used to re-present the event provided was a sense of its evanescence. It appeared impossible to tell any single authoritative story about what really happened – which meant that one could tell any number of possible stories about it."[13] Also, whereas historians traditionally learn to dissociate themselves as much as possible from the past they investigate, modernist events cause traumas and shocks that cannot easily be overcome. Another reason, then, why the Holocaust cannot be historicized in the way historians like to do is that we are emotionally too much involved in it. Unlike most events in history, the Holocaust is

> only virtually finished, not actually over and done with, but still alive in some sense, alive in the present as an after-effect, a presence which produces effects by virtue of its absence, or virtual absence, an

absence which presents itself to the present as distanced, withdrawn, still degenerating rather than totally obliterated.[14]

Do these three definitional elements provide a clear demarcation line between modernist events and other catastrophes, including especially those happening prior to the twentieth century? White was prepared to admit that such a line can probably never be precisely drawn.[15] What the foregoing suggests, though, is that White believed the twentieth century to have produced a type of event that is "unimaginable" or "incredible" to the degree that it challenges the modes of realism (still) prevailing in Western culture. This may give a clue as to why modernist events aroused White's fascination. The notion of "inconceivable" events allowed White to launch another attack on nineteenth-century modes of realism.

It cannot be overlooked, though, that this strategy raised some serious questions. For example, in speaking about events in which agency could not possibly be attributed, was White prepared to sacrifice his humanist assumption that human individuals must be held responsible for their own deeds? If modernist events blurred the distinction between event (in reality) and fact (in discourse), then could White maintain his critical dichotomy between a meaningless reality and the historian's meaning-imposing operations (chapter 5, this volume)? Was it possible that, at least occasionally, historians could not position themselves autonomously over against a sublime, meaningless reality, but would remain enmeshed in the ambiguities of (traumatic) relationships to a past whose burden they could not throw off?

Intransitive writing

In order to find out whether White indeed changed his mind in matters of meaning-imposition, let us first examine how he suggested that modernist events could be adequately represented. As we have seen, in White's view, attempts to describe the gruesome world of Auschwitz or Buchenwald are doomed to failure as long as they merely employ the Walter Scott-like story forms that Ranke had popularized in the historical discipline. Because such narratives require heroes and villains that can be held responsible for their own deeds, modernist events resist such treatment and require a mode of representation better attuned to their incomprehensibility. In White's own words, "the phenomena of Hitlerism, the Final

Solution, total war, nuclear contamination, mass starvation, and ecological suicide" confront us with "a profound sense of the incapacity of our sciences to *explain* them" and with a total "incapacity of our traditional modes of representation even to *describe* them adequately." Fortunately, however, we not only have the sciences and traditional story forms; we also have certain non-traditional modes of representation, developed by that literary movement that, among other things, saw itself as a response to such a modernist event as World War I:

> In point of fact I do not think that the Holocaust, Final Solution, Shoah, Churban, or German genocide of the Jews is any more unrepresentable than any other event in human history. It is only that its representation, whether in history or in fiction, requires the kind of style, the modernist style, that was developed in order to represent the kind of experiences which social modernism made possible, the kind of style met with in any number of modernist writers.[16]

In particular, White argued that "the stylistic innovations of modernism" are more appropriate for the representation of modernist events than the story-telling techniques that historians traditionally use. Compared to the sort of narratives usually written about the past, modernist techniques enable writer and reader much better "for that process of mourning which alone can relieve the 'burden of history' and make a more, if not totally realistic perception of current problems possible."[17]

How could this be achieved? White had some examples in mind. Following a suggestion made by philosopher Berel Lang, he invoked Roland Barthes's concept of "intransitive writing" as designating a modernist form of representation that might be quite appropriate for modernist events. Intransitive writing was Barthes's term for a form of prose, found in modernist authors such as Virginia Woolf, which consciously sought to erase distinctions between form and content, subject and object, past and present. In White's summary, intransitive writing challenged the borders between events and their representation in discourse, documents and (literary) texts, (literary) texts and their social contexts, literal and figurative speech, referent and subject of a discourse, fact and fiction, and history and literature. A concrete example is the stream of consciousness in Woolf's novel, *Between the Acts*, in which the protagonist, Isabella Oliver, pondering about the social ills of her time, reads in the newspaper about a rape case and day-dreamingly projects this scene on the door of the library through which, all of a sudden, Mrs. Swithin, one of Isabella's older relatives, enters the room. The scenes blend into each other, with the effect that it is impossible to determine where the past ends and the present begins, or at which point the girl being raped metamorphoses into Mrs. Swithin.[18]

Intransitive writing – or the conscious employment of a "middle voice," which is "neither subjective nor objective," but represents a mode of mediation between subject and object[19] – was one of the modernist stylistic practices that White, back in 1966, had recommended as sources of inspiration for historians tired of the narrative preferences of the historical discipline. On the occasion of Friedlander's conference in Los Angeles, White turned again to this stylistic practice because such intransitive writing, with its tendency to position itself between the event and the writer, neatly corresponded to how he defined the modernist event. After all, both modernist events and intransitive writing challenge the event/fact distinction, call into question the past/present divide, and obscure the line between reality and representation. Intransitive writing is an appropriate way of representing modernist events because it does not iron out the difficulties they pose to the human imagination, but deals as much with these representational problems as with the events themselves. Intransitive writing simultaneously refers to what happened in the past and to what happens in the process of trying to represent a "past that does not go away."

Concretely, White told his audience in Los Angeles that such an intransitive treatment of the Holocaust could be found in Art Spiegelman's *Maus*, a much-debated comic book about an artist interrogating his father about his memories of Auschwitz. In a complex interplay between words and drawings, Spiegelman shows that any attempt to tell a "straight" story about the camp is doomed to fail, if only because of (a) the traumatic character of the artist's father's recollections, (b) the gaps and inconsistencies in what the father remembers, and (c) the utterly "inhuman" behavior the father ascribes not merely to the German perpetrators, but also to victims and bystanders in the camp. Spiegelman's solution to this problem is to write and draw not only about Auschwitz or about his father's memories of the camp, but also, simultaneously, about the processes of remembering, repressing, recounting, and representation that both he and his father went through. In *Maus*, then, the voices of the father, those of the perpetrators, victims, and bystanders remembered by the father, and those of the artist mingle into a textual and visual discourse that deals as much with the Holocaust as it does with our present-day difficulties in determining what to think of this event. For this reason, White believed *Maus* to be so "critically self-conscious" as to raise "all of the crucial issues regarding the limits of representation in general."[20]

Indeed, instead of solving the problem of how to deal with modernist events, intransitive writing articulates an intensified awareness of it and provides a way of dealing with it. Intransitive writing "points to a way of questioning and thinking," rather than to a remedy for the problem of representation.[21] This is also apparent from the other examples White had in store, all of which are forms of highly self-reflective discourse that mixes first-order statements about the past with second-order observations about its own attempts at representation. In Jacques Rancière's *Les noms de l'histoire*, for example, White encountered a mode of discourse that "is to be taken neither literally nor figuratively; his own mode of address is to be taken as neither active nor passive; and his assertions are to be taken as neither denotative nor connotative."[22] In the Italian-Jewish Auschwitz survivor Primo Levi, too, White found examples of "writing in the middle voice." As a participant in the events he tried to describe in *I sommersi e i salvati*, Levi knew that his attempt at telling the truth about the concentration camp would inevitably be hampered by his psychic inclination to repress his most terrible recollections. It is this amalgamation of careful attempts at representation and critical reflections on the limits of that endeavor which, in White's view, best characterizes the middle voice:

> He [Levi] is on the one hand much too much a subject of his own writings to be considered merely a passive receiver of impressions and, on the other, much too deferential to detail and nuance to be identified as the Promethean "author." Fortunately, modern critical theory gives us a way of thinking about Levi's relationships to his subject (the experience of the Lager), on the one side, and to his own writing practices, on the other, which avoids the manichean choice between the poles of action and passion, or active and passive voices. This is found in the idea of a "middle voice."[23]

So, indeed, in Levi, the narrator's voice is not that of an autonomous interpreter, able to oversee the past and "grasp it together" in a meaningful story. Likewise, the intransitivity of *Maus* is more than an effect that Spiegelman, the artist, skillfully orchestrates. For better or for worse, middle voices only emerge when authors cannot get hold of the past, when events refuse to be comprehended, when shocks and traumas hamper the author's attempts to interpret the past in accordance with his or her moral and aesthetic principles (White's usual criterion).

A turning point?

The question, then, is how this relates to White's conviction that historians ought to position themselves autonomously vis-à-vis a meaningless historical reality. Did White maintain his belief that the past is sublime and only becomes meaningful if historians or others impose some meaning upon it (chapter 5, this volume)? A number of critics have argued that White did not. For example, in Los Angeles, historian Martin Jay chided White for undercutting what was "most powerful in his celebrated critique of naive historical realism." Didn't that critique stand or fall with the very distinction between subject (historian) and object (past) that Barthes's intransitive writing deliberately challenged? Wulf Kansteiner, too, identifies the middle voice with a "turning point" in White's oeuvre: "White's decision to introduce a more dialectical element into his structuralist methodology implies a renegotiation of the status of the fact with regard to the plot structures of the historical text."[24]

Such observations, however, easily miss the point. For one thing, both Jay and Kansteiner forget that White did not at all speak about historians. He illustrated his reflections on the mingling of subject and object voices, not with works of historiography, but with examples of witness literature, written by survivors (Levi) and their children (Spiegelman). Although "stream of consciousness" can be seen as a genre or literary technique that any historian with sufficient literary skills can learn to master, White did not summon historians to apply this technique or write about the Holocaust in the way that Woolf did about Isabella Oliver and Mrs. Swithin. He even explicitly noted that "such versions of history are seldom produced by professional historians."[25] His point, then, was different. Not historians, but survivors such as Levi engage in intransitive writing. Not historiography, with its tendency "to clothe the chaos of the phenomenal world in stable images,"[26] but witness literature, with its (traumatic) inability to dissociate itself from the past it purports to describe, offers a mode of dealing with modernist events. Accordingly, in reply to Jay or Kansteiner, or in response to the question how a work of history modeled after the example of *Maus* might look,[27] White could hold up his copy of *Maus* and declare: this is how we can relate to modernist events. Spiegel-man does not need to be "translated" into something historians might recognize; *Maus* itself shows us, better than any historio-graphical account, the ambiguities that modernist events confront us with.

Second, if White, in hermeneutic fashion, had claimed intransi-tive writing to be the result of a "fusion of horizons" between subject and object, Jay's point would have been correct. Such a Gadamerian approach to interpretation, which considers meaning not as made exclusively by the interpreting subject, but as stem-ming from a playful and unpredictable encounter between subject and object, would indeed be incompatible with White's constructiv-ism. However, White never even thought of such a fusion of hori-zons. Although Gadamer's work has been characterized in terms of the middle voice,[28] White used the term for his own purpose. In his view, the harsh reality of Auschwitz, Hiroshima, or Nagasaki does not neatly "fuse" with present-day concerns to produce a "meaning" that is the result of this productive "encounter." On the contrary, if Levi's or Spiegelman's "encounter" with the Holocaust yields any-thing, it is a *lack* of meaning. Modernist events resist interpretation; they call into question any attempt to endow them with meaning. Auschwitz, then, is as sublime – that is, as meaningless – as any other event in history. The only difference is that, comparatively speaking, the meaninglessness of such a modernist event can less easily be covered by narrative means. So, for White, modernist events are no sources of meaning; they rather thwart any effort to impose the past with meaning.

Accordingly, if intransitive writing mingles subject and object voices, it does not combine meanings offered by "reality" and meanings offered by "representation" (how could a sublime reality ever be a source of meaning?). Intransitive writing rather shows that Levi's or Spiegelman's efforts to say something meaningfully about the world of Auschwitz are doomed to failure. Intransitive writing is a mode of discourse dealing in gaps, incomprehensibilities, con-tradictions, and inconsistencies. To be sure, it does allow the author to impose meaning on the past, if only because it presents an occa-sion for mourning. But, simultaneously, it wrestles with such meaning, denies it, and calls it into question. Intransitive writing is as ironic a mode as one can think of.

Third, modernist events and middle voices can be interpreted as a turning point only if one overlooks what we have seen in previous chapters: that from the 1960s onwards, White had consistently criticized the domesticating effects caused by historical interpretation in more traditional forms. That is to say, long before the 1990s, White had claimed that modernist modes of representation allow historians to recognize the inherent meaninglessness of the past better than the "*bad* art" historians usually prefer. Also, White's contention that modernist writing "liberates the historical event from the domesticating suasions of 'plot' by doing away with 'plot' itself" was entirely consistent with the anti-narrativism exhibited in his essay on the sublime. And if he recommended treating modernist events by non-narrative means, so as to enable a "concentration on the fragment" that "finely-wrought narratives" never allow for, he was repeating, in a louder voice, his long-running critique of the realist novel as a model for historical representation:[29]

> What you get, then, in modernist writing, is a discovery of the depths behind things, not as meaning, but as chaos, as sublime, as that in confrontation with which you're thrown back upon the incapacities of the mind to grasp the conditions of your existence. That's why writing in modernism increasingly becomes the failure of the writer, the failure of the writer to do what the writer had traditionally been charged to do.[30]

Only this last sentence conveyed a thought that was relatively new. Never before had White displayed such a hesitation about whether, in confrontation with the sublimities of the past, people would be *capable* of performing the task of interpretation. If much of his previous work had portrayed the (ideal) historian as an almost heroic producer of meaning – armed with a rich stylistic repertoire, possessing a *totum simul* view of what had happened in the past, and devoted to a cause greater than him- or herself, the image now became somewhat less valiant. Presumably, White still subscribed to his ideal, but realized that especially in relation to such modernist events as the Holocaust, a past without burdens is an illusion. Yet, whereas for others this might have been a reason to insist less fiercely on liberation from the past, White did not stop being the liberation historiographer that he was. As we shall see in the remainder of this chapter, the modernist event did not erode his belief in the possibility of getting "out of history"; it rather underscored the need for contemporary individuals to abandon their historical attitudes towards realities they had involuntarily inherited.

Figural realism

This became particularly clear in White's reflections on another theme he addressed during the 1990s in a great many of the lectures he was invited to deliver at campuses around the globe: the figure-fulfillment model of historical interpretation. For audiences that had just absorbed the modernist event and/or the middle voice, this was a rather complicated theme, if only because it was less directly related to Spiegelman and Levi than suggested in such texts as "Figural Realism in Witness Literature." Given that this article presented Primo Levi *both* as an author of intransitive prose *and* as a writer using a figure-fulfillment model of historical interpretation, one would be forgiven for assuming that the word-pair of figure and fulfillment described one of the peculiarities of that modernist, non-narrative prose that White considered appropriate for the representation of modernist events. Careful readers may have noted, though, that in this very essay, White presented "figural realism," or the use of figure-fulfillment models, as the power of literary writing to endow facts with passions, feelings, and values – which is a much broader power than the capacity of intransitive writing to reckon with gaps and ruptures in the past. Indeed, as I will argue in this section, whereas Levi's *I sommersi e i salvati* – together with Spiegelman's *Maus* – initially served as White's favorite example of intransitive writing, he subsequently employed this same book for making a point he could have illustrated with any other work of prose: that it is impossible to endow the past with meaning without employing some version of the figure-fulfillment model. (Why *I sommersi* was nonetheless an interesting example will be explained below.)

One might wonder: what does this model entail and where did it come from? To start with the latter, White borrowed the idea from Erich Auerbach, the German-American philologist whose classic study of realism, *Mimesis*, White had frequently cited in his earlier work.[31] In Auerbach's terminology, *figura* referred to an interpretative practice that Christian theologians had introduced in the West. Typical of such figural interpretation is that it treats historical events as types or anticipations of later events. For example, it interprets King David as a *figura Christi*, that is, as a "figure" that finds its "fulfillment" in Jesus Christ. Along these lines, generations of Christians saw Noah's Ark as a *figura* of the New Testament church, and the people of Israel's passage through the Red Sea as anticipating the sacrament of baptism. This interpretative practice allowed them to read the Hebrew Bible not merely as a collection of Jewish poems, laws, and histories, but also as texts that figuratively speak about Jesus. In Auerbach's assessment, this "figural realism" had left ineradicable traces in the Western literary tradition, if only because it allowed for a multiple-level reading of history. While, at a literal level, David had been King of Israel and father of Salomon, he could figuratively be interpreted as anticipating the "great son of David" and King of heaven and earth, Jesus Christ. It was on this basis that medieval exegetes had distinguished between multiple "senses of Scripture." Without this tradition, *Mimesis* had shown, authors such as Dante, who had tried to interpret their own life-world through figural lenses, could not be understood.[32]

Unsurprisingly, White was not particularly interested in the theological aspects of this *Figuraldeutung*. His eagerness to adopt Auerbach's vocabulary rather stemmed from the hope that a figure-fulfillment model could be developed into a "peculiarly 'historical' mode of causation, different from ancient teleological notions, on the one side, and modern scientific, mechanistic notions, on the other." Following up on his 1967 lecture in Denver, on invention of traditions, choice of father-figures, and "retroactive ancestral substitution" (chapter 2 of this volume), White explained that figuralism allowed for a transfer of meaning between events that were not, scientifically speaking, causally related. There was no direct sense, for example, in which the Renaissance had been "caused" by the sort of classical ideals White had portrayed in *The Greco-Roman Tradition*. Yet the Renaissance had preferably seen itself, not merely as a "rebirth" of classical Antiquity, but also, more ambitiously, as a fulfillment or "consummation" of classical ideals. In White's words, then, the Renaissance had been a fulfillment of classical Antiquity insofar as the former had *chosen* the latter as its figure. In more general terms, one might say that a "given historical event can be viewed as the fulfillment of an earlier and apparently utterly unconnected event when the agents responsible for the occurrence of the later event link it 'genealogically' to the earlier one."[33] Indeed, figuralism might be called genealogical in so far as it provides an alternative to the genetic modes of reasoning that White had rejected as early as 1967. What counts is not biological inheritance or influence, but the choice of a culture from which one would wish to be descended. This, indeed, was a variation on the old Whitean theme of "choosing a past" (chapter 2 of this volume).

New, however, was that White began to employ the word-pair of figure and fulfillment for even more creative purposes (which

Auerbach, the cautious philologist, may never have envisioned, though, in a generous act of "creative correction," White attributed several of them to the author of *Mimesis*).[34] Dante's *La divina commedia*, for example, which had served as a figure for Balzac's *La comédie humaine*, was said to fulfill Virgil's *Aeneid*, so that "the diachronic 'plot' of the history of western literature" might be conceived of "as a sequence of figure-fulfillment relations."[35] Second, White suggested that not only this particular story-line, but all plot-structures distinguished in *Metahistory* and afterwards employ figurative means, since they endow historical events with meaning that is only revealed when the reader sighs, near the end of the narrative: "Oh, *now* I see what was *really* happening after all" (chapter 4 of this volume).

> Such is the work of narrativity, the differential distribution of events across a timeline in which the meaning of beginnings can only be discerned from the vantage point of a putative ending. This meaning is always the meaning of an ending only partially, imperfectly, and incompletely realized in comparison with the fullness of being displayed in the ending. It is a conceit of narrativity that the characters in the story can never foresee the ending from the vantage point of any position prior to its manifestation as ending, either as catastrophe or consummation and fulfillment.[36]

Also, anatomizing a passage from Proust's *A la recherche*, White reflected on four garden scenes (written, respectively, in the modes of metaphor, metonymy, synecdoche, and irony), the three last of which he claimed to be "a 'fulfillment' of the 'figures' of the scenes that precede it."[37] And so it went on, as if every (cross-) reference between texts, images, or events that was not causally related could be interpreted in terms of figure and fulfillment. Indeed, for White, every referential relationship between two texts, images, or events in which the latter retroactively determines the meaning of the former could be described in such terms.

This allows us to see why, appearances notwithstanding, figural realism cannot be equated with intransitive writing. Figure-fulfillment models generate meaning. They deal in meaning that is hidden and provisional at one point in time, but at a later moment becomes visible and fully disclosed. This, however, is by no means what intransitive writing is all about. In fact, such a creative production of meaning is precisely what is *lacking* in the modernist types of discourse that White recommended for their respectful toleration of gaps, incomprehensibilities, and absence of meaning. Admittedly,

Proust was a modernist, especially in so far as his discourse was not framed in a single trope, but utilized all "modalities of figuration."[38] But Levi, in White's reading, was not modernist at all, at least not consciously so. Indebted to what White called "a banal conception of poetry," Levi had suggested that only "literal" adherence to the "facts" could produce a mode of discourse appropriate to the horrors of Auschwitz. Any poetic speech or figurative language would lead to an "aesthetization" of the Holocaust (a scandal that Spiegelman sometimes found himself accused of).[39] Of course, White denied outright the possibility of such literalism. Hadn't he argued for decades that figurative language is impossible to avoid, that writing is an act of myth-making, and that even the most sincere attempts at "factual representation" cannot do without "fictions" (chapter 4, this volume)?

Accordingly, what may cause surprise is not that White took *I sommersi* to show that, despite the author's intentions, its prose "is consistently (and brilliantly) figurative throughout."[40] It is more surprising, perhaps, that White dropped the language of fiction and spoke about figuralism instead. He seems to have realized that the difference between "factual" and "fictional" literature only makes sense at an ideal-typical level. Precisely insofar as his own attempts to uncover the "fictions of factual representation" were successful, so that there was no factual discourse that was not at the same time fictional, the dichotomy between "factual" and "fictional" was rendered obsolete. This could not be said, however, of the distinction between literal and figurative language. Even though White did not believe one could produce meaning without using the latter, that is, without figuration of the world, he did not deny that literal language exists. Among other reasons, this was why White exchanged the language of fiction for that of figuration.[41]

The point, then, White sought to illustrate with Levi's book in hand was that figurative language, defined as the use of tropes, necessarily employs a figure-fulfillment model. For what figurative language does – think only of the metaphor "my love is a rose" – is to relate two things that are not causally related in such a way as to realize a transfer of meaning. More specifically, White speculated that Levi also (unconsciously) presented himself – that is, his own hopes, griefs, and anxieties – as fulfillments of figures in his text. For example, when he compared a fellow-inmate named Henri to Il Sodoma's painting of *St. Sebastian*, to a cat, to a wasp-like insect, and finally to the snake in the Garden of Eden, these comparisons not merely brought about a transfer of meaning between the

painting or the animals and the young man imprisoned in Auschwitz, but simultaneously also revealed something about Levi's
own attitudes towards Henri: "[W]hile these characterizations may
be more or less true in a factual sense, surely it is less their factuality
than their function in revealing something about their author, whose
emotional investment in his subject is manifested in the excessive-
ness of the imagery he uses to depict him." In White's reading, Levi
must have felt an "irrepressible desire" for the boyish man he figuratively described as homosexual (Sodoma's *St. Sebastian* had a
certain reputation in this regard). The figure of the Serpent, moreover, suggested that, in spite of this desire, Levi morally disap-
proved of Henri's seductive powers, at the time of writing at least.
For this reason, White suggested that the metaphors describing
Henri functioned as figures that found their fulfillment in how Levi
looked back upon the man while writing *I sommeri*. This is to say
that, for White, the "manifest" content of Levi's book found its
fulfillment in a "latent content" readers needed to grasp if they were
to understand the meaning of the figures.[42]

The practical past

As technical as this may sound, White's analysis of Levi's prose in
terms of figure and fulfillment paved the way for what White in the
2000s announced as his new and most important topic: the "practical past." What is more, all three threads distinguished so far in this
chapter – modernist events, intransitive writing, and figural realism
– came together in this idea of a "practical past." One might even
say that in this notion, White managed to integrate a number of key
ideas developed during his 50 years' career as a historical theorist:
moral deliberation vis-à-vis a burdensome past, the inability of
professional historical scholarship to provide moral orientation in
the present, and the need for modernist-inspired alternatives that
help us cope with our attitudes, emotions, and responsibilities
towards the past. However, when the final pages of this chapter
describe how White in some of his most recent (sometimes still
unpublished) writings elaborated on this "practical past," it is
important to realize that this elaboration has not yet come to an end.
At the time of writing, White was working enthusiastically on a
volume tentatively titled *The Practical Past*.[43] Accordingly, this final
section must be somewhat more exploratory and more open-ended
than the rest of this book. The reader may do worse than take

this as a recommendation to consult White's own most recent publications.

Most important, then, in White's reflections during the first decade of the present century, was the question of how we can morally relate to modernist events. Obviously, such events as the Final Solution cannot be fulfilled in the way classical Antiquity founds its fulfillment in the Renaissance, Dante in Balzac, or *St. Sebastian* in Henri. Any morally responsible person will reject out of hand the idea of finding inspiration in the horrors of the 1940s. Also, if modernist events resist interpretation, as White claimed they do, it is impossible to treat them as figures of later events. Yet there must be some way to handle the burden that such events as the Holocaust place upon us – a way to begin "anew," not by naively throwing off that burden, but by transforming it so as to stimulate creative action rather than mere passive contemplation. The ability to inspire such new beginnings was what White, in a 2005 interview, said he admired in Christian figural hermeneutics: "The pagans did not have such a concept; hence, they were unable to escape from Vico's eternal cycles. However, long before Kant and the Frankfurt School, the early Christians invented a concept that enabled them to transform – to transubstantiate, if you want – their Jewish past in such a way as to make the old look new."[44] What White hoped to achieve, then, was something similar. How to survive the monstrosities that twentieth-century technology had borne? How to live a morally responsible life in the shadows of Auschwitz and Hiroshima? Such a life, said White, requires not a historical, but a practical past.

The "historical" and the "practical" past had first been distinguished by the British philosopher Michael Oakeshott. Following Oakeshott, White understood the historical past to be the preserve of historians "interested in 'disinterested' study of the past 'as it really was' and 'as an end in itself'" – professional historiography in its most caricatural form – while, by contrast, the practical past rather serves as "a storehouse of memory, ideals, examples, events worthy of remembrance and repetition."[45] This reminds one of Nietzsche's distinction between critical and monumental historiography (discussed in chapter 2 of this volume) insofar as the former tries to keep contemporary problems away from the study of the past, whereas the latter values historical studies only insofar as they illuminate such problems – be they social, cultural, political, or religious. As a consistent advocate of the second approach, White not only opted for the "practical past," but also argued for the right of people to search the past for new, inspiring figures. For example, speaking about Eastern European countries after the fall of communism, White left no doubt that he applauded their efforts at "reinventing" the twentieth-century past, even if such reinventions sometimes tended towards idolization of former resistance heroes: "[C]ommunities have a right to determine the meaning or significance of their own pasts."[46]

As this example illustrates, the most striking difference between the historical and the practical past lies in the attitudes people bring to them, or in the questions they expect the past to answer for them. Whereas historians are typically interested in knowledge *about* the past, others often worry more how to deal *with* the past. While historians wonder "is it true?," the rest of society is usually more concerned about the question "what must be done?" The practical past, then, is practical in the sense of Kant's *praktische Vernunft*: it wonders "what should I (or we) do?"[47] For readers familiar with White's earlier work, this distinction between cognitive and moral relationships to the past is a familiar one. New, however, was White's observation that the question "is it true?" corresponds to a type of discourse operating in what he called the mode of "simple declaration." Simple declarations are statements of the type "the cat is on the mat" and "Archduke Franz Ferdinand of Austria was assassinated on June 28, 1914." Such statements are true or false, indeed, depending on whether they can be justified with appropriate documentation. But discourse can operate in other modes, too: in an interrogative, in an imperative, or in a subjunctive mode, for instance. Speech-acts such as "close the door!" and "I now pronounce you husband and wife" are examples of such non-declarative discourse. They do not solicit a response like "this is true," but rather "yes, sir" or "thanks be to God."[48]

Now, whereas the historical past corresponds to a declarative mode of discourse, the practical past prefers alternative, non-declarative modes, because it is concerned not with knowledge, but with that practical question of what must be done with "burdens" that people have involuntarily inherited. This is especially true for modernist events. Precisely because their shadows are so long and heavy, they are better dealt with in intransitive writing, that is, in a mode of discourse that cannot be reduced to simple declarations. For White, this increasingly became a matter of principle. Is it appropriate, he wondered, to represent the Holocaust in a declarative mode, which favors the question "is it true?" over questions such as "how to live with this?" or "how can we prevent this from happening again?" More specifically, if Levi's *I sommersi e i salvati* presents us with a non-declarative mode of dealing with the Final Solution, is it right to respond with the query whether Levi's account is true in a correspondence sense of the word? "I am interested in the question, is it proper to forego asking the question 'Is it true or false?' in the presence of a specific kind of discourse in which witness literature would be a paradigm and a modernist literary treatment (such as Sebald's *Austerlitz* or Ann Michael's *Fugitive Pieces*) of the Holocaust would be instances."[49]

Obviously, White's answer was affirmative. Much of his work after *Figural Realism* focused on such authors as Levi, whose *Se questo è un uomo* explicitly "instructs the reader to meditate upon the significance of life in Auschwitz for what it tells us about the capacity of human beings to humiliate their own kind."[50] This was as practical a past as Oakeshott could have imagined. White devoted special attention, moreover, to such modernist novelists as W. G. Sebald, whose *Austerlitz* he considered as important a specimen of intransitive writing as Spiegelman's *Maus*. The novel "raises more problems than it solves when it is a matter of seeking a meaning for an individual life or existence." That is because Sebald's book consistently refuses to conceptualize, to draw story lines, or to narrativize in the way historical novels from Walter Scott to Lev Tolstoy used to do. *Austerlitz* abandons any sense of continuity and rejects cheap meaning. It teaches us, said White, "to see in 'pictures' rather than in concepts."[51]

Seeing in "pictures," finally, is not without obligations: it solicits moral and political response. Admittedly, it is difficult to grasp why a lack of meaning, or a failed attempt to attribute a modernist event with meaning, invites a special kind of moral or political engagement. Hadn't White insisted that "modes of ideological implication" are impossible to avoid? Indeed, the point is not that the black holes of modernist events ask for more moral or political commitment, but rather that they solicit a particular type of response. White substantiated this idea with reference to Walter Benjamin, the modernist philosopher *par excellence*. "Seeing in pictures" refers to Benjamin's opaque formula "history does not break down into stories but into images," which became one of White's favorite lines in the late 1990s.[52] I call these words opaque, because even Benjamin scholars agree that "image" (or "dialectical image") is one of the most difficult concepts in Benjamin's philosophy.[53] Nonetheless, White accepted the dialectical image as a welcome tool in his struggle against historical realism of a nineteenth-century sort: "For him

[Benjamin], the images which we can find 'caught' in the record like a fly in amber are not those that figure forth an unambiguous and internally consistent social reality, but those which capture as in the still photograph a moment of tension and change, an intermittency between two moments of putative presence."[54]

Whereas historians, professionally in search of the historical past, subject such relics to "source criticism" and examine how they represent the "social circumstances" of their days, modernist thinkers or writers, concerned about the practical past, examine how we, present-day readers, may relate to remnants of a past that continues to horrify us. Like Sebald in *Austerlitz*, they confront us with images, that is, with relics that resist conceptualization and narrativization. They remind us that we have to relate to these images – to that famous photo of a young girl staring from between two train doors on the brink of deportation, or to a farewell letter from a concentration camp inmate, written several hours before his death – and urge us to respond to these images, not merely with horror or condemnation, but with morally responsible action. Although these images resist the sort of meaning that narratives provide, they can invoke in us a sense of "never again," that is, a sense of moral duty and commitment to make the world a slightly better place.

If this relation between images from the past and moral behavior in the present can be described in terms of figure and fulfillment, it may be most appropriate to say that White would like to see the past, not as *already* fulfilled, but as *awaiting* fulfillment (in what Benjamin, in quasi-theological language, called a "messianic" mode).[55] Images of people treated as second-rank beings may, or should, inspire us to protest against similar practices in our own life-world. They may stimulate us to work towards fulfillment, that is, to act towards change. Images, then, become like the Jewish Yom Kippur prayer, "Next year in Jerusalem!" We are not yet in the holy city, we still live in the Diaspora, but we hope and pray and do whatever we can to make the dream come true. In White's more mundane version, the image points towards a future we do not yet inhabit, but one day hope to enter. It keeps that hope alive, summons us not to resign ourselves to the realities of our time, and inspires us to "rebel," in Camus's sense of the word.

> We study the past not in order to find out what really happened there or to provide a genealogy of and thereby a legitimacy for the present, but [to] find out what it takes to face a future we should like to inherit rather than one that we have been forced to endure. I think that

something like that was what Benjamin had in mind when he spoke about "messianic" history as fulfillment – what he called the "explosion" of some bit of forgotten past in a present in such a way as to open out a future rather than sealing the present off from the past.[56]

In a sense, many of White's long-time ideals and preoccupations come together in this last quotation. In these words, we encounter White as a critic of the "historical past" and of the disciplinary practices developed in order to study the past "for its own sake." If there is one continuing thread in White's philosophy of history, it is a fierce rejection of a scientification of history, in the name of what White held to be a higher cause: moral orientation and political commitment. After the death of God and the end of metaphysics, only the past, if properly approached, can offer meaning, inspiration, and direction.[57] Accordingly, what ultimately matters is not the historical past, but the practical one – the struggle to liberate oneself and others from unsolicited heritages, false traditions, and repressive "burdens of history": "History is not something that one understands, it is something one endures – if one is lucky."[58] For this reason, White increasingly turned away from the historical discipline in which he had started his career to engage almost exclusively with writers more closely related to his liberation project.[59]

Moreover, against all "historical realism" that seeks to maintain the social status quo by depicting revisionist and revolutionary visions as "unrealistic" or "utopian," the words just quoted show how White, as fiercely as in *Metahistory*, insisted that the real is essentially contested and dependent, among other things, on moral and political beliefs. As always, White made no secret of his own desire to define the real in such a way as to encourage "modernist utopian thinking" in Benjamin's messianic mode. More concretely, he showed his continued indebtedness to a 1960s New Left kind of Marxism by declaring himself against "the imperatives of a capitalist system gone amuck with the desire to consume." He hoped and kept arguing for "fundamental changes in our social system," that is, for "a better world for our children and their progeny."[60] Although his optimism for the prospect of a socially progressive revolution tempered over the years,[61] White did not stop believing that history ought to inspire dreams of social change. Not unlike those early twentieth-century modernists who had worried how "to build a future out of the stuff that had been left to them in form of a historical legacy that was as insubstantial as it was glossy," White kept searching for "what is living" in history, looking for a past that could inspire, and yearning for meanings that one could live by.[62]

Finally, this modernist inspiration – which can be detected throughout White's work but found its most explicit articulation in the texts discussed in this chapter – fitted neatly with the existentialist-inspired kind of humanism that we have found to underlie, especially, White's views of human nature and morality. Whereas, for White, modernist writing expressed the need for what this study has called liberation historiography, the existentialists – modernist philosophers *par excellence*[63] – helped White articulate his conviction that liberation requires individual acts of will. Liberation does not take place without dedicated individuals whose sense of moral responsibility, to themselves and to others, urges them to rebel against traditions that prevent the individual from deciding for him- or herself what counts as real, possible, and desirable. Arguably, there is no other twentieth-century philosopher of history who has pushed this voluntarist claim as hard as White. No one else has so robustly sought to rethink philosophy of history out of such a concern for liberation from traditions that equate the real with history.

Epilogue

Since the early 1970s, White's work has served as a source of inspiration for scholars across the humanities. Among philosophers of history, historians, and literary scholars in particular, one now frequently hears about metahistory, tropes, and emplotment. At least part of White's terminology has entered everyday parlance among students of discourse and representation. Also, in the study of historical writing, Whitean influences have become so pervasive that some now speak about "historiography after Hayden White" or find it impossible to reflect on metahistory "in a pre-Hayden White sense."[1] It is important to realize, though, that the ideas attributed with such a classic status are not necessarily those most precious to White himself. Of course, White is very sympathetic to the constructivism that nowadays permeates so much of academic discourse in the humanities (due, not least, to his own influence). Likewise, the quadruple tetrad that many graduate students nowadays learn to associate with White ranks high among the most innovative aspects of his oeuvre. None of these issues, however, really touches the heart of his philosophy of history, which the present study has identified as an existentially driven attempt to put historical studies into the service of human self-determination.[2]

In the six preceding chapters, I have argued that White's often meandering oeuvre found its center of gravity in this essentially humanist project. No matter how eagerly White played with new ideas and jumped into new territories, the central aim behind his philosophy of history was to encourage individuals to map out their lives themselves and to choose a past in accordance with the

<u>future they desire</u>. By way of epilogue, then, it may be appropriate to suggest that something similar applies to how White's oeuvre invites us, readers, to respond. Of course, I do not wish to say that evaluations of White's philosophy of history must necessarily take their point of departure in the author's moral agenda or under-standing of the human subject. I would like to suggest, however, that White's humanist commitments play such a pivotal role in his philosophy of history that they elicit the reader's response in the first place. Precisely because White's historiographical and theoreti-cal considerations almost invariably stemmed from his humanist commitments, <u>there is nothing in his work that more urgently solic-its the reader's response than his devotion to the cause of human self-determination.</u>

Taking White seriously therefore implies asking ourselves: how convincing is his humanist and quasi-existentialist understanding of the human subject? How persuasive is his voluntarist approach to human agency? <u>Is there a sense in which White may have fallen victim to the myth of anthropocentrism</u>? To what extent are we, (hopefully) cured from some illusions of the 1960s, still able to share his anti-authoritarianism and anti-traditionalism? <u>What is gained and lost in White's prioritizing of meaning over knowledge, or his preference for the "practical" past as distinguished from the "his-torical" one</u>? And how appropriate is it to accept as a matter of course that historical interpretation revolves around the historian's wishes and desires – even if modernist events sometimes frustrate such presentism?

Perhaps there is some wisdom in David Harlan's hesitation, expressed near the end of a prolonged attempt to understand some of the twists and turns of White's deeply voluntarist philosophy of history:

> Can the plunge into irony really be stopped by a simple exertion of the will? Can the threat of irony be broken by simply deciding to break it? White's assurance that it can is essentially the assurance of a Pelagian. Jonathan Edwards – or Pascal or Melville or Kierkegaard or Dostoyevsky or any number of other writers – might have sug-gested to White that the historian can no more will her way out of irony than the melancholic can will her way out of depression, or the young Luther could reason himself into belief, or even the most fervent and devout believers can call down an outpouring of grace on their upturned faces.[3]

Notes

Introduction: How to Read Hayden White

1   LaCapra, "Poetics," p. 72.
2   Ermarth, review of *Metahistory*, p. 962.
3   Vann, "Reception," pp. 146, 155. Cf. Valera, "Ragioni della storia";
    Weber, "Hayden White."
4   For an interesting comparison between White and LaCapra, see
    Kramer, "Literature, Criticism and Imagination."
5   An accessible introduction is Day, *Philosophy of History*.
6   Popper, *Poverty of Historicism*.
7   Walsh, *Introduction*.
8   See Eskildsen, "Ranke's Archival Turn."
9   Novick, *That Noble Dream*, pp. 600, 625, 599.
10 By way of methodological clarification, let me point out that I do
    not subscribe to naive forms of intentionalism. Intentions are
    motives of persons (authors) in the past that are as such inacces-
    sible to historians in the present. What historians have is only the
    (written) expressions of these persons (authors), for example in a
    text entitled *Metahistory*. However, in explaining those expressions,
    historians may sometimes postulate intentions as hypotheses for
    understanding why those expressions took the form they did.
    Therefore, following Mark Bevir, I conceive of intentions as "infer-
    ences to the best possible explanation." In a less technical vocabu-
    lary: intentions are motives that historians attribute to persons
    (authors) in the past in order to explain why they said what they
    said. See Bevir, *Logic of the History of Ideas*.
11 Some recollections of White at Rochester can be found in Kellner,
    "Introduction," pp. 1–3.

12 On White's characteristic *modus operandi*, see Megill, "Rhetorical Dialectic."
13 Vann, "Reception," p. 145.
14 Doran, "Editor's Introduction," p. xiv.
15 Vann, "Reception," p. 144.
16 Bahners, "Ordnung der Geschichte," p. 519; Atkinson, *Inventing Inventors*, p. 16.
17 Methodologically, this approach is indebted both to Collingwood's "logic of question and answer" and to Gadamer's understanding of "the hermeneutic priority of the question." See Gadamer, *Truth and Method*, esp. pp. 362–79.
18 Ankersmit, *Narrative Logic*. For Ankersmit's own interpretation of White, see his "White's Appeal."
19 As far as I know, this is the first book-length study in English on White's philosophy of history. However, there are two foreign-language books: one by Roberto Dami, in Italian, and another by Torbjörn Gustafsson Chorell, in Swedish. See Dami, *I tropi della storia*, and Gustafsson Chorell, *Studier i Hayden Whites historietänkande*.
20 I adopt this terminology from Tucker, "Introduction," pp. 2–4.
21 "Future of Utopia" (2007), p. 16. The most important publications emphasizing this core element in White's philosophy of history are Kellner, "Bedrock"; Domańska, "Hayden White" (1997); Harlan, "Return"; and Moses, "Hayden White."
22 Novick, *That Noble Dream*, p. 601.
23 Unless otherwise indicated, all translations from foreign languages are my own.

1 Humanist Historicism: The Italian White

1 In 1996, White donated these volumes to the University of California at Santa Cruz, where they are currently known as the "Hayden White Collection."
2 Murphy, "Discussion," p. 23.
3 As a younger faculty member wrote in the early 1970s: "[N]o student who left a classroom where Professor William Bossenbrook lectured was ever the same again. When Professor Bossenbrook talked about the trade routes to the East you could almost see the sails of the great spice ships and hear the camels grunt by the walls of Trebizond. You saw, or almost saw, the ceiling of the Sistine Chapel being painted and felt the agony and genius of the creator. You almost saw Thomas Becket murdered in the gloom of a vast cathedral." Smith, "Gates of Excellence," p. 27. See also

Danto, *Analytical Philosophy of History*, p. viii; Domańska, "Arthur C. Danto," pp. 166–7, 176.

4 Megill, "Rhetorical Dialectic," p. 197. The GI Bill of Rights (1944), officially known as the Servicemen's Readjustment Act, opened the doors of higher education to millions of American soldiers, most of them World War II veterans.
5 "Preface" (1968), p. 10. For reasons of brevity, White's publications will hereafter be cited without the author's name.
6 Jenkins, "Conversation," p. 72; Rogne, "Aim of Interpretation," p. 64.
7 Jenkins, "Conversation," p. 70; Rogne, "Aim of Interpretation," p. 63.
8 Megill, "Rhetorical Dialectic," p. 197.
9 "Preface" (1968), p. 11.
10 Page numbers in parentheses refer to "Conflict of Papal Leadership Ideals" (1955).
11 Novick, *That Noble Dream*, p. 440; Erdelyi, *Max Weber in Amerika*, pp. 102, 128.
12 Throop, *Criticism of the Crusade*; Grace, *Concept of Property*.
13 "Tellenbach's study demonstrated, among other things, the heuristic value of Max Weber's typology of leadership when applied with caution by a sensitive and competent historian," wrote White in 1960 ("Gregorian Ideal," p. 325).
14 Cappai, *Modernisierung*, pp. 54–64; Roberts, *Benedetto Croce*, pp. 12–19.
15 "Pontius of Cluny" (1958), pp. 200–4; "Gregorian Ideal" (1960), pp. 327, 340; "Pontius of Cluny," p. 207.
16 Kennan, "De Consideratione," esp. pp. 92 n. 79, 93 nn. 80–81, 100, 107; Chodorow, *Christian Political Theory*, pp. 260–5; Sommerfeldt, "Charismatic and Gregorian Leadership"; Zerbi, "Intorno allo scisma," esp. pp. 316, 336, 338, 359–60, 363–4; Bredero, *Cluny et Cîteaux*, pp. 65–6 n. 109, 89 n. 41, 305; Stroll, *Jewish Pope*, pp. 24, 27–8 n. 20; Tellenbach, "Sturz des Abtes Pontius," p. 39. Judging by the book reviews White produced in the 1950s and early 1960s, Tellenbach's judgment was not necessarily unwelcome to White. "[I]t is as important for the historian to raise new questions through a fresh look at the data as to resolve old ones," he declared in a 1959 review (of *Les moines blancs*, p. 308).
17 Mannheim, "Nature of Economic Ambition," pp. 265–71; Toynbee, *Study of History*, vol. I, pp. 53–7, 271–99; Weber, *Wirtschaft und Gesellschaft*, pp. 142–8, 661–3. In an interview with Angelica Koufou and Margarita Miliori, White said: "I was inspired by Max Weber and my work in medieval history was meant to apply Weberian concepts to problems of church leadership" (Koufou and Miliori, "Ironic Poetics," p. 192).

18 Hempel, "Function of General Laws," pp. 35, 42, 37.
19 Novick, *That Noble Dream*, p. 394; "Ibn Khaldūn" (1959), p. 115; review of Lekai (1958), p. 308; "What is Living" (1969), pp. 385–9; "Foucault Decoded" (1973), p. 51; *Metahistory* (1973), pp. 38–42. "The Hempelians," White still declared in 1972, "are right to insist that [the] historian's arguments must stand or fall by the tests of adequacy that we apply to any scientific argument" ("Structure of Historical Narrative," p. 19).
20 Kluckhohn, "Values and Value-Orientations," p. 395.
21 Carlsnaes, *Concept of Ideology*, pp. 43–9, 180–97; Childe, *What Happened*, pp. 15–17.
22 In "Printing Industry" (1957), p. 74, White paid more attention to the "socioeconomic and cultural" factors that had stimulated early modern printing industries in Europe. In emphasizing the contribution these industries had made to the spread of Renaissance and Reformation thought, White's brief (and often overlooked) essay anticipated a major theme in Elizabeth L. Eisenstein's classic, *The Printing Press as an Agent of Change*.
23 Paul, "Weberian Medievalist," pp. 84–5.
24 Weber, *Roscher and Knies*, p. 192; Weber, "Science as a Vocation," p. 137.
25 Paul, "Beslissend moment," p. 590.
26 See, however, White's harsh judgments about the "irrational and intuitionist" figure of Bernard (pp. 508–9, 520, 569).
27 Weber, "Science as a Vocation," p. 153.
28 "Collingwood and Toynbee" (1957), pp. 175–7; "Religion" (1958), pp. 279, 284–5. Speaking about Collingwood's alleged "relativism," White made a rather insinuating reference to Giovanni Gentile and his "Fascist thought" ("Collingwood and Toynbee," p. 168). In the early 1990s, Carlo Ginzburg would criticize White with similar means (see ch. 5).
29 "Religion," pp. 280, 283, 283–4.
30 "Religion," pp. 282, 281, 282, 286–7.
31 Marianne Weber, *Max Weber*, p. 541; Weber, "Politics as a Vocation," p. 128. My interpretation of Weber is indebted to Patrick Dassen's fine study, *De onttovering van de wereld*.
32 Seerveld, *Croce's Earlier Aesthetic Theories*, p. 109.
33 "Translator's Preface" (1959), p. xi.
34 Antoni, *From History to Sociology*, pp. 8, 16, 37–8, 167–8, 64.
35 Jacoby, "New Intellectual History," p. 408.
36 Iggers, "Image of Ranke." White was indebted to this distorted image when he wrote that "Ranke, poor soul, spent a lifetime in his study and ruined his sight attempting to 'tell how it really happened'" ("Translator's Introduction" [1959], p. xxiv). In his review

in the journal *History and Theory*, Bruce Mazlish rebuked White for this statement, as well as for his generally "insufficient" translation of Antoni's book.

37 "Translator's Introduction," pp. xix–xxv (with quotations at p. xx).

38 "Translator's Introduction," p. xxii; *Metahistory* (1973), pp. 334, 372–3; Golob, "Irony of Nihilism," pp. 58, 65; "Translator's Introduction," p. xxi.

39 *Social Science Research Council Annual Report 1960–1961*, p. 76.

40 *Emergence*, p. xi; Segal, "Western Civ."

41 Unless one counts a book review of Wilkins, published in 1962.

42 Roberts, "Croce in America"; Novick, *That Noble Dream*, pp. 154–6, 263, 290, 403.

43 Mandelbaum, *Problem of Historical Knowledge*, pp. 39–57; Burks, "Benedetto Croce," p. 99. For White's recollections of Mandelbaum as a visiting professor at Michigan, see Domańska, "Hayden White" (1998), p. 18; Jenkins, "Conversation," p. 74. In later decades, Mandelbaum would turn into one of White's sharpest critics (see his "Presuppositions of *Metahistory*").

44 Croce, "Storia ridotta." White discussed this piece in *Metahistory*, pp. 381–6.

45 "Abiding Relevance" (1963), p. 122.

46 See Roberts, *Benedetto Croce*, pp. 79–81, 238–40, 252–60.

47 "Abiding Relevance," pp. 110, 115.

48 "Abiding Relevance," p. 118. A few years later, White attributed a similar view to Collingwood: "The function of the historian was to provide materials for the inculcation of a peculiarly human ethical sense in man, one which told men, not what they generally did in this or that hypothetical situation, but what they had done in specific situations in the past, and what, *therefore*, they ought to do in the situation in which they found themselves in the present. This did not mean that history provided a specific moral code or a ready-made solution to contemporary problems. Rather, it educated men to what acting morally was *in the society of which they were members*." Review of Donagan (1965), p. 248.

49 Croce, *Storia d'Europa*, pp. 354, 361–2; "Abiding Relevance" (1963), p. 123.

50 Roberts, "Stakes of Misreading," p. 243. Speaking about White's 1963 article, Roberts notes: "Nothing in English had better shown why history for Croce transcends naturalism to become the story of liberty, or why Croce's historicism entails broadly liberal implications" (p. 243).

51 Weber, "Science as a Vocation," p. 155; "Abiding Relevance," p. 116.

52 Roberts, *Benedetto Croce*, pp. 187, 188, 190. To be sure, Roberts also signals some important differences between Croce and Camus,

which have, among other things, to do with their understanding of the individual in history, the importance of personal subjectivity, and the existentialist concern with nothingness (pp. 190–8).

53 Jacoby, "New Intellectual History," p. 407; Kellner, "Bedrock," p. 219.
54 Kellner, "Hayden White."
55 White borrowed this distinction from Patrick Gardiner ("Collingwood and Toynbee" [1957], p. 150).
56 Review of Drew and Seyward Lear, p. 110.

2 Liberation Historiography: The Politics of History

1 *Emergence*, pp. vi, v. J. Salwyn Schapiro was listed as third author because of his contribution to the planning of the book. Coates's and White's "idealist" mode of explanation – illustrated in their treatment of Oswald Spengler, Martin Heidegger, and Ernst Jünger as thinkers contributing to the rise of National Socialism – is paralleled in Bossenbrook, *German Mind*. According to Richard T. Vann, *The Emergence of Liberal Humanism* and its sequel volume "display qualities that historians admire – broad erudition, novel insights, lucid style, and narrative skill; but they are not exactly samples of the program for historiography adumbrated in 'The Burden of History'" (Vann, "Hayden White, Historian," p. 308).
2 Novick, *Holocaust*, p. 144.
3 *Ordeal* (1970), pp. 459, 448, 449, 289, 450.
4 Review of Finberg and Weiss (1963), p. 387.
5 Review of Higham (1965), pp. 5–6.
6 Vann, "Turning Linguistic," p. 64 n. 107.
7 Review of Morton White (1966), p. 422.
8 "Burden of History" (1966), pp. 116, 124–5.
9 "Burden of History," pp. 125, 134.
10 "Burden of History," p. 116.
11 "Burden of History," pp. 116, 123, 124.
12 "Burden of History," pp. 132, 133, 117.
13 "Burden of History," pp. 123, 113, 112, 126, 127.
14 "Burden of History," pp. 128–9.
15 Harlan, "Return," p. 106.
16 Kellner, "Introduction," p. 2.
17 Bolkosky, "From the Book," p. 2. In a television interview with Harry Kreisler (December 5, 2001), Ruth Rosen told a similar story. See the transcript at http://globetrotter.berkeley.edu/people/Rosen/rosen-con1.html (retrieved November 30, 2010).

18 "Historical System?" (1972), pp. 235–6, 242. In "Literary History" (1970), p. 180, White made a similar point with regard to literary classics: "A 'classic' is made by the choices of successive generations to treat it as a valid approach to the problem of relating consciousness to experience. And 'tradition' is simply the history of these choices."

19 "Historical System," pp. 239, 240, 239, 241; "Burden of History" (1966), p. 123.

20 Allan Megill provides some information about this series in "Rhetorical Dialectic," pp. 204, 214, but misses *The Enlightenment Tradition* (1967) by Robert E. Anchor.

21 This may have been due to White's working on *Metahistory*, which also interfered with other projects. As Georg G. Iggers reports: "I visited him in Rochester for the first time shortly after I arrived in Buffalo [in 1964], and we then met occasionally to discuss our work. We both signed a contract to co-author a small book on the idea of progress in which each of us was supposed to write a longer essay and then reply to the other. I soon completed my essay, but White never wrote his. He was busy with work on his book, *Metahistory*" (Iggers and Iggers, *Two Lives*, p. 126).

22 *Greco-Roman Tradition* (1973), pp. xii–xiii, x.

23 *Greco-Roman Tradition*, pp. 6, 7.

24 Thompson, review of *Greco-Roman Tradition*, p. 304.

25 *Greco-Roman Tradition*, p. 8.

26 Nietzsche, *Untimely Meditations*, p. 67; Paul, "Hayden White and the Crisis of Historicism," p. 69.

27 Bossenbrook, "Introduction," pp. 6, 9, 11; "German Nationalism," p. 27; "United States," pp. 51, 52, 57.

28 "Editor's Introduction" (in the 1967 Weiss volume), pp. xii, xiv, xi, xv. Also typical, in this context, was White's praise for George Kelly's *Idealism, Politics, and History*: "Like any good book, it raises more questions than it answers; but it is more than good, it is brilliant – a tour de force, as intimidating as it is compelling, as irritating as it is comforting. My disagreements are more with the mood that suffuses it than with its thesis; but I should have been proud to have written it. For it deals with living problems, and it illuminates many questions not yet consigned to 'history'" (review of Kelly [1970], p. 345).

29 *Ordeal* (1970), pp. 458–9.

30 *Ordeal*, pp. 465, 466, referring to Camus's *L'homme révolté*.

31 "Biographical Note" (1969), p. xxvi. In the same volume, White defended Vico's law of the *ricorsi* against Croce's criticism: "What is Living," esp. pp. 387–9.

32 "Tasks of Intellectual History" (1969), pp. 620, 613, 614.

33 "Tasks of Intellectual History," pp. 626, 621, 615, 616.
34 Cantor, *American Century*, p. 304; "Tasks of Intellectual History," p. 625.
35 Goldmann, *Dieu caché*, pp. 118, 123–4, 157. Such a view on the relation between Jansenism and *noblesse de robe* was proposed earlier by Franz Borkenau. In turn, Goldmann's metaphor of tragedy was indebted to Georg Lúkacs.
36 "Tasks of Intellectual History," p. 625. This issue has been hotly debated. Whereas Serge Doubrovsky, the French existentialist, criticized Goldmann for undervaluing individual human responsibility, Goldmann himself sympathized with Sartre's criticism of dogmatic Marxism and his emphasis on human freedom. See Doubrovsky, *Pourquoi la nouvelle critique*, p. 199; Cohen, *Wager of Lucien Goldmann*, pp. 212, 220.
37 Accordingly, White strongly rejected a politics that "in the face of technological means to alleviate human suffering, contents itself with piecemeal planning and sets a Scandinavian sharing of the wealth as the outer limits of its oneiric aspirations" (review of Kelly [1970], p. 362).
38 Butler et al., "On Vietnam," p. 208; Veliz, "History as an Alibi," p. 21; Amsden et al., "Vladimir Bukovsky," p. 46. This was not White's last confrontation with the authorities. Among lawyers in the United States, his name remains associated with *White* v. *Davis* (13 Cal. 3d 757, 1975), a lawsuit White filed against the Los Angeles Police Department for violating the First Amendment right of speech. As reported in the *New York Times*, White charged "that undercover Los Angeles police officers had been sitting in on his classes and submitting reports to the police departments while posing as students." The California Supreme Court unanimously found for White and thereby set significant limits to state surveillance in California (Anon., "High Court in California," p. 12).
39 "Culture of Criticism" (1971), p. 69.
40 "You see, I never thought that Marxism constituted a real science of society. It seemed to me that its main strength was its demand for justice for the working class, an ethical socialism," White said in Jenkins, "Conversation," p. 72. For some of the responses that White's self-professed Marxism elicited, see Partner, "Hayden White" (1997), pp. 105, 108.
41 "Printing Industry" (1957), pp. 61–2, 73–4.
42 Publications addressing these issues include "The Irrational" (1972), "Forms of Wildness " (1972), and "Noble Savage Theme" (1976). Inspiration from Foucault is also evidenced in "Tasks of Intellectual History" (1969), pp. 621–2.
43 See the program in Anon., "The Chronicle Section," p. 322.

44 "Politics of Contemporary Philosophy of History" (1973), pp. 41, 48. In fact, metahistory was also used as a synonym of "speculative philosophies of history," which included the systems of conservative thinkers such as Spengler. See Yolton, "History and Meta-History," pp. 477–92. As for the term itself, White also appeared indebted to Frye, *Fables of Identity*, which borrowed it in turn from Underhill, "Arnold Toynbee."
45 "Politics of Contemporary Philosophy of History," p. 44; Dray, "Politics," p. 73.
46 "Politics of Contemporary Philosophy of History," pp. 48, 52.
47 Murdoch, *Sartre*, p. 42.
48 Rowland, *Cambridge Companion*; Gandolfo, "Liberation Philosophy." Liberation historiography is a term also employed by Ernest, *Liberation Historiography*.
49 The distinction between "positive" and "negative" freedom was famously drawn in Berlin, *Two Concepts*.
50 Harlan, "Return," p. 123.

3 The Historical Imagination: Four Modes of Realism

1 Reportedly, a draft of the book had been rejected by several publishing houses. White's colleague Lionel Gossman eventually persuaded Johns Hopkins University Press to publish a much-revised version of the book. Since 1973, it has sold more than 50,000 copies. See Jenkins, "Conversation," p. 74.
2 In this chapter, page numbers in parentheses refer to *Metahistory*.
3 Ankersmit, "White's Appeal," p. 253.
4 Kansteiner, "White's Critique," p. 278.
5 Kellner, "Twenty Years After," p. 109.
6 Although the chapter was intended for a monograph entitled *Modern Schools of Historical Thought* ("Hegel" [1966], p. 10), a book with this title never appeared. In all likelihood, White's reflections on the tasks of intellectual history (analyzed in ch. 2, this volume) caused the author to rethink whether the sort of analyses his work so far had provided – relatively straightforward summaries of "ideas" and "positions" – still met his standard. As we have seen, White's late 1960s essays suggested a more in-depth analysis of metahistorical paradigms.
7 Collini, "Discipline History," p. 388.
8 See chapter 1 in this volume, n. 36.
9 For White's appreciation of Foucault, see ch. 4 of this volume.
10 "Structure of Historical Narrative" (1972), p. 12.
11 Iggers, *German Conception*; Gay, *Style in History*.

12 O'Brien, *From the Heart*, p. 8.
13 Kansteiner, "White's Critique," p. 278.
14 Nelson, review of *Metahistory*, p. 81.
15 I borrow this expression from Roth, *Ironist's Cage*.
16 See the literature discussed in Paul, "Ironic Battle against Irony."
17 Nietzsche, *Untimely Meditations*, p. 103.
18 Contra Peters, "Voorbij de ironie," p. 231.
19 Nelson, "Tropal History," p. 85; Harlan, "Return," p. 119.
20 Kellner, "Twenty Years After," p. 115. Kellner's "Hayden White" dwells at greater length on the primacy of the will in White, emphasizing especially its Kantian background.
21 What follows draws on Paul, "Metahistorical Prefigurations."
22 I will discuss the charge of relativism in ch. 4.
23 This term has been put forward by Mali, *Mythistory*.
24 Review of Kelly (1970), p. 344.
25 On the "Promethean politics" and its "realism" in an age that had almost "fallen victim to an incapacity to dream at all," see review of Kelly, p. 362.
26 Nelson, review of *Metahistory*, p. 88. See also ch. 4, this volume.
27 For a more detailed version of this argument, see Paul, "Tegen zure regen."
28 White admitted as much in 1976: "I want to make clear that I am myself using these terms [metaphor, metonymy, synecdoche, and irony] as metaphors for the different ways we construe fields or sets of phenomena in order to 'work them up' into *possible objects of narrative representation* and *discursive analysis*" ("Fictions," p. 33). Cf. Domańska, "Hayden White" (1998), p. 25: "I only used the concept of tropes metaphorically. It's not supposed to be taken literally."
29 Vann, "Reception," p. 150 n. 22.
30 Jameson, "Figural Realism," p. 153.
31 Kellner, "Bedrock," p. 204. See also ch. 4 of this volume, n. 17.
32 LaCapra, "Poetics," p. 81.
33 I borrow this phrase from Dominick LaCapra (personal communication).
34 Cf. Dosse, *History of Structuralism*, vol. I, pp. 52–8.
35 For Jakobson's influence on Lévi-Strauss, see Dosse, *History of Structuralism*, vol. I, pp. 21–4.
36 The twentieth-century metaphor–metonymy debate is helpfully summarized in Dirven, "Metonymy and Metaphor."
37 Lévi-Strauss, "Structural Study," p. 84.
38 Kellner, "Bedrock," p. 223.
39 In a 1995 response to Roger Chartier, White still took the same position: "I do not see any contradiction between the idea that the

codes (linguistic and otherwise) circulating in a given culture *set limits* on what one can say and the idea that *choices* among the codes can be made with more or less freedom, more or less self-consciously." "Rejoinder," p. 63.

40 Kellner, "Bedrock," p. 219; Harlan, "Return," p. 121.
41 *Fiction of Narrative* (2010), p. ix.
42 For example, Crane, "Language," p. 330; Ankersmit, "Linguistic Turn," p. 30.
43 Ermarth, review of *Metahistory*, p. 962.

4 The Power of Discourse: White's Structuralist Adventure

1 Anon., "UCLA Prof. White," pp. 1–2; Chanin, "Hayden White," p. 7.
2 "Structuralism and Popular Culture" (1974), p. 774.
3 This echoes the title of Geoffrey Hartman's essay, "Structuralism: The Anglo-American Adventure."
4 According to James, "Louis Mink," p. 171, Mink and White had come to know each other "through their joint involvement in antiwar activity in the late 1960s."
5 Gallie, *Philosophy*, pp. 22–50.
6 Mink, "History and Fiction," pp. 47–8, 50, 53, 57.
7 White to Mink, October 3, 1970, as quoted in Vann, "Mink's Linguistic Turn," p. 6. Whereas Williams ("Geschichte," p. 349) argues that Mink's linguistic turn "is difficult to imagine without White's work," it is more appropriate to argue, as does Samuel James, that White was deeply influenced by Mink ("Louis Mink," p. 156).
8 Mink did not necessarily disagree with this. In an unpublished lecture, "Interpretation and Historical Understanding," delivered to the American Historical Association in December 1973, Mink explained that all three modes of comprehension can be found in historical studies. Yet, unlike White, Mink believed that each of these modes had a certain affinity with a particular type of historiography: "Social scientific historiography is to different degrees the attempt to put data in the service of theoretical comprehension. At the other extreme, both *Geisteswissenschaftliche* history and the history of ideas on the models of Lovejoy and Boas can be seen as aiming at the categoreal comprehension of the changes and continuities of cultures. But the primary mode of historical understanding which is *sui generis*, I believe, is that which is satisfied by configurational comprehension." (I am indebted to Terry Mink for his permission to consult and quote his father's unpublished writings.)

9 Vann calls "event" the "most under-analyzed term" in White's vocabulary ("Reception," p. 154).

10 "Fictions" (1976), p. 43; *Tropics of Discourse* (1978), p. 2.

11 This argument was indebted to Frye, *Anatomy*, pp. 52–3.

12 "Structure of Historical Narrative" (1972), pp. 15–17.

13 "Structure of Historical Narrative," pp. 17–18.

14 "Structure of Historical Narrative," p. 18.

15 "Structure of Historical Narrative," pp. 18, 14.

16 "Structure of Historical Narrative," p. 19.

17 Note in passing that this strategy was strikingly similar to that of Erich Auerbach's *Mimesis*, a book often compared to *Metahistory* (White himself was the first to draw this parallel: *Metahistory*, p. 3 n. 4). Indeed, in terms of aim and subject-matter, these studies closely resembled each other. Both *Mimesis* and *Metahistory* focused on "realistic" representations of the world (in literature and history, respectively). Both sought to show that "realism" is an essentially contested concept and provided a history of changing paradigms of realism, highlighting the discontinuities between these paradigms by classifying them typologically. But whereas *Mimesis* proceeded from selected fragments – a page from the *Iliad*, a paragraph or two from *A la recherche du temps perdu* – and subjected these fragments to careful rhetorical analysis, *Metahistory* did not do so. White adopted this Auerbachian procedure only as late as 1975 (and brought it to full maturity in his 1988 essay "The Rhetoric of Interpretation").

18 "Historicism" (1975), pp. 57, 58.

19 "Historicism," p. 58.

20 "Interpretation" (1973), p. 292; "Historical Text" (1974), p. 295.

21 "Fictions" (1976), p. 28; "Historical Text," p. 296.

22 "Fictions," p 28. The phrase "events under description" was proposed by Danto, in his *Analytical Philosophy of History*, and further elaborated by Mink, especially in his essay "Narrative Form."

23 "Fictions," pp. 22, 28.

24 "Rhetoric and History" (1978), p. 7; "Historical Text," p. 296.

25 "Historicism" (1975), pp. 52–3; "Problem of Style" (1979); "Rhetoric and History," p. 3; Barthes, "Reality Effect."

26 "Introductory Comments" (1976), p. 1; Gossman, "Augustin Thierry"; Bann, *Clothing of Clio*, p. 4; Bann, *Romanticism*, pp. 16, 34–6; Orr, *Headless History*, p. 13.

27 James, "Louis Mink," p. 182 n. 162.

28 "Historicism" (1975), p. 51; "Interpretation" (1973), p. 294; "Historical Text" (1974), p. 283; "Interpretation," p. 296.

29 Review of Droysen (1980), p. 81.

30 "Historicism," p. 58; Barthes, "Discourse of History," esp. pp. 128–9.
31 "Historical Text," p. 301.
32 "Historical Text," p. 278.
33 "Interpretation," p. 295; "Historical Text," pp. 292, 283.
34 "Fictions" (1976), pp. 25, 28.
35 For a rather different and perhaps more accurate view on the relation between history and literature among historians of Ranke's generation, see Fulda, *Wissenschaft aus Kunst*.
36 *Metahistory*, p. 1.
37 On the ancient roots of this question: Hadot, *Philosophy*, esp. pp. 49–70.
38 Bernstein, *Beyond Objectivism and Relativism*, p. 8; Lorenz, "Can Histories Be True?" A similar point is made in Golob, "Irony of Nihilism," pp. 56–7.
39 *Tropics of Discourse* (1978), p. 21.
40 *Tropics of Discourse*, p. 4.
41 "Historicism" (1975), p. 65; Paz Soldán, "Interview," p. 4.
42 Lorenz, "Historical Knowledge," p. 315.
43 "Interpretation" (1973), p. 294.
44 "Historical Text" (1974), pp. 282–3.
45 "Historical Text," pp. 298–9.
46 "Historicism," pp. 66, 65.
47 E.g., Kohlhammer, "Welt im Viererpack."
48 Although, in later years, White would become less obsessive about the number 4, he continued to defend the view that "the number of versions of any given set of events which any given audience can adjudge plausible is limited to the set of emplotting procedures known to the audience in question" ("Historical Pluralism" [1986], p. 488).
49 Himmelfarb, "Telling It as You Like It."
50 "Historicism" (1975), p. 66; "Fictions" (1976), p. 44; "Interpretation" (1973), p. 312.
51 "Foucault Decoded" (1973), p. 24; Foucault, *Order of Things*, p. 387.
52 "Foucault Decoded," p. 32.
53 "Foucault Decoded," p. 45; "Structuralism and Popular Culture" (1974), p. 761. Cf. Browne, *Against Academia*, pp. 26–7.
54 *Fiction of Narrative*, p. ix.
55 Jameson, *Prison-House*.
56 *Tropics of Discourse* (1978), pp. 5, 13, 23.
57 "Foucault Decoded," p. 44.
58 "Criticism as Cultural Politics" (1976), pp. 10, 8. Hence White's sharp criticism of Leon Pompa's attempt to transform Vico into a

social scientist *avant la lettre*: review of Pompa (1976), esp. pp. 186–90.
59 *Tropics of Discourse*, p. 22.
60 "Absurdist Moment" (1976), pp. 398, 379–80, 381, 388, 398. The Derrida quote comes from "Structure, Sign, and Play," p. 267.
61 Krieger, "Introduction," pp. 311–17; LaCapra, "Poetics," p. 78.
62 In 1993, White creatively reinterpreted his attack on Derrida by saying: "I meant that he was a philosopher of the absurd. I did not mean that he was absurd. You know what I mean? I was using an existentialist term, *absurdism*. And I characterized him as the philosopher of paradox, or of the absurd. But people thought I meant that I was hostile to him, but I did not see it that way" (Domańska, "Hayden White" [1998], pp. 32–3).
63 *Tropics of Discourse* (1978), p. 21.
64 "Historicism" (1975), p. 66.
65 "Historicism," p. 66.
66 "Historicism," p. 66.
67 Think only of White's former colleague at Rochester, the Marxist historian of American slavery, Eugene D. Genovese, whose prize-winning *Roll, Jordan, Roll* (1974) challenged conventional standards of historical interpretation in a more direct manner than White ever did. See also Van der Linden, *Revolt against Liberalism*.
68 "Structuralism and Popular Culture" (1974), p. 762.
69 "Structuralism and Popular Culture," pp. 759, 769, 775, 770, 771.
70 This refers to a famous remark by Levi-Strauss – "As we say of certain careers, history may lead to anything, provided you get out of it" – which supplied White with a title for his 1982 piece on Frederic Jameson. See Lévi-Strauss, *Savage Mind*, p. 262, and White's "Getting Out of History" (1982), p. 2.

5 Masks of Meaning: Facing the Sublime

1 Under White's leadership, this program became especially well known for its interdisciplinary study of "theory." Among its faculty were such renowned figures as the anthropologist James Clifford, and the feminist theorist Donna Haraway. See Schneider, *Donna Haraway*, p. 11.
2 White discussed the *Annalistes* at some length in "Question of Narrative" (1984), pp. 7–9. For the broader context, see Stone, "Revival."
3 "Value of Narrativity" (1980), pp. 12, 13.
4 "Value of Narrativity," pp. 10, 14, 20.
5 "Value of Narrativity," pp. 16, 18.
6 "Value of Narrativity," p. 27.

7 *Content of the Form* (1987), p. ix; "Value of Narrativity," p. 24. In passing, it is worth observing how much this argument depended on a correspondence theory of truth. White even explicitly invoked the concept of truth when he claimed "that real life can never be truthfully represented as having the kind of formal coherency met with in the conventional, well-made or fabulistic story" (*Content of the Form*, p. ix). Indeed, how can one make metaphysical claims without a correspondence theory of truth?

8 *Content of the Form*, p. ix; Partner, "Hayden White" (1998), p. 167; "Value of Narrativity" (1980), p. 26.

9 "In this world, reality wears the mask of a meaning, the completeness and fullness of which we can only *imagine*, never experience" ("Value of Narrativity," p. 24). The mask metaphor also appears in Munz, *Shapes of Time*, p. 17, and provided the title of my 2006 Ph.D. dissertation on White.

10 Dray, "Narrative and Historical Realism," pp. 133–5, 156–7. A good introduction to the debate, as well as a representative sample of contributions to it, can be found in Roberts, *History and Narrative Reader*.

11 Mink, "History and Fiction," p. 60. Mink's statement that life has no endings should not be misunderstood. Alisdair MacIntyre's often-quoted question, "But have you never heard of death?" (*After Virtue*, p. 197), misses the point, since Mink used the notion of "ending" as an equivalent to what literary theorists call closure, or "the sense of an ending" (Frank Kermode). Ending is not an abrupt break-off, as death sometimes is, but a rounding-off that retrospectively gives meaning to what came before.

12 Whereas Ankersmit first made this point in *Narrative Logic*, he has elaborated and amplified it ever since. See, for example, Ankersmit, "Use of Language," and, more recently, "Representation and Reference."

13 See, e.g., White's review of Ankersmit (1984) and his "Reply to Professor Ankersmit" (2003).

14 "Value of Narrativity" (1980), p. 24.

15 "Politics of Historical Interpretation" (1982), p. 128.

16 Carr, "Narrative and the Real World," esp. pp. 127–31. Along the same lines: Carroll, "Interpretation."

17 In fact, there is nothing contradictory between (1) Carr's claim that story-like experience exists, (2) Mink's and Ankersmit's insistence that the sort of narrative coherence historians offer has no equivalent in the past, and (3) White's morally inspired objection against narrative closure. Carr admitted as much when he acknowledged that historians "may tell a story about a community which is very different from the story the community

(through its leaders, journalists, and others) tells about itself."
This is precisely what Mink and Ankersmit observed and White
encouraged historians to do. Carr's addition, "The form, nonetheless, remains the same," is of no particular relevance: formal
similarities between the discursive forms of what he calls first-
and second-level narratives are compatible with the idea of a
radical dissimilarity between the semantic contents these narratives offer. See Carr, "Narrative and the Real World," p. 131, and
Norman's perceptive comments in "Telling It Like It Was," p. 127.

18   "Rhetoric and History" (1978), p. 24.
19   Weiskel, *Romantic Sublime*; Ankersmit, *Sublime Historical Experience*.
20   Bloom, *Anxiety of Influence*, p. 30.
21   "Politics of Historical Interpretation" (1982), pp. 137, 135; Pease,
     "Sublime Politics," pp. 38, 39.
22   "Burden of History" (1966), p. 134. In 1973, White had praised
     Lessing's *Geschichte als Sinngebung des Sinnlosen* as a "brilliant"
     (though neglected) attempt to invoke an "awareness of the
     strangeness of ordinary things" ("Foucault Decoded" [1973],
     pp. 51–2).
23   "Politics of Historical Interpretation," p. 128.
24   "Politics of Historical Interpretation," pp. 135, 136.
25   "Politics of Historical Interpretation," p. 128.
26   "Politics of Historical Interpretation," pp. 129, 128.
27   Review of Droysen (1980), pp. 91–2; Jenkins, "Beyond the Old
     Dichotomies," p. 14.
28   "Politics of Historical Interpretation," p. 130. In fact, however,
     continuity in terms of *Blut und Boden* was a far more important
     theme in Nazi and fascist historiography than White acknowl-
     edged. See Fogu, "Actualism," p. 198.
29   Review of Kelly (1970), p. 362.
30   Chartier, "Four Questions," pp. 36–8; "Rejoinder" (1995), p. 66.
31   Ginzburg, "Just One Witness," p. 91.
32   Domańska, "Hayden White" (1998), p. 16.
33   Ginzburg, "Just One Witness," p. 94.
34   See, for example, Roberts, "Stakes of Misreading," pp. 28–52;
     Peters, "Voorbij de ironie," pp. 229–32; Cohen, "Historiography,"
     p. 133; Davidson, "Carlo Ginzburg," pp. 309–11; Varon, "Probing
     the Limits," pp. 90–103; Young, "Toward a Received History,"
     pp. 27–9; Young, "Hayden White," pp. 145–9; Ricoeur, *La mémoire*,
     pp. 333–5; Fogu, "Actualism," pp. 196–8.
35   Gregor, *Giovanni Gentile*, p. 21.
36   Moses, "Hayden White," p. 311.
37   Moses, "Hayden White," pp. 319, 320. "Hypergood" is Charles
     Taylor's term for core value or ultimate goal.

38 "Public Relevance" (2005), p. 337.
39 Review of Kelly (1970), p. 362.
40 "Ethnological Lie" (1978), p. 8.
41 Perniola, "Difference."
42 "Italian Difference" (1984), pp. 121–2, 118.
43 Rogne, "Aim of Interpretation," p. 70.
44 "Getting Out of History" (1982), p. 6.
45 "Getting Out of History," p. 9.
46 This formulation is adopted from Xie and Wang, "Hayden White,"
    p. 253.
47 "Getting Out of History," p. 13.
48 "Getting Out of History," pp. 11, 12–13. Although White in the
    1980s no longer joined political demonstrations, as he had done
    in the 1960s, his aversion to grand narratives had nonetheless an
    unmistakably political dimension: "It may well be that the decline
    of narrative reflects, less a condition of decadence [as Jameson
    argued] than a sickness unto death with the stories that repre-
    sentatives of official culture are always invoking to justify the
    sacrifices and sufferings of the citizenry. One alternative to 'col-
    lective unity' is anarchy, and this alternative becomes more attrac-
    tive as an ideal, the more 'collective unity' is enforced upon us
    by a combination of 'master-narratives' and instruments of
    control backed by weapons" ("Getting Out of History," p. 13).
49 On White's affinities with Sartre in these matters, see Flynn,
    Sartre, vol. I, esp. p. 221.
50 Momigliano, "Rhetoric of History," p. 56.

6 Figuring History: The Modernist White

1 Levitt, "Colonization," p. 267.
2 Kellner, "Does the Sublime," p. 216.
3 Steiner, "K," p. 123.
4 "Truth and Circumstance" (unpub.), p. 19.
5 On the American context of this debate, see Novick, *Holocaust*.
    For a critical discussion of Holocaust uniqueness claims, see Van
    den Berghe, *Uitbuiting van de Holocaust*, pp. 140–73.
6 "Historical Emplotment" (1992), pp. 37–8.
7 "Modernist Event" (1995), pp. 102, 117, 119; "*Comparare*" (2001),
    p. 498; "Literature against Fiction" (1997), p. 204.
8 "Modernist Event" (1995), p. 120. Cf. Bauman, *Modernity and the
    Holocaust*.
9 "Modernist Event" (1995), p. 103.
10 "Modernist Event" (1996), p. 21.

11   Koufou and Miliori, "Ironic Poetics," pp. 193–4 (with correction of a spelling mistake).
12   "Modernist Event" (1995), p. 102.
13   "Modernist Event" (1996), p. 24. For media events more generally: Couldry, Hepp, and Krotz, *Media Events*.
14   "Figural Realism" (2004), p. 114; "Metaphysics" (2004), p. 4. On the traumatic effects of modernist events, see also "Historical Event" (2008), pp. 26–30.
15   "[I]f modernist events appear infinitely complex and at the same time insubstantial due to the ways in which the media can be used to manipulate images and indices of them, one has only to look for a moment at past events – such as battles and revolutions or famines or the fall of empires – to realize that they are similarly complex and insubstantial and that their seeming substantiality and openness to perception were primarily functions of the paucity of the documents we have for them and the crudity with which they were recorded by their witnesses" ("Postmodernism and Textual Anxieties" [1999], p. 31).
16   "Historical Emplotment" (1992), p. 52. For literary modernism as a response to World War I, see White's remarks in Murphy, "Discussion," pp. 22–3.
17   "Modernist Event" (1996), p. 32.
18   "Literature against Fiction" (1997), pp. 202–3; "Modernist Event" (1995), pp. 110–12. White saw the process metaphorically described in Primo Levi's story "of how an atom of carbon which turns up in a glass of milk which he, Levi, drinks, migrated into a cell in his own brain – 'the brain of *me* who is writing, and [how] the cell in question, and within it the atom in question, is in charge of my writing, in a gigantic minuscule game which nobody has yet described'" ("Historical Emplotment" [1992], p. 53). For Barthes's own view on intransitive writing, see his classic piece, "To Write."
19   "Historical Emplotment," p. 47. An excellent introduction to the notion is Eberhard, *Middle Voice*, pp. 7–30. Pecora, "Ethics," offers a nice overview of how thinkers from Émile Benveniste to Jacques Derrida have reflected on the middle voice.
20   "Historical Emplotment," p. 42. See Spiegelman, *Maus*.
21   Eberhard, *Middle Voice*, p. 7.
22   "Foreword" (1994), p. xix.
23   *"Comparare"* (2001), pp. 499–500.
24   Jay, "Plots," pp. 101, 97; Kansteiner, "White's Critique," p. 286.
25   "Literature against Fiction" (1997), p. 201.
26   "Burden of History" (1966), p. 132.
27   Carroll, "Tropology and Narration," p. 402; Young, "Hayden White," p. 157.

28 Eberhard, *Middle Voice*, pp. 62–108.
29 "Burden of History," p. 127; "Historical Event" (2008), p. 25; Murphy, "Discussion," p. 21.
30 Rogne, "Aim of Interpretation," p. 69.
31 See, for example, "Abiding Relevance" (1963), p. 109; "Romanticism" (1968), pp. 46–7; "Culture of Criticism" (1971); and *Tropics of Discourse* (1978), p. 5. As I noted in ch. 3, White even presented *Metahistory* as a study modeled after *Mimesis* (p. 3 n. 4).
32 Besides *Mimesis*, pp. 77–80, see esp. Auerbach, "Figura." It is worth noting that some of White's favorite literary theorists, such as Fredric Jameson, had also picked up Auerbach's theme, thereby setting the terms for White's rather unorthodox interpretation of Auerbach. See esp. Jameson, *Political Unconscious*, pp. 29–32.
33 "Auerbach's Literary History" (1996), pp. 125, 126. In "Metaphysics" (2004), p. 13, and "Frye's Place" (1994), p. 37, White also argued that the figure-fulfillment model "bestows genealogical meaning" and provides "a notion of genealogical affiliation" that might serve "as an historically responsible alternative to the physical and biological conception of a genetic relationship." Although White (in "Auerbach's Literary History," n. 6) claimed that this use of the term "genealogy" conformed to "the usage by Nietzsche and Foucault," it by no means shared the iconoclastic agenda for which the two earlier thinkers had employed it (cf. Nietzsche, *Genealogy of Morals*; Foucault, "Nietzsche"). Most notably, unlike Nietzsche and Foucault, White understood genealogy not as a method for *deconstructing* meaning, but as a means for *generating* it.
34 "Creative correction" is Bloom's term in *Anxiety of Influence*, p. 30.
35 "Auerbach's Literary History" (1996), pp. 129, 128.
36 "Metaphysics" (2004), pp. 14–15.
37 "Rhetoric of Interpretation" (1988), p. 273.
38 "Rhetoric of Interpretation," p. 255.
39 "Figural Realism" (2004), pp. 123, 115.
40 "Figural Realism," p. 116.
41 On the problematic relationship between literalist and figurative speech in representation, see "Rhetoric of Interpretation," esp. pp. 254–5. Cf. Murphy, "Discussion," p. 21: "I made a mistake in saying there's factual discourse, and there's fictional discourse. Because fictional discourse turns out to be just another version of factual discourse and history. Or the factual discourse turns out to be a particular kind of convention that will call itself non-fictional even thought its products are fictional in nature."
42 "Figural Realism," pp. 122, 120.
43 Personal communication from Hayden White (October 29, 2010).
44 Paul, "Beslissend moment," pp. 581–2.

45 "Public Relevance" (2005), p. 334. See also "Historical Event" (2008), pp. 10–11. For the original distinction: Oakeshott, "Present."
46 Domańska, "Conversation," p. 17. Cf. Murphy, "Discussion," pp. 27–8.
47 "Practical Past" (unpub.), p. 12.
48 "Truth and Circumstance" (unpub.), pp. 6, 11.
49 "Truth and Circumstance," p. 7.
50 "Truth and Circumstance," p. 16.
51 "Practical Past," pp. 5, 3.
52 "Modernist Event" (1996), p. 17.
53 Pensky, "Method and Time," p. 178.
54 "Constructing Pasts" (2000).
55 Pensky, "Method and Time," pp. 193–5.
56 Domańska, "Conversation," p. 19.
57 Paul, "Beslissend moment," p. 590.
58 "Against Historical Realism" (2007), p. 110.
59 In Rogne, "Aim of Interpretation," p. 75, White declared: "I'm not really concerned about the discipline. I'm much more interested in the way creative writers, literary writers, are dealing with history." For White's interest in Lev Tolstoy and W. G. Sebald, see also "Against Historical Realism," and Paul, "Mogelijkheidszin."
60 "Future of Utopia" (2007), pp. 15, 16.
61 "Politics of Historical Interpretation" (1982), p. 119; Aldama, "Hayden White," p. 15.
62 "Future of Utopia," p. 14.
63 White agreed with this: "existentialism is *the* modernist philosophy" (Rogne, "Aim of Interpretation," p. 69).

Epilogue

1 Phillips, "Historiography after Hayden White"; Antohi, "Narratives Unbound," p. xii.
2 Moses makes a similar observation in "Hayden White," p. 316.
3 Harlan, "Return," p. 119.

Bibliography

This bibliography consists of two parts. White's own publications are listed under "Primary titles." Although this list does not pretend to completeness, it is the most extensive bibliography of White currently available. Translations of White's work are not included, with the exception of foreign-language articles that never appeared in English. Interviews conducted with White are included under "Secondary titles." To avoid inordinate length, this second list is limited to titles referred to in the endnotes.

Primary Titles

Unpublished

"The Conflict of Papal Leadership Ideals from Gregory VII to St. Bernard of Clairvaux with Special Reference to the Schism of 1130" (Ph.D. thesis, University of Michigan, 1955).

"Truth and Circumstance: What (If Anything) Can Be Properly Said about the Holocaust?" (draft chapter, to appear in a volume tentatively titled *The Practical Past*).

"The Practical Past" (draft chapter, to appear in a volume tentatively titled *The Practical Past*; available at http://haydenwhite.blogspot.com/2010/08/near-beginning-of-w.html [retrieved November 30, 2010]).

Books, articles, and reviews

"Collingwood and Toynbee: Transitions in English Historical Thought," *English Miscellany*, 8 (1957), pp. 147–78.

"The Printing Industry from Renaissance to Reformation and from Guild to Capitalism," *Stechert-Hafner Book News*, 11 (1957), pp. 61–2, 73–4.

"Pontius of Cluny, the *Curia Romana* and the End of Gregorianism in Rome," *Church History*, 27 (1958), pp. 195–219.

"Religion, Culture and Western Civilization in Christopher Dawson's Idea of History," *English Miscellany*, 9 (1958), pp. 247–87.

"Ibn Khaldūn in World Philosophy of History." Review of *The Muqaddimah: An Introduction to History* by Ibn Khaldūn, *Comparative Studies in Society and History*, 2 (1959), pp. 110–25.

Review of *Church, Kingship and Lay Investiture in England, 1089–1135* by Norman F. Cantor, *Church History*, 28 (1959), pp. 208–9.

Review of *Les moines blancs: histoire de l'ordre cistercien* by Louis J. Lekai, *Speculum*, 34 (1959), pp. 304–8.

"Translator's Introduction: On History and Historicisms," in Antoni, *From History to Sociology*, pp. xv–xxviii.

"Translator's Preface," in Antoni, *From History to Sociology*, pp. ix–xii.

"The Gregorian Ideal and Saint Bernard of Clairvaux," *Journal of the History of Ideas*, 21 (1960), pp. 321–48.

Review of *Études sur la "Vita prima" de Saint Bernard* by Adriaan Hendrik Bredero, *Speculum*, 36 (1961), pp. 641–2.

Review of *Life of Petrarch* by Ernest Hatch Wilkins, *The American Historical Review*, 67 (1962), pp. 687–8.

Review of *The English Mystical Tradition* by David Knowles and *The Mediaeval Mystics of England*, ed. Eric Colledge, *Speculum*, 37 (1962), pp. 447–8.

Review of *Approaches to History*, ed. H. P. R. Finberg and *History: Written and Lived* by Paul Weiss, *Journal of Modern History*, 35 (1963), pp. 387–8.

"The Abiding Relevance of Croce's Idea of History," *Journal of Modern History*, 35 (1963), pp. 109–24.

Review of *Medieval History: The Life and Death of a Civilization* by Norman F. Cantor, *Political Science Quarterly*, 79 (1964), pp. 593–7.

Review of *Perspectives in Medieval History*, ed. Katherine Fischer Drew and Floyd Seyward Lear, *The American Historical Review*, 70 (1964), pp. 109–10.

Review of *History* by John Higham (in collaboration with Leonard Krieger and Felix Gilbert), *AHA Newsletter*, 3, 5 (1965), pp. 5–6.

Review of *The Later Philosophy of R. G. Collingwood* by Alan Donagan, *History and Theory*, 4 (1965), pp. 244–52.

"Editor's Introduction," in Milton Covensky, *The Ancient Near Eastern Tradition* (New York: Harper & Row, 1966), pp. vii–xv.

"Hegel: Historicism as Tragic Realism," *Colloquium*, 5, 2 (1966), pp. 10–19.

"Introduction," in D. A. Miller, *The Byzantine Tradition* (New York: Harper & Row, 1966), pp. vii–xvi.

Review of *Foundations of Historical Knowledge* by Morton White, *Journal of Modern History*, 38 (1966), pp. 422–3.

Review of *Great Historical Enterprises: Problems in Monastic History* by David Knowles, *Speculum*, 41 (1966), pp. 146–7.

Review of *Shapes of Philosophical History* by Frank E. Manuel, *Journal of Modern History*, 38 (1966), pp. 59–60.

"The Burden of History," *History and Theory*, 5 (1966), pp. 111–34.

The Emergence of Liberal Humanism: An Intellectual History of Western Europe, vol. I, with Willson H. Coates and J. Salwyn Schapiro (New York: McGraw-Hill, 1966).

"Editor's Introduction," in Robert Anchor, *The Enlightenment Tradition* (New York: Harper & Row, 1967), pp. ix–xix.

"Editor's Introduction," in John Weiss, *The Fascist Tradition: Radical Right-Wing Extremism in Modern Europe* (New York: Harper & Row, 1967), pp. vii–xv.

"Feuerbach, Ludwig Andreas," in *The Encyclopedia of Philosophy*, ed. Paul Edwards, vol. III (New York: Macmillan, 1967), pp. 190–2.

"Gobineau, Comte Joseph Arthur de," in *The Encyclopedia of Philosophy*, ed. Paul Edwards, vol. III (New York: Macmillan, 1967), pp. 342–3.

"Klages, Ludwig," in *The Encyclopedia of Philosophy*, ed. Paul Edwards, vol. IV (New York: Macmillan, 1967), pp. 343–4.

"Strauss, David Friedrich," in *The Encyclopedia of Philosophy*, ed. Paul Edwards, vol. VIII (New York: Macmillan, 1967), pp. 25–6.

"Windelband, Wilhelm," in *The Encyclopedia of Philosophy*, ed. Paul Edwards, vol. VIII (New York: Macmillan, 1967), pp. 320–2.

"Preface," in *The Uses of History: Essays in Intellectual and Social History Presented to William J. Bossenbrook*, ed. Hayden V. White (Detroit: Wayne State University Press, 1968), pp. 9–13.

Review of *The Riddle of History: The Great Speculators from Vico to Freud* by Bruce Mazlish, *Journal of Modern History*, 40 (1968), pp. 278–9.

"Romanticism, Historicism, and Realism: Toward a Period Concept for Early 19th Century Intellectual History," in *The Uses of History: Essays in Intellectual and Social History Presented to William J. Bossenbrook*, ed. Hayden V. White (Detroit: Wayne State University Press, 1968), pp. 45–58.

"Vico, Giovanni Battista," in *International Encyclopedia of the Social Sciences*, ed. David L. Sills, vol. XVI (New York: Macmillan, 1968), pp. 313–16.

"Biographical Note," in *Giambattista Vico: An International Symposium*, ed. Giorgio Tagliacozzo and Hayden V. White (Baltimore, MD: Johns Hopkins University Press, 1969), pp. xxv–xxvi.

Review of *The Transfer of Ideas: Historical Essays*, ed. C. D. W. Goodwin and I. B. Holley, Jr. and *The Emergence of the Eastern World: Seven Essays on Political Ideas* by G. L. Seidler, *The American Historical Review*, 74 (1969), pp. 1243–5.

"The Tasks of Intellectual History," *The Monist*, 53 (1969), pp. 606–30.

"What is Living and What is Dead in Croce's Criticism of Vico," *Giambattista Vico: An International Symposium*, ed. Giorgio Tagliacozzo and Hayden V. White (Baltimore, MD: Johns Hopkins University Press, 1969), pp. 379–89.

"Literary History: The Point of It All," *New Literary History*, 2 (1970), pp. 173–85.

Review of *Idealism, Politics and History: Sources of Hegelian Thought* by George Armstrong Kelly, *History and Theory*, 9 (1970), pp. 343–63.

The Ordeal of Liberal Humanism: An Intellectual History of Western Europe, vol. II, with Willson H. Coates (New York: McGraw-Hill, 1970).

"Croce and Becker: A Note on the Evidence of Influence," *History and Theory*, 10 (1971), pp. 222–7.

"The Culture of Criticism," in *Liberations: New Essays on the Humanities in Revolution*, ed. Ihab Hassan (Middletown, CT: Wesleyan University Press, 1971), pp. 55–69.

"Editor's Introduction," in John B. Christopher, *The Islamic Tradition* (New York: Harper & Row, 1972), pp. xvii–xxii.

Review of *History, Man, and Reason* by Maurice Mandelbaum, *The Pacific Historical Review*, 41 (1972), pp. 527–9.

"The Forms of Wildness: Archaeology of an Idea," in *The Wild Man Within: An Image in Western Thought from the Renaissance to Romanticism*, ed. Edward Dudley and Maximillian E. Novak (Pittsburgh, PA: University of Pittsburgh Press, 1972), pp. 3–38.

"The Irrational and the Problem of Historical Knowledge in the Enlightenment," in *Irrationalism in the Eighteenth Century*, ed. Harold E. Pagliaro (Cleveland, OH: Press of Case Western Reserve University, 1972), pp. 303–21.

"The Structure of Historical Narrative," *Clio*, 1, 3 (1972), pp. 5–20.

"What is a Historical System?," in *Biology, History, and Natural Philosophy*, ed. Allen D. Breck and Wolfgang Yourgrau (New York: Plenum Press, 1972), pp. 233–42.

"Foucault Decoded: Notes from Underground," *History and Theory*, 12 (1973), pp. 23–54.

"Interpretation in History," *New Literary History*, 4 (1973), pp. 281–314.

Metahistory: The Historical Imagination in Nineteenth-Century Europe (Baltimore, MD: Johns Hopkins University Press, 1973).

The Greco-Roman Tradition (New York: Harper & Row, 1973).

"The Politics of Contemporary Philosophy of History," *Clio*, 3 (1973), pp. 35–53.

Review of *Kurt Breysig: Geschichtswissenschaft zwischen Historismus und Soziologie* by Bernhard vom Brocke, *Journal of Modern History*, 45 (1973), pp. 161–3.

Review of *Historism: The Rise of a New Historical Outlook* by Friedrich Meinecke, *The Pacific Historical Review*, 43 (1974), pp. 597–8.

"Structuralism and Popular Culture," *Journal of Popular Culture*, 7 (1974), pp. 759–75.

"The Historical Text as Literary Artifact," *Clio*, 3 (1974), pp. 277–303.

"Historicism, History, and the Figurative Imagination," *History and Theory*, Beiheft 14 (1975), pp. 48–67.

"The Problem of Change in Literary History," *New Literary History*, 7 (1975), pp. 97–111.

Review of *Praxis der Geschichtswissenschaft: Die Desorientiertheit des historischen Interesses* by Joachim Radkau and Orlinde Radkau, *Journal of Modern History*, 47 (1975), pp. 540–2.

Review of *Style in History* by Peter Gay, *Journal of Modern History*, 47 (1975), pp. 539–40.

"The Historian at the Bridge of Sighs." Review of *The Historian between the Ethnologist and the Futurologist*, ed. Jerôme Dumoulin and Dominique Moisi, *Reviews in European History*, 1 (1975), pp. 437–45.

"Criticism as Cultural Politics." Review of *Beginnings: Intention and Method* by Edward W. Said, *Diacritics*, 6, 3 (1976), pp. 8–13.

"Introductory Comments," *History and Theory*, Beiheft 15 (1976), pp. 1–2.

Review of *Vico: A Study of the "New Science"* by Leon Pompa, *History and Theory*, 15 (1976), pp. 186–202.

"The Absurdist Moment in Contemporary Literary Theory," *Contemporary Literature*, 17 (1976), pp. 378–403.

"The Fictions of Factual Representation," in *The Literature of Fact: Selected Papers from the English Institute*, ed. Angus Fletcher (New York: Columbia University Press, 1976), pp. 21–44.

"The Noble Savage Theme as Fetish," in *First Images of America: The Impact of the New World on the Old*, ed. Fredi Chiappelli (Berkeley: University of California Press, 1976), pp. 121–35.

"The Tropics of History: The Deep Structure of the *New Science*," in *Giambattista Vico's Science of Humanity*, ed. Giorgio Tagliacozzo and Donald Phillip Verene (Baltimore, MD: Johns Hopkins University Press, 1976), pp. 65–85.

Review of *Surveiller et punir: naissance de la prison* by Michel Foucault, *The American Historical Review*, 82 (1977), pp. 605–6.

Review of *Vico and Herder: Two Studies in the History of Ideas* by Isaiah Berlin, *Political Theory*, 5 (1977), pp. 124–7.

"The Archaeology of Sex." Review of *Histoire de la sexualité*, vol. I, by Michel Foucault, *The Times Literary Supplement* (May 6, 1977), p. 565.

"Ethnological 'Lie' and Mythical 'Truth.'" Review of *Violence and the Sacred* by René Girard, *Diacritics*, 8, 1 (1978), pp. 2–9.

"Power and the Word." Review of *Discipline and Punish: The Birth of the Prison* and *Language, Counter-Memory, Practice: Selected Essays and Interviews* by Michel Foucault, *Canto*, 2 (1978), pp. 164–72.

"Rhetoric and History," in Hayden White and Frank E. Manuel, *Theories of History: Papers Read at a Clark Library Seminar, March 6, 1976* (Los Angeles: William Andrews Clark Memorial Library, 1978), pp. 1–25.

Tropics of Discourse: Essays in Cultural Criticism (Baltimore, MD: Johns Hopkins University Press, 1978).

"Michel Foucault," in *Structuralism and Since: From Lévi-Strauss to Derrida*, ed. John Sturrock (Oxford: Oxford University Press, 1979), pp. 81–115.

"The Discourse of History," *Humanities in Society*, 2 (1979), pp. 1–15.

"The Problem of Style in Realistic Representation: Marx and Flaubert," in *The Concept of Style*, ed. Berel Lang (Philadelphia: University of Pennsylvania Press, 1979), pp. 213–29.

"Fiery Numbers and Strange Productions: A Cento of Thoughts on Ihab Hassan." Review of *The Right Promethean Fire: Imagination, Science and Cultural Change* by Ihab Hassan, *Diacritics*, 10, 4 (1980), pp. 50–9.

"Literature and Social Action: Reflections on the Reflection Theory of Literary Art," *New Literary History*, 11 (1980), pp. 363–80.

Review of *Historik* by Johann Gustav Droysen, *History and Theory*, 19 (1980), pp. 73–93.

Review of *The Origin of Table Manners* by Claude Lévi-Strauss, *Annals of Science*, 37 (1980), pp. 249–51.

"The Value of Narrativity in the Representation of Reality," *Critical Inquiry*, 7 (1980), pp. 5–27.

"A Critical Garden." Review of *Criticism in the Wilderness: The Study of Literature Today* by Geoffrey Hartman, *Partisan Review*, 48 (1981), pp. 646–9.

"Conventional Conflicts," *New Literary History*, 13 (1981), pp. 145–60.

"Critic, Critic." Review of *Allegories of Reading: Figural Language in Rousseau, Nietzsche, Rilke, and Proust* by Paul de Man, *Partisan Review*, 48 (1981), pp. 311–15.

"The Narrativization of Real Events," *Critical Inquiry*, 7 (1981), pp. 793–8.

"Getting Out of History," *Diacritics*, 12, 3 (1982), pp. 2–13.

"Method and Ideology in Intellectual History: The Case of Henry Adams," in *Modern European Intellectual History: Reappraisals and New*

Perspectives, ed. Dominick LaCapra and Steven L. Kaplan (Ithaca, NY: Cornell University Press, 1982), pp. 280–310.

"Preface," in *Representing Kenneth Burke*, ed. Hayden White and Margaret Brose (Baltimore, MD: Johns Hopkins University Press, 1982), pp. vii–ix.

Review of *Desire in Language: A Semiotic Approach to Literature and Art* by Julia Kristeva, *Journal of Modern History*, 54 (1982), pp. 777–8.

Review of *Karl Marx, Romantic Irony, and the Proletariat: The Mythopoetic Origins of Marxism* by Leonard P. Wessell, Jr., *Studies in Romanticism*, 21 (1982), pp. 105–7.

Review of *The Origin of Formalism in Social Science* by Jeffrey T. Bergner, *The American Historical Review*, 87 (1982), pp. 746–7.

"The Politics of Historical Interpretation: Discipline and De-Sublimation," *Critical Inquiry*, 9 (1982), pp. 113–37.

"Painting and Beholder." Review of *Absorption and Theatricality: Painting and Beholder in the Age of Diderot* by Michael Fried, *The Eighteenth Century*, 24 (1983), pp. 173–7.

Review of *Vico, Past and Present*, vols. I–II, ed. Giorgio Tagliacozzo, *Journal of the History of Philosophy*, 21 (1983), pp. 581–4.

"The Authoritative Lie." Review of *The Dialogic Imagination: Four Essays* by M. M. Bakhtin, *Partisan Review*, 50 (1983), pp. 307–12.

"The Limits of Relativism in the Arts," in *Relativism in the Arts*, ed. Betty Jean Craige (Athens, GA: University of Georgia Press, 1983), pp. 45–74.

"The Worm in the Apple." Review of *From Locke to Saussure: Essays on the Study of Language and Intellectual History* by Hans Aarsleff, *Partisan Review*, 50 (1983), pp. 618–22.

"Vico and the Radical Wing of Structuralist/Poststructuralist Thought Today," *New Vico Studies*, 1 (1983), pp. 63–8.

"He Merged Myth and History." Review of *Victor Hugo and the Visionary Novel* by Victor Brombert, *The New York Times Book Review* (December 23, 1984), p. 7.

Review of *Narrative Logic: A Semantic Analysis of the Historian's Language* by F. R. Ankersmit, *The American Historical Review*, 89 (1984), pp. 1037–8.

"The Interpretation of Texts," *Berkshire Review*, 19 (1984), pp. 7–23.

"The Italian Difference and the Politics of Culture," *Graduate Faculty Philosophy Journal*, 10, 1 (1984), pp. 117–22.

"The Question of Narrative in Contemporary Historical Theory," *History and Theory*, 23 (1984), pp. 1–33.

"From Faith to Fatalism." Review of *The Paradox of History: Stendhal, Tolstoy, Pasternak and Others* by Nicola Chiaromonte, *The New York Times Book Review* (September 22, 1985), p. 7.

Review of *Which Road to the Past? Two Views of History* by Robert William Fogel and G. R. Elton, *Pacific Historical Review*, 54 (1985), pp. 353–4.

"The Rule of Narrativity: Symbolic Discourse and the Experiences of Time in Ricoeur's Thought," *Revue de l'Université d'Ottawa*, 55, 4 (1985), pp. 287–99.

"Between Science and Symbol." Review of *Writing History: Essay on Epistemology* by Paul Veyne; *Justifying Historical Descriptions* by C. Behan McCullagh; *Historical Reason* by José Ortega y Gasset; and *History and Criticism* by Dominick LaCapra, *The Times Literary Supplement* (January 31, 1986), pp. 109–10.

"Historical Pluralism," *Critical Inquiry*, 12 (1986), pp. 480–93.

"Das Problem der Erzählung in der modernen Geschichtstheorie," in *Theorie der modernen Geschichtsschreibung*, ed. Pietro Rossi (Frankfurt am Main: Suhrkamp, 1987), pp. 57–106.

Review of *Futures Past: On the Semantics of Historical Time* by Reinhart Koselleck, *The American Historical Review*, 92 (1987), pp. 1175–6.

The Content of the Form: Narrative Discourse and Historical Representation (Baltimore, MD: Johns Hopkins University Press, 1987).

"'The Nineteenth-Century' as Chronotope," *Nineteenth-Century Contexts*, 11 (1987), pp. 119–29.

"Historiography and Historiophoty," *The American Historical Review*, 93 (1988), pp. 1193–9.

Review of *After Philosophy: End or Transformation?* ed. Kenneth Baynes, James Bohman, and Thomas McCarthy, *New Vico Studies*, 6 (1988), pp. 167–8.

Review of *The Growth of Minds and Cultures: A Unified Theory of the Structures of Human Experience* by Willem H. Vanderburg, *Isis*, 79 (1988), pp. 493–4.

"The Rhetoric of Interpretation," *Poetics Today*, 9 (1988), pp. 253–74.

Review of *Vico in the Tradition of Rhetoric* by Michael Mooney, *Eighteenth-Century Studies*, 22 (1988–9), pp. 219–22.

"'Figuring the Nature of the Times Deceased': Literary Theory and Historical Writing," in *The Future of Literary Theory*, ed. Ralph Cohen (New York: Routledge, 1989), pp. 19–43.

"Introduction," *Stanford Literature Review*, 6 (1989), pp. 5–14.

"New Historicism: A Comment," in *The New Historicism*, ed. H. Aram Veeser (New York: Routledge, 1989), pp. 293–302.

Review of *Anthropology through the Looking-Glass: Critical Ethnography in the Margins of Europe* by Michael Herzfeld, *New Vico Studies*, 7 (1989), pp. 126–9.

"Romantic Historiography," in *A New History of French Literature*, ed. Denis Hollier (Cambridge, MA: Harvard University Press, 1989), pp. 632–8.

"Introduction," in Thomas Mann, *Lotte in Weimar: The Beloved Returns*, trans. H. T. Lowe-Porter (Berkeley: University of California Press, 1990), pp. v–xi.

"Kermode and Theory." Review of *An Appetite for Poetry: Essays in Literary Interpretation* by Frank Kermode, *London Review of Books*, 12, 19 (October 11, 1990), pp. 14–15.

"Ideology and Counterideology in the *Anatomy*," in *Visionary Poetics: Essays on Northrop Frye's Criticism*, ed. Robert D. Denham and Thomas Willard (New York: Peter Lang, 1991), pp. 101–11.

"Vattimo's 'Weak' Thought and Vico's 'New' Science." Review of *The End of Modernity: Nihilism and Hermeneutics in Postmodern Culture* by Gianni Vattimo, *New Vico Studies*, 9 (1991), pp. 61–8.

"Form, Reference, and Ideology in Musical Discourse," in *Music and Text: Critical Inquiries*, ed. Steven Paul Scher (Cambridge: Cambridge University Press, 1992), pp. 288–319.

"Historical Emplotment and the Problem of Truth," in *Probing the Limits of Representation: Nazism and the "Final Solution,"* ed. Saul Friedlander (Cambridge, MA: Harvard University Press, 1992), pp. 37–53.

"History as Narration," in *Telling Facts: History and Narration in Psychoanalysis*, ed. Joseph H. Smith and Humphrey Morris (Baltimore, MD: Johns Hopkins University Press, 1992), pp. 284–99.

"The Real, the True, and the Figurative in the Human Sciences," *Profession*, 92 (1992), pp. 15–17.

"Writing in the Middle Voice," *Stanford Literature Review*, 9 (1992), pp. 179–87.

Review of *The Production of Space* by Henri Lefebvre, *Design Book Review*, 29–30 (1993), pp. 90–3.

"Foreword: Rancière's Revisionism," in Jacques Rancière, *The Names of History: On the Poetics of Knowledge*, trans. Hassan Melehy (Minneapolis, MN: University of Minnesota Press, 1994), pp. vii–xix.

"Frye's Place in Contemporary Cultural Studies," in *The Legacy of Northrop Frye*, ed. Alvin A. Lee and Robert D. Denham (Toronto: University of Toronto Press, 1994), pp. 28–39.

Review of *G. B. Vico: The Making of the Anti-Modern* by Mark Lilla, *Political Theory*, 22 (1994), pp. 509–11.

Review of *The Arbor Scientiae Reconceived and the History of Vico's Resurrection* by Giorgio Tagliacozzo, *New Vico Studies*, 12 (1994), pp. 114–21.

"The Modernist Event and the Flight from History," in *The Sheila Carmel Lectures, 1988–1993*, ed. Hana Wirth-Nesher (Tel Aviv: Tel Aviv University, 1995), pp. 99–123.

"Bodies and Their Plots," in *Choreographing History*, ed. Susan Leigh Foster (Bloomington, IN: Indiana University Press, 1995), pp. 229–34.

"A Rejoinder: A Response to Professor Chartier's Four Questions," *Storia della Storiografia*, 27 (1995), pp. 63–70.

182   Bibliography

"Response to Arthur Marwick," *Journal of Contemporary History*, 30 (1995), pp. 233–46.
"Auerbach's Literary History: Figural Causation and Modernist Historicism," in *Literary History and the Challenge of Philology: The Legacy of Erich Auerbach*, ed. Seth Lerer (Stanford: Stanford University Press, 1996), pp. 124–39.
"Commentary," *History of the Human Sciences*, 9, 4 (1996), pp. 123–38.
"Storytelling: Historical and Ideological," in *Centuries' Ends, Narrative Means*, ed. Robert Newman (Stanford: Stanford University Press, 1996), pp. 58–78.
"The Modernist Event," in *The Persistence of History: Cinema, Television, and the Modern Event*, ed. Vivian Sobchack (New York: Routledge, 1996), pp. 17–38.
"Literature against Fiction: Postmodernist History," *La Torre*, 2 (1997), pp. 193–207.
"The Suppression of Rhetoric in the Nineteenth Century," in *The Rhetoric Canon*, ed. Brenda Deen Schildgen (Detroit: Wayne State University Press, 1997), pp. 21–31.
"The End of Narrative Historiography," in *Świat historii: prace z metodologii historii i historii historiografii dedykowane Jerzemu Topolskiemu z okazji siedemdziesi ciolecia urodzin*, ed. Wojciech Wrzosek (Poznań: Instytutu Historii UAM, 1998), pp. 393–409.
"The Problem with Modern Patriotism," *2b*, 13 (1998), pp. 119–30.
"Afterword," in *Beyond the Cultural Turn: New Directions in the Study of Society and Culture*, ed. Victoria E. Bonnell and Lynn Hunt (Berkeley: University of California Press, 1999), pp. 315–24.
Figural Realism: Studies in the Mimesis Effect (Baltimore, MD: Johns Hopkins University Press, 1999).
"Kosmos, Chaos und Reihenfolge in der historiologischen Darstellung," in *Kontinuität und Wandel: Geschichtsbilder in verschiedenen Fächern und Kulturen*, ed. Evelyn Schulz and Wolfgang Sonne (Zürich: Hochschulverlag AG an der ETH, 1999), pp. 89–113.
"Postmodernism and Textual Anxieties," in *The Postmodern Challenge: Perspectives East and West*, ed. Bo Stråth and Nina Witoszek (Amsterdam: Rodopi, 1999), pp. 27–45.
"Postmodernism, Textualism, and History," in *Literaturforschung heute*, ed. Eckhart Goebel and Wolfgang Klein (Berlin: Akademie Verlag, 1999), pp. 173–84.
"An Old Question Raised Again: Is Historiography Art or Science? (Response to Iggers)," *Rethinking History*, 4 (2000), pp. 391–406.
"Catastrophe, Communal Memory, and Mythic Discourse: The Uses of Myth in the Reconstruction of Society," in *Myth and Memory in the Construction of Community: Historical Patterns in Europe and Beyond*, ed. Bo Stråth (Brussels: Peter Lang, 2000), pp. 49–74.

"Figura and Historical Subalternation," in *Kontaktzone Amerika: Literarische Verkehrsformen kultureller Übersetzung*, ed. Utz Riese (Heidelberg: C. Winter, 2000), pp. 31–9.

"Posthumanism and the Liberation of Humankind," *Design Book Review*, 41–2 (2000), pp. 10–13.

"Przedmowa do wydania polskiego," in Hayden White, *Poetyka pisarstwa historycznego*, ed. Ewa Domańska and Marek Wilczyński (Kraków: TAiWPN Universitas, 2000), pp. 32–8.

"The Discourse of Europe and the Search for a European Identity," in *Europe and the Other and Europe as the Other*, ed. Bo Stråth (Brussels: Peter Lang, 2000), pp. 67–86.

"*Comparare*: Considerations on a Levian Practice," in *Perspectives on Early Modern and Modern Intellectual History: Essays in Honor of Nancy S. Struever*, ed. Joseph Marino and Melinda W. Schlitt (Rochester, NY: University of Rochester Press, 2001), pp. 492–501.

"Constructing Pasts," in *Traces of the Past, Eyes of the Present: Papers from the Nordic Seminar in Ebeltoft, April 2000*, ed. Mads Mordhorst and Anne Katrine Gjerløff (n. p.: Netværk for Historieteori og Historiografi, 2001), consulted at www.tulane.edu/~isn/hwkeynote.htm (retrieved November 30, 2010).

"Foreword," in Reinhart Koselleck, *The Practice of Conceptual History: Timing History, Spacing Concepts*, trans. Todd Samuel Presner et al. (Stanford: Stanford University Press, 2002), pp. ix–xiv.

"Prefacio," in *Historiografía y memoria colectiva: tiempos y territorios*, ed. Cristina Godoy (Madrid: Miño y Dávila, 2002), pp. 9–12.

"The Westernization of World History," in *Western Cultural Thinking: An Intercultural Debate*, ed. Jörn Rüsen (New York: Berghahn, 2002), pp. 111–18.

"Anomalies of Genre: The Utility of Theory and History for the Study of Literary Genres," *New Literary History*, 34 (2003), pp. 597–615.

"Commentary: Good of their Kind," *New Literary History*, 34 (2003), pp. 367–76.

"Reply to Professor Ankersmit," *Groniek*, 36 (2003), p. 465.

"Imperiale Träume: Hat utopische Geschichte eine Zukunft?" *Frankfurter Allgemeine Zeitung* (February 12, 2003), p. N3.

"On Transcommunality and Models of Community," in *Transcommunality: From the Politics of Conversion to the Ethics of Respect*, ed. John Brown Childs (Philadelphia: Temple University Press, 2003), pp. 165–72.

"Figural Realism in Witness Literature," *Parallax*, 10 (2004), pp. 113–24.

"The Metaphysics of Western Historiography," *Taiwan Journal of East Asian Studies*, 1 (2004), pp. 1–16.

"Introduction: Historical Fiction, Fictional History, and Historical Reality," *Rethinking History*, 9 (2005), pp. 147–57.

Review of *The New History* by Alun Munslow, *Rethinking History*, 9 (2005), pp. 129–37.

"The Public Relevance of Historical Studies: A Reply to Dirk Moses," *History and Theory*, 44 (2005), pp. 333–8.

"Historical Discourse and Literary Writing," in *Tropes for the Past: Hayden White and the History/Literature Debate*, ed. Kuisma Korhonen (Amsterdam: Rodopi, 2006), pp. 25–33.

"Afterword: Manifesto Time," in *Manifestos for History*, ed. Keith Jenkins, Sue Morgan, and Alun Munslow (London: Routledge, 2007), pp. 220–31.

"Against Historical Realism: A Reading of 'War and Peace,'" *New Left Review*, 46 (2007), pp. 89–110.

"Foreword," in Aziz Al-Azmeh, *The Times of History: Universal Topics in Islamic Historiography* (Budapest: Central European University Press, 2007), pp. ix–xiii.

"Foreword," in Geoffrey Hartman, *Criticism in the Wilderness: The Study of Literature Today*, 2nd edn. (New Haven, CT: Yale University Press, 2007), pp. xi–xvii.

"Guilty of History? The *longue durée* of Paul Ricoeur," *History and Theory*, 46 (2007), pp. 233–51.

"Response: The Dark Side of Art History," *The Art Bulletin*, 89 (2007), pp. 21–5.

"The Future of Utopia in History," *Historein*, 7 (2007), pp. 11–19.

"Commentary: 'With no particular place to go': Literary History in the Age of the Global Picture," *New Literary History*, 39 (2008), pp. 727–45.

"The Historical Event," *Differences*, 2 (2008), pp. 9–34.

"Foreword: The Postmodern Messenger," in Keith Jenkins, *At the Limits of History: Essays on Theory and Practice* (London: Routledge, 2009), pp. 1–3.

"Przedmowa," in Hayden White, *Proza historyczna*, ed. Ewa Domańska (Kraków: TAiWPN Universitas, 2009), pp. 9–18.

"Reflections on 'Gendre' in the Discourses of History," *New Literary History*, 40 (2009), pp. 867–77.

The Fiction of Narrative: Essays on History, Literature, and Theory, 1957–2007, ed. Robert Doran (Baltimore, MD: Johns Hopkins University Press, 2010).

Translations

Antoni, Carlo, *From History to Sociology: The Transition in German Historical Thinking*, trans. Hayden V. White (Detroit: Wayne State University Press, 1959).

Lucien,

Badaloni, Nicola, "Ideality and Factuality in Vico's Thought," trans. Hayden V. White, in *Giambattista Vico: An International Symposium*, ed. Giorgio Tagliacozzo and Hayden V. White (Baltimore, MD: Johns Hopkins University Press, 1969), pp. 391–400.

Goldmann, Lucien, *The Human Sciences and Philosophy*, trans. Hayden V. White and Robert Anchor (London: Jonathan Cape, 1969).

Grassi, Ernesto, "Critical Philosophy or Topical History? Meditations on the *De Nostri Temporis Studiorum Rationae*," trans. Hayden V. White, in Tagliacozzo and White, *Giambattista Vico*, pp. 39–50.

Piovani, Pietro, "Vico without Hegel," trans. Hayden V. White, in Tagliacozzo and White, *Giambattista Vico*, pp. 103–23.

Secondary Titles

Aldama, Frederick, "Hayden White Talks Trash," *Bad Subjects*, 55 (2001), pp. 12–17.

Amsden, Jon, Joseph E. Emonds, Samuel Farber et al., "Vladimir Bukovsky," *The New York Review of Books*, 18, 7 (April 20, 1972), p. 46.

Ankersmit, F. R., *Narrative Logic: A Semantic Analysis of the Historian's Language* (The Hague: Martinus Nijhoff, 1983).

Ankersmit, F. R., "The Use of Language in the Writing of History," in Ankersmit, *History and Tropology: The Rise and Fall of Metaphor* (Berkeley: University of California Press, 1994), pp. 75–96.

Ankersmit, F. R., "The Linguistic Turn: Literary Theory and Historical Theory," in Ankersmit, *Historical Representation* (Stanford: Stanford University Press, 2001), pp. 29–74.

Ankersmit, F. R., "Hayden White's Appeal to the Historians," in Ankersmit, *Historical Representation* (Stanford: Stanford University Press, 2001), pp. 249–61.

Ankersmit, F. R., *Sublime Historical Experience* (Stanford: Stanford University Press, 2005).

Ankersmit, Frank, "Representation and Reference," *Journal of the Philosophy of History*, 4 (2010), 375–409.

Ankersmit, Frank, Ewa Domańska, and Hans Kellner, eds., *Re-Figuring Hayden White* (Stanford: Stanford University Press, 2009).

Anon., "The Chronicle Section," *Man and World*, 2 (1969), pp. 319–27.

Anon., "UCLA Prof. White Named Center Head," *The Wesleyan Argus* (March 2, 1973), pp. 1–2.

Anon., "High Court in California Scores Police Classroom Surveillance," *The New York Times* (March 31, 1975), p. 12.

Antohi, Sorin, "Narratives Unbound: A Brief Introduction to Post-Communist Historical Studies," in *Narratives Unbound: Historical Studies in Post-Communist Eastern Europe*, ed. Sorin Antohi, Balázs

Trenscényi, and Péter Apor (Budapest: Central European University Press, 2007), pp. ix–xxiii.

Atkinson, Catherine, *Inventing Inventors in Renaissance Europe: Polydore Vergil's "De inventoribus rerum"* (Tübingen: Mohr Siebeck, 2007).

Auerbach, Erich, *Mimesis: Dargestellte Wirklichkeit in der abendländischen Literatur* (Bern: Francke, 1946).

Auerbach, Erich, "Figura," in Auerbach, *Gesammelte Aufsätze zur romanischen Philologie*, ed. Gustav Konrad (Bern: Francke, 1967), pp. 55–92.

Bahners, Patrick, "Die Ordnung der Geschichte: Über Hayden White," *Merkur*, 46 (1992), pp. 506–21.

Bann, Stephen, *The Clothing of Clio: A Study of the Representation of History in Nineteenth-Century Britain and France* (Cambridge: Cambridge University Press, 1984).

Bann, Stephen, *Romanticism and the Rise of History* (New York: Twayne and Maxwell Macmillan, 1995).

Barthes, Roland, "The Discourse of History," in Barthes, *The Rustle of Language*, trans. Richard Howard (Berkeley: University of California Press, 1989), pp. 127–40.

Barthes, Roland, "The Reality Effect," in Barthes, *The Rustle of Language*, trans. Richard Howard (Berkeley: University of California Press, 1989), pp. 141–8.

Barthes, Roland, "To Write: An Intransitive Verb?" in Barthes, *The Rustle of Language*, trans. Richard Howard (Berkeley: University of California Press, 1989), pp. 11–21.

Bauman, Zygmunt, *Modernity and the Holocaust* (Ithaca, NY: Cornell University Press, 1989).

Berlin, Isaiah, *Two Concepts of Liberty* (Oxford: Clarendon Press, 1958).

Bernstein, Richard J., *Beyond Objectivism and Relativism: Science, Hermeneutics, and Praxis* (Philadelphia: University of Pennsylvania Press, 1983).

Bevir, Mark, *The Logic of the History of Ideas* (Cambridge: Cambridge University Press, 1999).

Bloom, Harold, *The Anxiety of Influence: A Theory of Poetry* (New York: Oxford University Press, 1973).

Bolkosky, Sidney M., "From the Book to the Survivor," in *Working to Make a Difference: The Personal and Pedagogical Stories of Holocaust Educators Across the Globe*, ed. Samuel Totten (Lanham, MD: Lexington, 2003), pp. 1–30.

Bossenbrook, William J., "The United States, the Soviet Union, and Western Nationalism," in *American Foreign Policy and American Democracy*, ed. Alfred H. Kelly (Detroit: Wayne University Press, 1954), pp. 43–62.

Bossenbrook, William J., *The German Mind* (Detroit: Wayne State University Press, 1961).

Bossenbrook, William J., "Introduction," in *Mid-Twentieth Century Nationalism*, ed. William J. Bossenbrook (Detroit: Wayne State University Press, 1965), pp. 5–12.

Bossenbrook, William J., "German Nationalism and Fragmentation," in *Mid-Twentieth Century Nationalism*, ed. William J. Bossenbrook (Detroit: Wayne State University Press, 1965), pp. 15–32.

Bredero, Adriaan H., *Cluny et Cîteaux au douzième siècle: l'histoire d'une controverse monastique* (Amsterdam: Holland University Press, 1985).

Browne, Ray B., *Against Academia: The History of the Popular Culture Association / American Culture Association and the Popular Culture Movement, 1967–1988* (Bowling Green, OH: Bowling Green State University Popular Press, 1989).

Burks, Richard V., "Benedetto Croce (1866–)," in *Some Historians of Modern Europe: Essays in Historiography by Former Students of the Department of History of the University of Chicago*, ed. Bernadotte E. Schmitt (Chicago: University of Chicago Press, 1942), pp. 66–99.

Butler, Thorpe, Donald R. Fletcher, Jonathan S. Golan et al., "On Vietnam," *The New York Times* (June 5, 1966), pp. 207–9.

Camus, Albert, *L'homme révolté* (Paris: Gallimard, 1951).

Cantor, Norman F., *The American Century: Varieties of Culture in Modern Times* (New York: HarperCollins, 1997).

Cappai, Gabriele, *Modernisierung, Wissenschaft, Demokratie: Untersuchungen zur italienischen Rezeption des Werkes von Max Weber* (Baden-Baden: Nomos, 1994).

Carignan, Michael I., "Fiction as History or History as Fiction? George Eliot, Hayden White, and Nineteenth-Century Historicism," *Clio*, 29 (2000), pp. 395–415.

Carlsnaes, Walter, *The Concept of Ideology and Political Analysis: A Critical Examination of Its Usage by Marx, Lenin, and Mannheim* (Westport, CT: Greenwood Press, 1981).

Carr, David, "Narrative and the Real World: An Argument for Continuity," *History and Theory*, 25 (1986), pp. 117–31.

Carroll, Noël, "Interpretation, History and Narrative," *The Monist*, 73 (1990), pp. 134–66.

Carroll, Noël, "Tropology and Narration," *History and Theory*, 39 (2000), pp. 396–404.

Chanin, Clifford, "Hayden White Seeks an American Humanities," *The Wesleyan Argus* (September 7, 1973), pp. 3, 7.

Chartier, Roger, "Four Questions for Hayden White," in Chartier, *On the Edge of the Cliff: History, Language, and Practices*, trans. Lydia G. Cochrane (Baltimore, MD: Johns Hopkins University Press, 1997), pp. 28–38.

Childe, Gordon, *What Happened in History* (Harmondsworth: Penguin, 1942).

Chodorow, Stanley, *Christian Political Theory and Church Politics in the Mid-Twelfth Century: The Ecclesiology of Gratian's Decretum* (Berkeley: University of California Press, 1972).

Cohen, Mitchell, *The Wager of Lucien Goldmann: Tragedy, Dialectics, and a Hidden God* (Princeton: Princeton University Press, 1994).

Cohen, Sande, "Historiography, Scholarship and Mastery," in Cohen, *Passive Nihilism: Cultural Historiography and the Rhetorics of Scholarship* (New York: St. Martin's Press, 1998), pp. 127–61.

Collini, Stefan, " 'Discipline History' and 'Intellectual History': Reflections on the Historiography of the Social Sciences in Britain and France," *Revue de Synthèse*, 109 (1988), pp. 387–99.

Couldry, Nick, Andreas Hepp, and Friedrich Krotz, eds., *Media Events in a Global Age* (London: Routledge, 2010).

Crane, Susan A., "Language, Literary Studies, and Historical Thought," in *A Companion to Western Historical Thought*, ed. Lloyd Kramer and Sarah Maza (Malden, MA: Blackwell, 2002), pp. 319–36.

Croce, Benedetto, *Storia d'Europa nel secolo decimonono*, 2nd edn. (Bari: Gius. Laterza & Figli, 1932).

Croce, Benedetto, "La storia ridotta sotto il concetto generale dell'arte," in Croce, *Primi saggi*, 3rd edn. (Bari: Gius. Laterza & Figli, 1951), pp. 1–41.

Dami, Roberto, *I tropi della storia: la narrazione nella teoria della storiografia di Hayden White* (Milan: FrancoAngeli, 1994).

Danto, Arthur C., *Analytical Philosophy of History* (Cambridge: Cambridge University Press, 1965).

Dassen, Patrick, *De onttovering van de wereld: Max Weber en het probleem van de moderniteit in Duitsland, 1890–1920* (Amsterdam: G. A. van Oorschot, 1999).

Davidson, Arnold I., "Carlo Ginzburg and the Renewal of Historiography," in *Questions of Evidence: Proof, Practice, and Persuasion across the Disciplines*, ed. James Chandler, Arnold I. Davidson, and Harry Harootunian (Chicago: University of Chicago Press, 1994), pp. 304–20.

Day, Mark, *The Philosophy of History: An Introduction* (London: Continuum, 2008).

Derrida, Jacques, "Structure, Sign, and Play in the Discourse of the Human Sciences," in *The Languages of Criticism and the Sciences of Man: The Structuralist Controversy*, ed. Richard Macksey and Eugenio Donato (Baltimore, MD: Johns Hopkins University Press, 1970), pp. 247–72.

Dirven, René, "Metonymy and Metaphor: Different Mental Strategies of Conceptualisation," in *Metaphor and Metonymy in Comparison and*

Contrast, ed. René Dirven and Ralf Pörings (Berlin: Mouton de Gruyter, 2002), pp. 75–111.

Domańska, Ewa, "Hayden White: Beyond Irony," in Stückradt and Zbinden, *Metageschichte* (1997), pp. 104–24.

Domańska, Ewa, "Arthur C. Danto," in Domańska, *Encounters: Philosophy of History after Postmodernism* (Charlottesville, VA: University Press of Virginia, 1998), pp. 166–87.

Domańska, Ewa, "Hayden White," in Domańska, *Encounters: Philosophy of History after Postmodernism* (Charlottesville, VA: University Press of Virginia, 1998), pp. 13–38.

Domańska, Ewa, "A Conversation with Hayden White," *Rethinking History*, 12 (2008), pp. 3–21.

Doran, Robert, "Editor's Introduction: Humanism, Formalism, and the Discourse of History," in White, *Fiction of Narrative* (2010), pp. xiii–xxxii.

Dosse, François, *History of Structuralism*, vol. I: *The Rising Sign, 1945–1966*, trans. Deborah Glassman (Minneapolis, MN: University of Minnesota Press, 1997).

Doubrovsky, Serge, *Pourquoi la nouvelle critique: critique et objectivité* (Paris: Mercure de France, 1966).

Dray, W. H., "The Politics of Contemporary Philosophy of History: A Reply to Hayden White," *Clio*, 3 (1973), pp. 55–76.

Dray, William H., "Narrative and Historical Realism," in Dray, *On History and Philosophers of History* (Leiden: E. J. Brill, 1989), pp. 131–63.

Eberhard, Philippe, *The Middle Voice in Gadamer's Hermeneutics: A Basic Interpretation with Some Theological Implications* (Tübingen: Mohr Siebeck, 2004).

Eisenstein, Elizabeth L., *The Printing Press as an Agent of Change: Communications and Cultural Transformations in Early-Modern Europe* (Cambridge: Cambridge University Press, 1979).

Erdelyi, Agnes, *Max Weber in Amerika: Wirkungsgeschichte und Rezeptionsgeschichte Webers in der anglo-amerikanischen Philosophie und Sozialwissenschaft*, trans. Klara Bodnar (Vienna: Passagen Verlag, 1992).

Ermarth, Michael, review of *Metahistory*, *The American Historical Review* 80 (1975), pp. 961–3.

Ernest, John, *Liberation Historiography: African American Writers and the Challenge of History, 1794–1861* (Chapel Hill, NC: University of North Carolina Press, 2004).

Eskildsen, Kasper Risbjerg, "Leopold Ranke's Archival Turn: Location and Evidence in Modern Historiography," *Modern Intellectual History*, 5 (2008), pp. 425–53.

Flynn, Thomas R., *Sartre, Foucault, and Historical Reason*, vol. I: *Toward an Existentialist Theory of History* (Chicago: University of Chicago Press, 1997).

Fogu, Claudio, "Actualism and the Fascist Historic Imaginary," *History and Theory*, 42 (2003), pp. 196–221.

Foucault, Michel, *The Order of Things: An Archaeology of the Human Sciences*, trans. Alan Sheridan (New York: Vintage Books, 1973).

Foucault, Michel, "Nietzsche, Genealogy, History," in *The Foucault Reader*, ed. Paul Rabinow (New York: Pantheon, 1984), pp. 76–100.

Friedlander, Saul, ed., *Probing the Limits of Representation: Nazism and the "Final Solution"* (Cambridge, MA: Harvard University Press, 1992).

Frye, Northrop, *Anatomy of Criticism: Four Essays* (Princeton: Princeton University Press, 1957).

Frye, Northrop, *Fables of Identity: Studies in Poetic Mythology* (New York: Harcourt, 1963).

Fulda, Daniel, *Wissenschaft aus Kunst: Die Entstehung der modernen deutschen Geschichtsschreibung, 1760–1860* (Berlin: Walter de Gruyter, 1996).

Gadamer, Hans-Georg, *Truth and Method*, trans. Joel Weinsheimer and Donald G. Marshall, 2nd edn. (New York: Continuum, 1998).

Gallie, W. B., *Philosophy and Historical Understanding*, 2nd edn. (New York: Schocken, 1968).

Gandolfo, David Ignatius, "Liberation Philosophy," in *A Companion to Latin American Philosophy*, ed. Susanne Nuccetelli, Ofelia Schutte, and Otávio Bueno (Malden, MA: Blackwell, 2010), pp. 185–98.

Gay, Peter, *Style in History* (New York: Basic Books, 1974).

Genovese, Eugene D., *Roll, Jordan, Roll: The World the Slaves Made* (New York: Pantheon Books, 1974).

Ginzburg, Carlo, "Just One Witness," in Friedlander, *Probing the Limits* (1992), pp. 82–96.

Goldmann, Lucien, *Le dieu caché: étude sur la vision tragique dans les Pensées de Pascal et dans le théâtre de Racine* (Paris: Gallimard, 1955).

Golob, Eugene O., "The Irony of Nihilism," *History and Theory*, Beiheft 19 (1980), pp. 55–65.

Gossman, Lionel, "Augustin Thierry and Liberal Historiography," *History and Theory*, 15 (1976), pp. 3–83.

Grace, Frank, *The Concept of Property in Modern Christian Thought* (Urbana, IL: University of Illinois Press, 1953).

Gregor, A. James, *Giovanni Gentile: Philosopher of Fascism* (New Brunswick, NJ: Transaction, 2001).

Gustafsson Chorell, Torbjörn, *Studier i Hayden Whites historietänkande* (Skellefteå: Norma, 2003).

Hadot, Pierre, *Philosophy as a Way of Life: Spiritual Exercises from Socrates to Foucault*, trans. Michael Chase (Oxford: Blackwell, 1995).

Harlan, David, "The Return of the Moral Imagination," in Harlan, *The Degradation of American History* (Chicago: University of Chicago Press, 1997), pp. 105–26.

Hartman, Geoffrey, "Structuralism: The Anglo-American Adventure," *Yale French Studies*, 36–7 (1966), pp. 148–68.

Hempel, Carl G., "The Function of General Laws in History," *The Journal of Philosophy*, 39 (1942), 35–48.

Himmelfarb, Gertrude, "Telling It as You Like It: Postmodernist History and the Flight from Fact," in *The Postmodern History Reader*, ed. Keith Jenkins (London: Routledge, 1997), pp. 158–74.

Iggers, Georg G., "The Image of Ranke in American and German Historical Thought," *History and Theory*, 2 (1962), pp. 17–40.

Iggers, Georg G., *The German Conception of History: The National Tradition of Historical Thought from Herder to the Present* (Middletown, CT: Wesleyan University Press, 1968).

Iggers, Wilma, and Georg Iggers, *Two Lives in Uncertain Times: Facing the Challenges of the Twentieth Century as Scholars and Citizens* (New York: Berghahn Books, 2006).

Jacoby, Russell, "A New Intellectual History?" *The American Historical Review*, 97 (1992), pp. 405–24.

James, Samuel, "Louis Mink, 'Postmodernism,' and the Vocation of Historiography," *Modern Intellectual History*, 7 (2010), pp. 151–84.

Jameson, Fredric, *The Prison-House of Language: A Critical Account of Structuralism and Russian Formalism* (Princeton: Princeton University Press, 1972).

Jameson, Fredric, *The Political Unconscious: Narrative as a Socially Symbolic Act* (Ithaca, NY: Cornell University Press, 1981).

Jameson, Fredric, "Figural Realism, or the Poetics of Historiography," in Jameson, *The Ideologies of Theory: Essays, 1971–1986*, vol. I (London: Routledge, 1988), pp. 153–65.

Jay, Martin, "Of Plots, Witnesses, and Judgments," in Friedlander, *Probing the Limits* (1992), pp. 97–107.

Jenkins, Keith, "Beyond the Old Dichotomies: Some Reflections on Hayden White," *Teaching History*, 74 (1994), pp. 10–16.

Jenkins, Keith, "A Conversation with Hayden White," *Literature and History*, 7, 1 (1998), pp. 68–82.

Kansteiner, Wulf, "Hayden White's Critique of the Writing of History," *History and Theory*, 32 (1993), pp. 273–95.

Kellner, Hans, "A Bedrock of Order: Hayden White's Linguistic Humanism," in Kellner, *Language and Historical Representation: Getting the Story Crooked* (Madison, WI: University of Wisconsin Press, 1989), pp. 193–227.

Kellner, Hans, "Hayden White and the Kantian Discourse: Freedom, Narrative, History," in *The Philosophy of Discourse*, vol. I, ed. Chip Sills and George H. Jensen (Portsmouth, NH: Boynton and Cook, 1992), pp. 246–67.

Kellner, Hans, "Twenty Years After: A Note on *Metahistories* and Their Horizons," *Storia della Storiografia*, 24 (1993), pp. 109–17.

Kellner, Hans, "Does the Sublime Price Explanation out of the Historical Marketplace?" in Ankersmit, Domańska, and Kellner, *Re-Figuring Hayden White* (2009), pp. 216–30.

Kellner, Hans, "Introduction: A Distinctively Human Life," in Ankersmit, Domańska, and Kellner, *Re-Figuring Hayden White* (2009), pp. 1–8.

Kennan, Elizabeth, "The 'De Consideratione' of St. Bernard of Clairvaux and the Papacy in the Mid-Twelfth Century: A Review of Scholarship," *Traditio*, 23 (1967), pp. 73–115.

Kluckhohn, Clyde, "Values and Value-Orientations in the Theory of Action: An Exploration in Definition and Classification," in *Toward a General Theory of Action*, ed. Talcott Parsons and Edward A. Shils (Cambridge, MA: Harvard University Press, 1951), pp. 388–433.

Kohlhammer, Siegfried, "Die Welt im Viererpack: Zu Hayden White," *Merkur*, 52 (1998), pp. 898–907.

Koufou, Angelica, and Margarita Miliori, "The Ironic Poetics of Late Modernity," *Historein*, 2 (2000), pp. 183–200.

Kramer, Lloyd S., "Literature, Criticism and Imagination: The Literary Challenge of Hayden White and Dominick LaCapra," in *The New Cultural History*, ed. Lynn Hunt (Berkeley: University of California Press, 1989), pp. 97–128.

Krieger, Murray, "Introduction: A Scorecard for the Critics," *Contemporary Literature*, 17 (1976), pp. 297–326.

LaCapra, Dominick, "A Poetics of Historiography: Hayden White's *Tropics of Discourse*," in LaCapra, *Rethinking Intellectual History: Texts, Contexts, Language* (Ithaca, NY: Cornell University Press, 1983), pp. 72–83.

Lévi-Strauss, Claude, "The Structural Study of Myth," in *Myth: A Symposium*, ed. Thomas Sebeok (Indiana University Press, 1958), pp. 81–106.

Lévi-Strauss, Claude, *The Savage Mind*, trans. John Weightman and Doreen Weightman (Chicago: University of Chicago Press, 1966).

Levitt, Norman, "The Colonization of the Past and the Pedagogy of the Future," in *Archaeological Fantasies: How Pseudoarchaeology Misrepresents the Past and Misleads the Public*, ed. Garrett G. Fagan (London; New York: Routledge, 2006), pp. 259–85.

Lorenz, Chris, "Historical Knowledge and Historical Reality: A Plea for 'Internal Realism,'" *History and Theory*, 33 (1994), pp. 297–327.

Lorenz, Chris, "Can Histories Be True? Narrativism, Positivism, and the 'Metaphorical Turn,'" *History and Theory*, 37 (1998), pp. 309–29.

MacIntyre, Alisdair, *After Virtue: A Study in Moral Theory* (London: Duckworth, 1981).

Mali, Joseph, *Mythistory: The Making of Modern Historiography* (Chicago: University of Chicago Press, 2003).

Mandelbaum, Maurice, *The Problem of Historical Knowledge: An Answer to Relativism* (New York: Liveright, 1938).

Mandelbaum, Maurice, "The Presuppositions of *Metahistory*," *History and Theory*, Beiheft 19 (1980), pp. 39–54.

Mannheim, Karl, "On the Nature of Economic Ambition and Its Significance for the Social Education of Man," in Mannheim, *Essays on the Sociology of Knowledge*, ed. Paul Kecskemeti (New York: Oxford University Press, 1952), pp. 230–75.

Mazlish, Bruce, review of *From History to Sociology* by Carlo Antoni, *History and Theory*, 1 (1961), pp. 219–27.

Megill, Allan, "The Rhetorical Dialectic of Hayden White," in Ankersmit, Domańska, and Kellner, *Re-Figuring Hayden White* (2009), pp. 190–215.

Mink, Louis O., "Interpretation and Historical Understanding," lecture delivered to the American Historical Association, December 1973 (unpublished).

Mink, Louis O., "History and Fiction as Modes of Comprehension," in Mink, *Historical Understanding*, ed. Brian Fay, Eugene O. Golob, and Richard T. Vann (Ithaca, NY: Cornell University Press, 1987), pp. 42–60.

Mink, Louis O., "Narrative Form as a Cognitive Instrument," in Mink, *Historical Understanding*, ed. Brian Fay, Eugene O. Golob, and Richard T. Vann (Ithaca, NY: Cornell University Press, 1987), pp. 182–203.

Momigliano, Arnaldo, "The Rhetoric of History and the History of Rhetoric: On Hayden White's Tropes," in Momigliano, *Settimo contributo alla storia degli studi classici e del mondo antico* (Rome: Edizioni di Storia e Letteratura, 1984), pp. 49–59.

Moses, A. Dirk, "Hayden White, Traumatic Nationalism, and the Public Role of History," *History and Theory*, 44 (2005), pp. 311–32.

Munz, Peter, *The Shapes of Time: A New Look at the Philosophy of History* (Middletown, CT: Wesleyan University Press, 1977).

Murdoch, Iris, *Sartre, Romantic Rationalist* (New Haven, CT: Yale University Press, 1967).

Murphy, Richard J., "A Discussion with Hayden White," *Sources*, 2 (1997), pp. 13–30.

Nelson, John S., review of *Metahistory*, *History and Theory*, 14 (1975), pp. 74–91.

Nelson, John S, "Tropal History and the Social Sciences: Reflections on Struever's Remarks," *History and Theory*, Beiheft 19 (1980), pp. 80–101.

Nietzsche, Friedrich, *On the Genealogy of Morals*, ed. Keith Ansell Pearson, trans. Carol Diethe (Cambridge: Cambridge University Press, 1994).

Nietzsche, Friedrich, *Untimely Meditations*, ed. Daniel Breazeale, trans. R. J. Hollingdale (Cambridge: Cambridge University Press, 1997).

Norman, Andrew P., "Telling it Like it Was: Historical Narratives on Their Own Terms," *History and Theory*, 30 (1991), pp. 119–35.

Novick, Peter, *That Noble Dream: The "Objectivity Question" and the American Historical Profession* (Cambridge: Cambridge University Press, 1988).

Novick, Peter, *The Holocaust in American Life* (Boston: Houghton Mifflin, 1999).

Oakeshott, Michael, "Present, Future and Past," in Oakeshott, *On History and Other Essays* (Oxford: Basil Blackwell, 1983), pp. 1–44.

O'Brien, David J., *From the Heart of the American Church: Catholic Higher Education and American Culture* (Maryknoll, NY: Orbis Books, 1994).

Orr, Linda, *Headless History: Nineteenth-Century French Historiography of the Revolution* (Ithaca, NY: Cornell University Press, 1990).

Partner, Nancy, "Hayden White (and the Content and the Form and Everyone Else) at the AHA," *History and Theory*, Theme Issue 36 (1997), pp. 102–10.

Partner, Nancy, "Hayden White: The Form of the Content," *History and Theory*, 37 (1998), pp. 162–71.

Paul, Herman, "Metahistorical Prefigurations: Towards a Reinterpretation of Tropology in Hayden White," *Journal of Interdisciplinary Studies in History and Archaeology*, 1, 2 (2004), pp. 1–19.

Paul, Herman, "Een beslissend moment van geschiedenis: Hayden White en de erfenis van het existentialisme," *Groniek*, 38 (2005), pp. 581–91.

Paul, Herman, "An Ironic Battle against Irony: Epistemological and Ideological Irony in Hayden White's Philosophy of History, 1955–1973," in *Tropes for the Past: Hayden White and the History/Literature Debate*, ed. Kuisma Korhonen (Amsterdam: Rodopi, 2006), pp. 35–44.

Paul, Herman, "Masks of Meaning: Existentialist Humanism in Hayden White's Philosophy of History" (Ph.D. thesis, University of Groningen, 2006).

Paul, Herman, "Mogelijkheidszin: Hayden White en het genre van de roman," *Dietsche Warande en Belfort*, 152 (2007), pp. 848–57.

Paul, Herman, "Tegen zure regen: Hayden White, anti-ironisme en existentialistisch humanisme," *Tijdschrift voor Geschiedenis*, 120 (2007), pp. 74–84.

Paul, Herman, "A Weberian Medievalist: Hayden White in the 1950s," *Rethinking History*, 12 (2008), pp. 75–102.

Paul, Herman, "Hayden White and the Crisis of Historicism," in Ankersmit, Domańska, and Kellner, *Re-Figuring Hayden White* (2009), pp. 54–73.

Paul, Herman, "Hayden White: The Making of a Philosopher of History," *Journal of the Philosophy of History*, 5 (2011), pp. 131–45.

Paz Soldán, José Edmundo, "Interview with Hayden White," *Lucero*, 6 (1995), pp. 3–7.

Pease, Donald, "Sublime Politics," in *The American Sublime*, ed. Mary Arensberg (Albany, NY: State University of New York Press, 1986), pp. 21–50.

Pecora, Vincent, "Ethics, Politics, and the Middle Voice," *Yale French Studies*, 79 (1991), pp. 203–30.

Pensky, Max, "Method and Time: Benjamin's Dialectical Images," in *The Cambridge Companion to Walter Benjamin*, ed. David S. Ferris (Cambridge: Cambridge University Press, 2004), pp. 177–98.

Perniola, Mario, "The Difference of the Italian Philosophical Culture," *Graduate Faculty Philosophy Journal*, 10, 1 (1984), pp. 103–16.

Peters, Rik, "Voorbij de ironie: Hayden White tussen Croce en Gentile," *Tijdschrift voor Geschiedenis*, 120 (2007), pp. 222–32.

Phillips, Mark, "Historiography after Hayden White: The Contribution of Genre-Studies," in *Explorations on Post-Theory: Toward a Third Space*, ed. Fernando de Toro (Frankfurt am Main: Vervuert Verlag, 1999), pp. 145–57.

Popper, Karl Raimund, *The Poverty of Historicism* (London: Routledge and Kegan Paul, 1957).

Ricoeur, Paul, *La mémoire, l'histoire, l'oubli* (Paris: Du Seuil, 2000).

Roberts, David D., *Benedetto Croce and the Uses of Historicism* (Berkeley: University of California Press, 1987).

Roberts, David D., "Croce in America: Influence, Misunderstanding, and Neglect," in Roberts, *Historicism and Fascism in Modern Italy* (Toronto: University of Toronto Press, 2007), pp. 81–113.

Roberts, David D., "The Stakes of Misreading: Hayden White, Carlo Ginzburg, and the Crocean Legacy," in Roberts, *Historicism and Fascism in Modern Italy* (Toronto: University of Toronto Press, 2007), pp. 237–64.

Roberts, Geoffrey, ed., *The History and Narrative Reader* (London: Routledge, 2001), pp. 1–21.

Rogne, Erlend, "The Aim of Interpretation is to Create Perplexity in the Face of the Real: Hayden White in Conversation with Erlend Rogne," *History and Theory*, 48 (2009), pp. 63–75.

Roth, Michael S., *The Ironist's Cage: Memory, Trauma, and the Construction of History* (New York: Columbia University Press, 1995).

Rowland, Christopher, ed., *The Cambridge Companion to Liberation Theology*, 2nd edn. (Cambridge: Cambridge University Press, 2007).

Schneider, Joseph, *Donna Haraway: Live Theory* (New York: Continuum, 2005).

Seerveld, Calvin G., *Benedetto Croce's Earlier Aesthetic Theories and Literary Criticism: A Critical Philosophical Look at the Development during His Rationalistic Years* (Kampen: J. H. Kok, 1958).

Segal, Daniel A., " 'Western Civ' and the Staging of History in American Higher Education," *The American Historical Review*, 105 (2000), pp. 770–805.

Smith, Goldwin, "The Gates of Excellence," in *The Professor and the Public: The Role of the Scholar in the Modern World*, ed. Goldwin Smith (Detroit: Wayne State University Press, 1972), pp. 13–42.

Social Science Research Council Annual Report 1960–1961 (New York: SSRC, [1961]).

Sommerfeldt, John R., "Charismatic and Gregorian Leadership in the Thought of Bernard of Clairvaux," in *Bernard of Clairvaux: Studies Presented to Dom Jean Leclercq* (Washington, DC: Consortium Press, 1973), pp. 73–90.

Spiegelman, Art, *Maus: A Survivor's Tale*, 2 vols. (London: Penguin, 1986–91).

Steiner, George, "K," in Steiner, *Language and Silence: Essays on Language, Literature, and the Inhuman* (New York: Atheneum, 1967), pp. 118–26.

Stone, Lawrence, "The Revival of Narrative: Reflections on a New Old History," *Past and Present*, 85 (1979), 3–24.

Stroll, Mary, *The Jewish Pope: Ideology and Politics in the Papal Schism of 1130* (Leiden: Brill, 1987).

Stückradt, Jörn, and Jürg Zbinden, eds., *Metageschichte: Hayden White und Paul Ricoeur: Dargestellte Wirklichkeit in der europäischen Kultur im Kontext von Husserl, Weber, Auerbach und Gombrich Zbinden* (Baden-Baden: Nomos, 1997).

Tellenbach, Gerd, "Der Sturz des Abtes Pontius von Cluny und seine geschichtliche Bedeutung," *Quellen und Forschungen aus Italienischen Archiven und Bibliotheken*, 42–3 (1963), pp. 13–55.

Thompson, Wesley E., review of *The Greco-Roman Tradition*, *The History Teacher*, 8 (1975), pp. 303–4.

Throop, Palmer A., *Criticism of the Crusade: A Study of Public Opinion and Crusade Propaganda* (Amsterdam: Swets & Zeitlinger, 1940).

Toynbee, Arnold J., *A Study of History*, vol. I, 2nd edn. (London: Oxford University Press, 1935).

Tucker, Aviezer, "Introduction," in *A Companion to the Philosophy of History and Historiography*, ed. Aviezer Tucker (Malden, MA: Wiley-Blackwell, 2009), pp. 1–6.

Underhill, Frank H., "Arnold Toynbee, Metahistorian," *The Canadian Historical Review*, 32 (1951), pp. 201–19.

Valera, Gabriella, "Le ragioni della storia. Ermeneutica, 'linguistic turn' e storiografia nella reazione italiana a *Metahistory* di Hayden White," *Storia della Storiografia*, 25 (1994), pp. 121–52.

Van den Berghe, Gie, *De uitbuiting van de Holocaust* (Antwerp: HouteKiet, 1990).

Van der Linden, A. A. M., *A Revolt against Liberalism: American Radical Historians, 1959–1976* (Amsterdam: Rodopi, 1996).

Vann, Richard T., "Louis O. Mink's Linguistic Turn," *History and Theory*, 26 (1987), pp. 1–14.

Vann, Richard T., "Turning Linguistic: History and Theory and *History and Theory*, 1960–1975," in *A New Philosophy of History*, ed. Frank Ankersmit and Hans Kellner (London: Reaktion Books, 1995), pp. 40–69.

Vann, Richard T., "The Reception of Hayden White," *History and Theory*, 37 (1998), pp. 143–61.

Vann, Richard T., "Hayden White, Historian," in Ankersmit, Domańska, and Kellner, *Re-Figuring Hayden White* (2009), pp. 304–31.

Varon, Jeremy, "Probing the Limits of the Politics of Representation," *New German Critique*, 72 (1997), pp. 83–114.

Veliz, Claudio, "History as an Alibi," *Quadrant*, 47, 3 (2003), pp. 21–4.

Walsh, W. H., *An Introduction to Philosophy of History* (London: Hutchinson, 1951).

Weber, Marianne, *Max Weber: Ein Lebensbild* (Tübingen: J. C. B. Mohr, 1926).

Weber, Max, "Politics as a Vocation," in *From Max Weber: Essays in Sociology*, trans. H. H. Gerth and C. Wright Mills (London: Kegan Paul, Trench, Trubner & Co., 1947), pp. 77–128.

Weber, Max, "Science as a Vocation," in *From Max Weber: Essays in Sociology*, trans. H. H. Gerth and C. Wright Mills (London: Kegan Paul, Trench, Trubner & Co., 1947), pp. 129–56.

Weber, Max, *Wirtschaft und Gesellschaft: Grundriss der verstehenden Soziologie*, ed. Johannes Winckelmann, 5th edn. (Tübingen: J. C. B. Mohr, 1972).

Weber, Max, *Roscher and Knies: The Logical Problems of Historical Economics*, trans. Guy Oakes (London: Collier Macmillan, 1975).

Weber, Wolfgang, "Hayden White in Deutschland," *Storia della Storiografia*, 25 (1994), pp. 89–102.

Weiskel, Thomas, *The Romantic Sublime: Studies in the Structure and Psychology of Transcendence* (Baltimore, MD: Johns Hopkins University Press, 1976).

Williams, Gerhild Scholz, "Geschichte und die literarische Dimension: Narrativik und Historiographie in der anglo-amerikanischen Forschung der letzten Jahrzehnte: Ein Bericht," *Deutsche Vierteljahrsschrift für Literaturwissenschaft und Geistesgeschichte*, 93 (1989), pp. 315–92.

Xie, Shaobo, and Fengzhen Wang, "Hayden White," in *Dialogues on Cultural Studies: Interviews with Contemporary Critics*, ed. Shaobo Xie and Fengzhen Wang (Calgary, AB: University of Calgary Press, 2002), pp. 253–61.

Yolton, John W., "History and Meta-History," *Philosophy and Phenomenological Research*, 15 (1955), pp. 477–92.

Young, James E., "Hayden White, postmoderne Geschichte und der Holocaust," in Stückradt and Zbinden, *Metageschichte* (1997), pp. 139–65.

Young, James E., "Toward a Received History of the Holocaust," *History and Theory*, 36 (1997), pp. 21–43.

Zerbi, Piero, "Intorno allo scisma di Ponzio, abate di Cluny (1122–26)," in Zerbi, *Tra Milano e Cluny: momenti di vita e cultura ecclesiastica nel secolo XII* (Rome: Herder, 1978), pp. 309–71.

Index

CPSIA information can be obtained at www.ICGtesting.com
Printed in the USA
BVOW06s0000211215

430686BV00008B/95/P